PAGODA
TOEFL
Actual Test Reading

3rd Edition

파고다교육그룹 언어교육연구소 | 저

PAGODA Books

3rd Edition
PAGODA
TOEFL
Actual Test
Reading

초 판	1쇄 발행	2014년 12월 15일
개정 2판	1쇄 발행	2021년 2월 26일
개정 3판	1쇄 인쇄	2025년 4월 21일
개정 3판	1쇄 발행	2025년 4월 30일

지 은 이 | 파고다교육그룹 언어교육연구소
펴 낸 이 | 박경실
펴 낸 곳 | PAGODA Books 파고다북스
출판등록 | 2005년 5월 27일 제 300-2005-90호
주　　소 | 06614 서울특별시 서초구 강남대로 419, 19층(서초동, 파고다타워)
전　　화 | (02) 6940-4070
팩　　스 | (02) 536-0660
홈페이지 | www.pagodabook.com

저작권자 | ⓒ 2021, 2025 파고다아카데미, 파고다에스씨에스

이 책의 저작권은 저자와 출판사에 있습니다. 서면에 의한 저작권자와 출판사의 허락 없이
내용의 일부 혹은 전부를 인용 및 복제하거나 발췌하는 것을 금합니다.

Copyright ⓒ 2021, 2025 by PAGODA Academy, PAGODA SCS

All rights reserved. No part of this publication may be reproduced, stored
in a retrieval system, or transmitted, in any form or by any means, electronic,
mechanical, photocopying, recording or otherwise, without the prior written
permission of the copyright holder and the publisher.

ISBN 978-89-6281-937-3 (13740)

파고다북스	www.pagodabook.com
파고다 어학원	www.pagoda21.com
파고다 인강	www.pagodastar.com
테스트 클리닉	www.testclinic.com

| 낙장 및 파본은 구매처에서 교환해 드립니다.

2023년 7월
New iBT TOEFL®의 시작!

TOEFL 주관사인 미국 ETS(Educational Testing Service)는 iBT TOEFL® 시험에서 채점되지 않는 더미 문제가 삭제되면서 시간이 개정 전 3시간에서 개정 후 2시간 이하로 단축됐으며, 새로운 라이팅 유형이 추가되었다고 발표했다. 새로 바뀐 iBT TOEFL® 시험은 2023년 7월 26일 정기 시험부터 시행된다.

- 총 시험 시간 기존 약 3시간 ⋯▶ 약 2시간으로 단축
- 시험 점수는 각 영역당 30점씩 총 120점 만점으로 기존과 변함없음

영역	2023년 7월 26일 이전	2023년 7월 26일 이후
Reading	지문 3~4개 각 지문 당 10문제 시험 시간 54~72분	지문 2개 각 지문 당 10개 시험 시간 36분
Listening	대화 2~3개, 각 5문제 강의 3~5개, 각 6문제 시험 시간 41~57분	28문제 대화 2개, 각 5문제 강의 3개, 각 6문제 시험 시간 36분
Speaking	*변함없음 4문제 독립형 과제 1개 통합형 과제 3개 시험 시간 17분	
Writing	2문제 통합형 과제 1개 독립형 과제 1개 시험 시간 50분	2문제 통합형 과제 1개 수업 토론형 과제 1개 시험 시간 30분

목차

이 책의 구성과 특징	5
4주 완성 학습 플랜	7
iBT TOEFL® 개요	8
iBT TOEFL® Reading 개요	15

PART 01 Question Types — 18

01 Sentence Simplification	20
02 Fact / Negative Fact	26
03 Vocabulary	32
04 Reference	36
05 Rhetorical Purpose	42
06 Inference	48
07 Insertion	54
08 Summary	60
09 Category Chart	66

PART 02 Actual Tests — 70

Actual Test 01	72
Actual Test 02	81
Actual Test 03	90
Actual Test 04	99
Actual Test 05	108
Actual Test 06	117
Actual Test 07	126

해설서

이 책의 구성과 특징

>> **New TOEFL 변경사항 및 최신 출제 유형 완벽 반영!**
2023년 7월부터 변경된 새로운 토플 시험을 반영, iBT TOEFL®의 출제 경향을 완벽하게 반영한 문제와 주제를 골고루 다루고 있습니다.

>> **예제를 통한 문제 유형별 공략법 정리!**
본격적으로 실전에 들어가기에 앞서, iBT TOEFL® Reading의 9가지 문제 유형을 정리해 자주 나오는 질문을 파악하고 예제를 풀어보면서 iBT TOEFL® 전문 연구원이 제시하는 문제풀이 필수 전략을 학습할 수 있도록 하였습니다.

>> **7회분의 Actual Test로 실전 완벽 대비!**
실제 시험과 동일하게 구성된 7회분의 Actual Test를 수록해 실전에 철저하게 대비할 수 있도록 구성하였습니다.

>> **추가 3회분의 Actual TEST 온라인으로 제공!**
교재 외에 추가 3회분의 Actual TEST를 파고다북스 홈페이지에서 PDF로 다운로드 받으실 수 있습니다. (총 10회분의 Actual TEST 제공)

>> **그룹 스터디와 독학에 유용한 단어 시험지 생성기 제공!**
자동 단어 시험지 생성기를 통해 교재를 학습하면서 외운 단어 실력을 테스트해 볼 수 있습니다.

▶ 사용 방법: 파고다북스 홈페이지(www.pagodabook.com)에 로그인한 후 상단 메뉴의 [모의테스트] 클릭 >모의테스트 메뉴에서 [단어 시험] 클릭 > TOEFL - PAGODA TOEFL Actual Test Reading를 고른 후 원하는 문제 수를 입력하고 문제 유형 선택 > '단어 시험지 생성'을 누르고 별도의 브라우저 창으로 뜬 단어 시험지를 PDF로 내려 받거나 인쇄

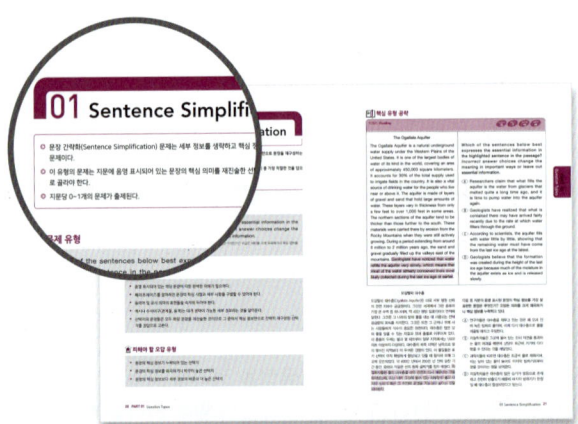

PART 01. Question Types

iBT TOEFL® 전문 연구원이 제안하는 9가지 문제 유형별 고득점 전략을 학습할 수 있습니다.

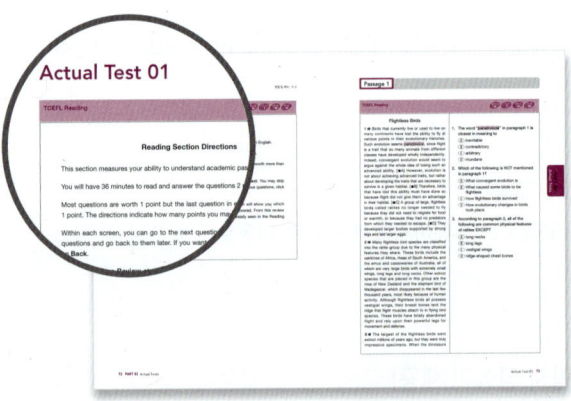

PART 02. Actual Tests

실제 시험과 동일하게 구성된 7회분의 Actual Test를 통해 실전에 대비합니다.

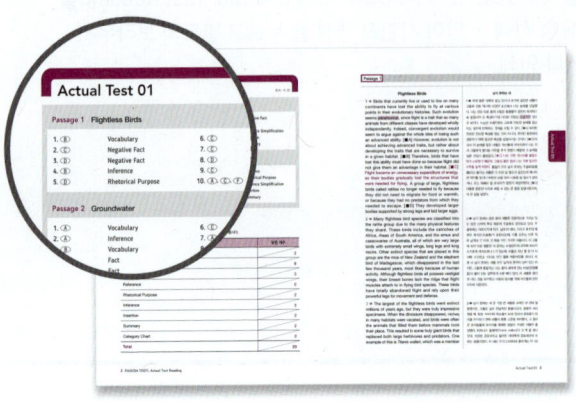

해설서

지문 및 문제에 대한 정답과 해석, 지문에서 등장한 주요 어휘 정리를 수록했습니다.

4주 완성 학습 플랜

DAY 1	DAY 2	DAY 3	DAY 4	DAY 5
PART 01				
01 Sentence Simplification • 문제 유형 및 전략 • Sample Questions	02 Fact / Negative Fact • 문제 유형 및 전략 • Sample Questions	03 Vocabulary • 문제 유형 및 전략 • Sample Questions	04 Reference • 문제 유형 및 전략 • Sample Questions	05 Rhetorical Purpose • 문제 유형 및 전략 • Sample Questions

DAY 6	DAY 7	DAY 8	DAY 9	DAY 10
PART 01				PART 02
06 Inference • 문제 유형 및 전략 • Sample Questions	07 Insertion • 문제 유형 및 전략 • Sample Questions	08 Summary • 문제 유형 및 전략 • Sample Questions	09 Category Chart • 문제 유형 및 전략 • Sample Questions	Actual Test 01 • 문제 풀이

DAY 11	DAY 12	DAY 13	DAY 14	DAY 15
PART 02				
Actual Test 02 • 문제 풀이	Actual Test 01~02 Review • 지문 다시 읽기 • 단락 요약하기 연습	Actual Test 03 • 문제 풀이	Actual Test 04 • 문제 풀이	Actual Test 03~04 Review • 지문 다시 읽기 • 단락 요약하기 연습

DAY 16	DAY 17	DAY 18	DAY 19	DAY 20
PART 02				
Actual Test 05 • 문제 풀이	Actual Test 06 • 문제 풀이	Actual Test 05~06 Review • 지문 다시 읽기 • 단락 요약하기 연습	Actual Test 07 • 문제 풀이	Actual Test 07 & Voca Review • 지문 다시 읽기 • 단락 요약하기 연습 • 학습한 단어 총정리

iBT TOEFL® 개요

1. iBT TOEFL® 이란?

TOEFL은 영어 사용 국가로 유학을 가고자 하는 외국인들의 영어 능력을 평가하기 위해 개발된 시험이다. TOEFL 시험 출제 기관인 ETS는 이러한 TOEFL 본연의 목적에 맞게 문제의 변별력을 더욱 높이고자 PBT(Paper-Based Test), CBT(Computer-Based Test)에 이어 차세대 시험인 인터넷 기반의 iBT(Internet-Based Test)를 2005년 9월부터 시행하고 있다. ETS에서 연간 30~40회 정도로 지정한 날짜에 등록함으로써 치르게 되는 이 시험은 Reading, Listening, Speaking, Writing 총 4개 영역으로 구성되며 총 시험 시간은 약 2시간이다. 각 영역별 점수는 30점으로 총점 120점을 만점으로 하며 성적은 시험 시행 약 4~8일 후에 온라인에서 확인할 수 있다.

2. iBT TOEFL®의 특징

1) 영어 사용 국가로 유학 시 필요한 언어 능력을 평가한다.

각 시험 영역은 실제 학업이나 캠퍼스 생활에 반드시 필요한 언어 능력을 측정한다. 평가되는 언어 능력에는 자신의 의견 및 선호도 전달하기, 강의 요약하기, 에세이 작성하기, 학술적인 주제의 글을 읽고 내용 이해하기 등이 포함되며, 각 영역에 걸쳐 고르게 평가된다.

2) Reading, Listening, Speaking, Writing 전 영역의 통합적인 영어 능력(Integrated Skill)을 평가한다.

시험이 4개 영역으로 분류되어 있기는 하지만 Speaking과 Writing 영역에서는 [Listening + Speaking], [Reading + Listening + Speaking], [Reading + Listening + Writing]과 같은 형태로 학습자가 둘 또는 세 개의 언어 영역을 통합해서 사용할 수 있는지를 평가한다.

3) Reading 지문 및 Listening 스크립트가 길다.

Reading 지문은 700단어 내외로 A4용지 약 1.5장 분량이며, Listening은 3~4분 가량의 대화와 6~8분 가량의 강의로 구성된다.

4) 전 영역에서 노트 필기(Note-taking)를 할 수 있다.

긴 지문을 읽거나 강의를 들으면서 핵심 사항을 간략하게 적어두었다가 문제를 풀 때 참고할 수 있다. 노트 필기한 종이는 시험 후 수거 및 폐기된다.

5) 선형적(Linear) 방식으로 평가된다.

응시자가 시험을 보는 과정에서 실력에 따라 문제의 난이도가 조정되어 출제되는 CAT(Computer Adaptive Test) 방식이 아니라, 정해진 문제가 모든 응시자에게 동일하게 제시되는 선형적인 방식으로 평가된다.

6) 시험 응시일이 제한된다.

시험은 주로 토요일과 일요일에만 시행되며, 시험에 재응시할 경우, 시험 응시일 3일 후부터 재응시 가능하다.

7) Performance Feedback이 주어진다.

온라인 및 우편으로 발송된 성적표에는 수치화된 점수뿐 아니라 각 영역별로 수험자의 과제 수행 정도를 나타내는 표도 제공된다.

3. iBT TOEFL®의 구성

시험 영역	Reading, Listening, Speaking, Writing
시험 시간	약 2시간
시험 횟수	연 30~40회(날짜는 ETS에서 지정)
총점	0~120점
영역별 점수	각 영역별 30점
성적 확인	응시일로부터 4~8일 후 온라인에서 성적 확인 가능

시험 영역	문제 구성	시간
Reading	● 독해 지문 2개, 총 20문제가 출제된다. ● 각 지문 길이 700단어 내외, 지문당 10개 문제	36분
Listening	● 대화(Conversation) 2개(각 5문제씩)와 강의(Lecture) 3개(각 6문제씩)가 출제된다.	36분
Break		10분
Speaking	● 독립형 과제(Independent Task) 1개, 통합형 과제(Integrated Task) 3개 총 4개 문제가 출제된다.	17분
Writing	● 통합형 과제(Integrated Task) 1개(20분) ● 수업 토론형 과제 (Writing for Academic Discussion) 1개(9분)	30분

4. iBT TOEFL®의 점수

1) 영역별 점수

Reading	0~30	Listening	0~30
Speaking	0~30	Writing	0~30

2) iBT, CBT, PBT 간 점수 비교

기존에 있던 CBT, PBT 시험은 폐지되었으며, 마지막으로 시행된 CBT, PBT 시험 이후 2년 이상이 경과되어 과거 응시자의 시험 성적 또한 유효하지 않다.

5. 시험 등록 및 응시 절차

1) 시험 등록

온라인과 전화로 시험 응시일과 각 지역의 시험장을 확인하여 신청할 수 있으며, 일반 접수는 시험 희망 응시일 7일 전까지 가능하다.

❶ 온라인 등록

ETS 토플 등록 사이트(https://www.ets.org/mytoefl)에 들어가 화면 지시에 따라 등록한다. 비용은 신용카드로 지불하게 되므로 American Express, Master Card, VISA 등 국제적으로 통용되는 신용카드를 미리 준비해 둔다. 시험을 등록하기 위해서는 회원 가입이 선행되어야 한다.

❷ 전화 등록

한국 프로메트릭 콜센터(00-7981-4203-0248)에 09:00~17:00 사이에 전화를 걸어 등록한다.

2) 추가 등록

시험 희망 응시일 3일(공휴일을 제외한 업무일 기준) 전까지 US $60의 추가 비용으로 등록 가능하다.

3) 등록 비용

2023년 현재 US $220(가격 변동이 있을 수 있음)

4) 시험 취소와 변경

ETS 토플 등록 사이트나 한국 프로메트릭(00-7981-4203-0248)으로 전화해서 시험을 취소하거나 응시 날짜를 변경할 수 있다. 등록 취소와 날짜 변경은 시험 날짜 4일 전까지 해야 한다. 날짜를 변경하려면 등록 번호와 등록 시 사용했던 성명이 필요하며 비용은 US $60이다.

5) 시험 당일 소지품

❶ 사진이 포함된 신분증(주민등록증, 운전면허증, 여권 중 하나)

❷ 시험 등록 번호(Registration Number)

6) 시험 절차

❶ 사무실에서 신분증과 등록 번호를 통해 등록을 확인한다.

❷ 기밀 서약서(Confidentiality Statement)를 작성한 후 서명한다.

❸ 소지품 검사, 사진 촬영, 음성 녹음 및 최종 신분 확인을 하고 연필과 연습장(Scratch Paper)을 제공받는다.

❹ 감독관의 지시에 따라 시험실에 입실하여 지정된 개인 부스로 이동하여 시험을 시작한다.

❺ Reading과 Listening 영역이 끝난 후 10분간의 휴식이 주어진다.

❻ 시험 진행에 문제가 있을 경우 손을 들어 감독관의 지시에 따르도록 한다.

❼ Writing 영역 답안 작성까지 모두 마치면 화면 종료 메시지를 확인한 후에 신분증을 챙겨 퇴실한다.

7) 성적 확인

응시일로부터 약 4~8일 후부터 온라인으로 점수 확인이 가능하며, 시험 전에 종이 사본 수령을 신청했을 경우 약 11-15일 후 우편으로 성적표를 받을 수 있다.

6. 실제 시험 화면 구성

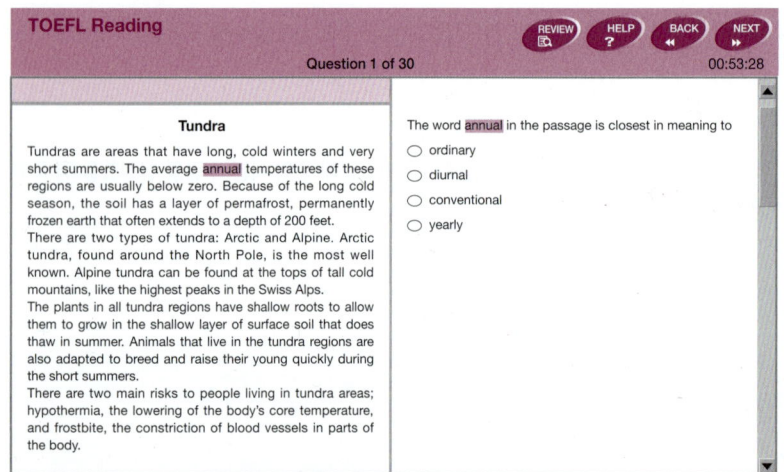

전체 Direction

시험 전체에 대한 구성 설명

Reading 영역 화면

지문은 왼쪽에, 문제는 오른쪽에 제시

Listening 영역 화면

수험자가 대화나 강의를 듣는 동안 사진이 제시됨

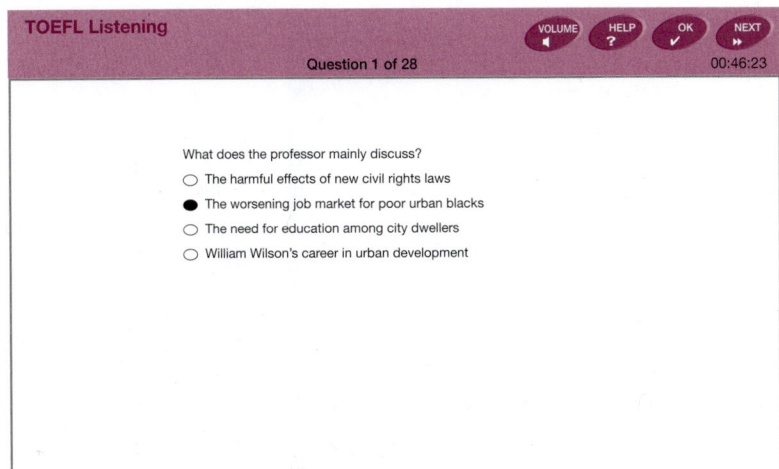

Listening 영역 화면

듣기가 끝난 후 문제 화면이 등장

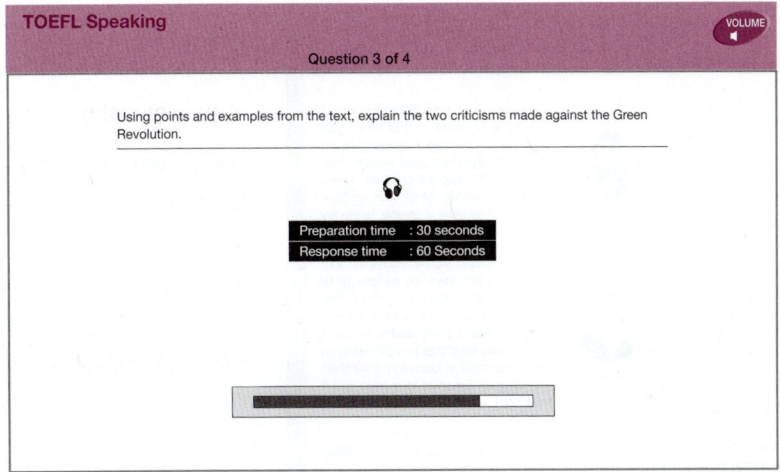

Speaking 영역 화면

문제가 주어진 후, 답변을 준비하는 시간과 말하는 시간을 알려줌

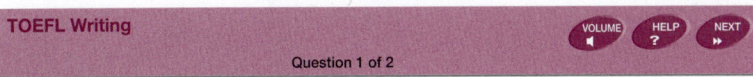

Writing 영역 화면

왼쪽에 문제가 주어지고 오른쪽에 답을 직접 타이핑할 수 있는 공간이 주어짐

복사(Copy), 자르기(Cut), 붙여넣기(Paste) 버튼이 위쪽에 위치함

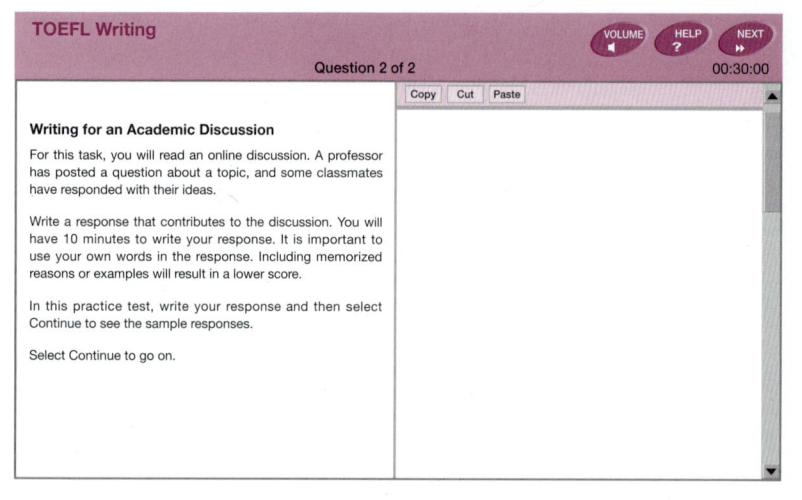

Writing 영역 화면

왼쪽에 문제가 주어지고 오른쪽에 답을 직접 타이핑할 수 있는 공간이 주어짐

복사(Copy), 자르기(Cut), 붙여넣기(Paste) 버튼이 위쪽에 위치함

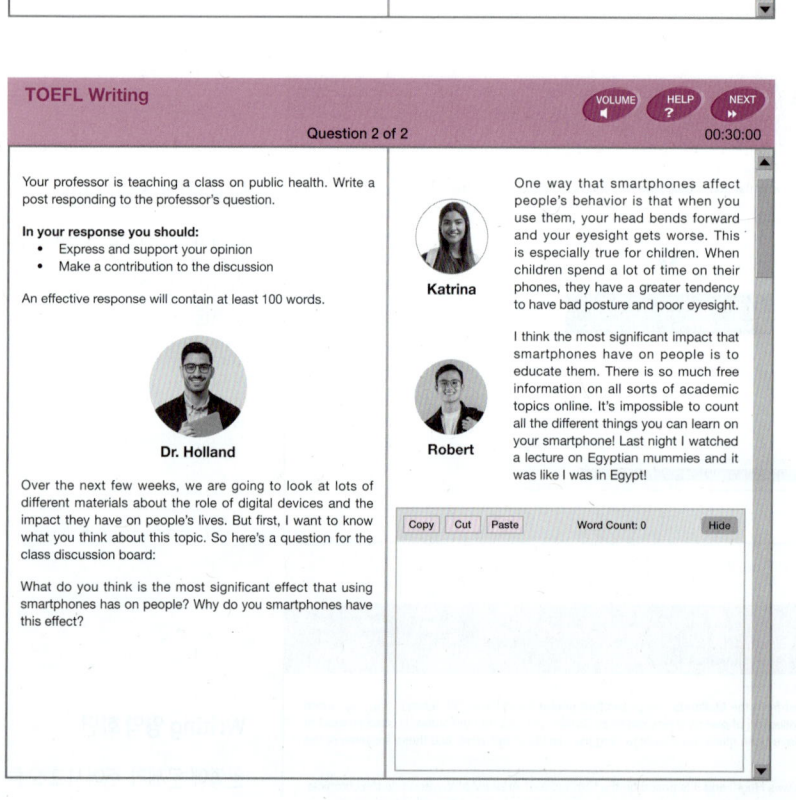

Writing 영역 화면

왼쪽에 문제가 주어지고 오른쪽에 답을 직접 타이핑할 수 있는 공간이 주어짐

복사(Copy), 자르기(Cut), 붙여넣기(Paste) 버튼이 타이핑하는 곳 위쪽에 위치함

iBT TOEFL® Reading 개요

1. Reading 영역의 특징

1. 지문의 특징

Reading 영역에서는 영어권 대학의 학습 환경에서 접할 수 있는 전공별 강좌의 입문 내지 개론 수준의 지문이 다뤄지며 다양한 분야의 주제가 등장한다.

① 자연 과학: 화학, 수학, 물리학, 생물학, 의학, 공학, 천문학, 지질학 등
② 인문: 역사, 문화, 정부 정책, 문학, 그림, 조각, 건축, 연극, 춤, 특정 인물의 일대기 또는 업적 등
③ 사회 과학: 사회학, 심리학, 인류학, 경제학 등

Reading 영역에서 출제되는 글의 종류는 크게 설명(Exposition), 논증(Argumentation), 역사적인 인물 혹은 역사적인 사건의 서술(Historical/Biographical Event Narratives)로 나눌 수 있으며, 수필이나 문학 작품은 포함되지 않는다. 각 지문은 논지가 매우 분명하며 객관적인 논조로 전개되는 잘 짜인 글이다. 각 지문에는 제목이 주어지며 때로는 지문과 관련된 그림이나 사진, 도표, 그래프, 지도 등이 포함되기도 한다. 또한 용어 설명(Glossary) 기능이 있어 지문에서 밑줄 표시가 된 어휘에 마우스를 갖다 대면 그 영어 뜻이 화면 하단에 제공된다. 이러한 어휘는 일반적으로 난이도가 매우 높거나 특수한 용어다.

2. 문제의 특징

각 지문당 10개의 문제가 주어지며 크게 3가지 유형으로 나뉜다.

① 사지선다형
② 지문에 문장 삽입하기
③ 지문 전반에 걸쳐 언급된 주요 사항을 분류하여 요약표(Summary)나 범주표(Category Chart)에 넣기

※ 하나의 지문에는 Summary와 Category Chart 중 한 가지 유형의 문제만 출제되며, 이 두 문제 유형에는 부분 점수(총점 2~3점)가 있다.

2. Reading 영역의 구성

Reading 영역에서는 총 10개의 문제 유형을 통해 지문에 대한 이해도를 다각도로 평가한다. 지문 길이가 700단어 내외로 상당히 긴 편이기 때문에 자칫 어렵다고 생각할 수 있지만, 문제 풀이에 필요한 정보는 모두 지문에서 찾을 수 있다. 따라서 다양한 주제의 지문을 접하면서 실제 시험 문제 유형에 익숙해지고 나면 TOEFL의 그 어느 영역보다도 고득점에 유리한 영역이다.

TOEFL 시험의 첫 번째 영역인 Reading 지문은 기존 3~4개에서 2개로 바뀌면서 시험 시간도 36분으로 줄었다.

Part 구성	지문 수	문제 수	시험 시간
Part 1	2개	20 문제	36분

3. Reading 영역의 문제 유형

Reading 영역을 통해 평가하고자 하는 기본 능력은 다음과 같다.

- Basic Comprehension: 지문에 대한 기초적인 이해도
- Reading to Learn: 문장/문단 전후 관계 파악 및 전체 지문과의 연관성에 대한 이해도
- Inferencing: 지문 전체의 흐름에 대한 이해에 기반한 저자 의도 파악 능력

<Reading 영역의 10가지 문제 유형>

문제 유형	문제 설명	문제 개수
Basic Comprehension		
어휘 (Vocabulary)	문맥 안에서 특정 어휘가 어떤 뜻으로 사용되었는지 선택지 가운데 가장 비슷한 유의어를 고르는 문제	1~2
지시어 (Reference)	문맥에서 대명사나 관계대명사 등이 지칭하는 명사를 고르는 문제	0~1
문장 요약 (Sentence Simplification)	지문에서 음영 표시된 문장을 가장 잘 간결하게 바꾸어 쓴 것을 선택지 중에서 고르는 문제	0~1
사실 정보 찾기 (Factual Information)	지문을 바탕으로 문제를 통해 특정 정보의 사실 여부를 파악하거나 육하원칙에 따라 묻는 정보를 찾는 문제	2~3
틀린 정보 찾기 (Negative Fact)	지문에서 언급되지 않았거나 지문의 정보에 비춰볼 때 잘못된 것을 가려내는 문제	1

	Reading to Learn		
요약 완성 (Summary)	제시된 지문에 대한 요약의 글을 완성시키는 문제로서 선택지의 6개 문장 가운데 요약에 포함되어야 할 문장 3개를 고르는 문제		0~1
분류 (Category Chart)	지문에서 언급된 요점 혹은 그 외 중요한 정보를 분류표의 카테고리에 맞게 분류하는 문제		0~1
	Inferencing		
추론 (Inference)	지문에서 명백하게 언급된 사실은 아니지만 지문의 내용을 통해 추론하는 문제		0~2
의도 파악 (Rhetorical Purpose)	글을 쓰는 방식에 대한 저자의 의도를 파악하는 문제		1~2
문장 삽입 (Insertion)	주어진 한 문장을 지문의 정해진 부분에 표시된 네 곳 중 가장 알맞은 위치에 끼워 넣는 문제		1
	총 문항 수		10

4. 기존 시험과 개정 시험 간 Reading 영역 비교

	기존 iBT (~2023년 7월 전)	개정 후 iBT (2023년 7월 이후)
지문 개수	3~4개	2개
지문당 문제 수	10문제	10문제
지문당 평균 시간	18분	18분
전체 시험 시간	54~72분	36분

• 지문 길이, 난이도, 문제 난이도에는 변화가 없다.

PART 01
Question Types

- 01 Sentence Simplification
- 02 Fact / Negative Fact
- 03 Vocabulary
- 04 Reference
- 05 Rhetorical Purpose
- 06 Inference
- 07 Insertion
- 08 Summary
- 09 Category Chart

01 Sentence Simplification

- 문장 간략화(Sentence Simplification) 문제는 세부 정보를 생략하고 핵심 정보만으로 문장을 재구성하는 문제이다.
- 이 유형의 문제는 지문에 음영 표시되어 있는 문장의 핵심 의미를 재진술한 선택지 중 가장 적절한 것을 답으로 골라야 한다.
- 지문당 0~1개의 문제가 출제된다.

📖 문제 유형

- Which of the sentences below best expresses the essential information in the highlighted sentence in the passage? *Incorrect* answer choices change the meaning in important ways or leave out essential information.
  다음 중 지문의 음영 표시된 문장의 핵심 정보를 가장 잘 표현한 문장은 무엇인가? 오답은 의미를 크게 왜곡하거나 핵심 정보를 누락하고 있다.

💡 문제 풀이 전략

- 음영 표시되어 있는 해당 문장에 대한 완벽한 이해가 필요하다.
- 패러프레이즈를 잘하려면 문장의 핵심 사항과 세부 사항을 구별할 수 있어야 한다.
- 동의어 및 유사 의미의 표현들을 숙지해 두어야 한다.
- 예시나 수식어구(관계절, 동격)는 대개 생략이 가능한 세부 정보라는 것을 알아둔다.
- 선택지의 문장들은 모두 해당 문장을 재진술한 것이므로 그 중에서 핵심 정보만으로 간략히 재구성된 선택지를 정답으로 고른다.

🚨 피해야 할 오답 유형

- 문장의 핵심 정보가 누락되어 있는 선택지
- 문장의 핵심 정보를 왜곡하거나 바꾸어 놓은 선택지
- 문장의 핵심 정보보다 세부 정보의 비중이 더 높은 선택지

핵심 유형 공략

TOEFL Reading

The Ogallala Aquifer

The Ogallala Aquifer is a natural underground water supply under the Western Plains of the United States. It is one of the largest bodies of water of its kind in the world, covering an area of approximately 450,000 square kilometers. It accounts for 30% of the total supply used to irrigate fields in the country. It is also a vital source of drinking water for the people who live near or above it. The aquifer is made of layers of gravel and sand that hold large amounts of water. These layers vary in thickness from only a few feet to over 1,000 feet in some areas. The northern sections of the aquifer tend to be thicker than those further to the south. These materials were carried there by erosion from the Rocky Mountains when they were still actively growing. During a period extending from around 6 million to 2 million years ago, the sand and gravel gradually filled up the valleys east of the mountains. ==Geologists have noticed that water refills the aquifer very slowly, which means that most of the water already contained there most likely collected during the last ice age or earlier.==

Which of the sentences below best expresses the essential information in the highlighted sentence in the passage? *Incorrect* answer choices change the meaning in important ways or leave out essential information.

(A) Researchers claim that what fills the aquifer is the water from glaciers that melted quite a long time ago, and it is time to pump water into the aquifer again.

(B) Geologists have realized that what is contained there may have arrived fairly recently due to the rate at which water filters through the ground.

(C) According to scientists, the aquifer fills with water little by little, showing that the remaining water must have come from the last ice age at the latest.

(D) Geologists believe that the formation was created during the height of the last ice age because much of the moisture in the aquifer exists as ice and is released slowly.

오갈랄라 대수층

오갈랄라 대수층(Ogallala Aquifer)은 미국 서부 평원 산하의 천연 지하수 공급원이다. 그것은 세계에서 그런 종류의 가장 큰 수역 중 하나이며, 약 45만 평방 킬로미터의 면적에 달한다. 그것은 그 나라의 밭에 물을 대는 데 사용되는 전체 공급량의 30%를 차지한다. 그것은 또한 그 근처나 위에 사는 사람들에게 식수의 중요한 원천이다. 대수층은 많은 양의 물을 담을 수 있는 자갈과 모래 층으로 이루어져 있다. 이 층들의 두께는 불과 몇 피트부터 일부 지역에서는 1,000 피트 이상까지 다양하다. 대수층의 북쪽 지역은 남쪽으로 멀리 떨어진 지역보다 더 두꺼운 경향이 있다. 이 물질들은 로키 산맥이 아직 활발하게 형성되고 있을 때 침식에 의해 그곳에 운반되었다. 약 600만 년에서 200만 년 전에 걸친 기간 동안, 모래와 자갈은 산의 동쪽 골짜기를 점차 메웠다. ==지질학자들은 물이 대수층을 매우 천천히 다시 채운다는 것을 알아냈는데, 이는 이미 그곳에 들어 있는 대부분의 물이 마지막 빙하기 혹은 그 이전에 모였을 가능성이 높다는 것을 의미한다.==

다음 중 지문의 음영 표시된 문장의 핵심 정보를 가장 잘 표현한 문장은 무엇인가? 오답은 의미를 크게 왜곡하거나 핵심 정보를 누락하고 있다.

(A) 연구자들은 대수층을 채우고 있는 것은 꽤 오래 전에 녹은 빙하의 물이며, 이제 다시 대수층으로 물을 퍼올릴 때라고 주장한다.

(B) 지질학자들은 그곳에 들어 있는 것이 지면을 통과하는 물의 여과율 때문에 상당히 최근에 거기에 다다랐을 수 있다는 것을 깨달았다.

(C) 과학자들에 따르면 대수층은 조금씩 물로 채워지며, 이는 남아 있는 물이 늦어도 마지막 빙하기로부터 왔을 것이라는 점을 보여준다.

(D) 지질학자들은 대수층의 많은 습기가 얼음으로 존재하고 천천히 방출되기 때문에 마지막 빙하기가 한창일 때 대수층이 형성되었다고 믿는다.

STEP 1 해당 문장에서 핵심 정보 파악하기

해당 문장을 읽으며 중요 핵심 정보와 주변 세부 정보를 구분하여 표시해 둔다.

> Geologists have noticed that ① water refills the aquifer very slowly, which means that ② most of the water already contained there most likely collected during the last ice age or earlier.
>
> 핵심 정보 ① 물이 대수층을 천천히 다시 채우고 있음
> 핵심 정보 ② 대수층의 물은 대부분 마지막 빙하기로부터 온 것임

STEP 2 정보가 모두 언급되어 있는 선택지 고르기

문장의 핵심 정보를 담고 있는 선택지가 한 개 이상이므로 꼼꼼히 읽고 비교하여 고른다.

> Geologists have noticed that ① water refills the aquifer very slowly, which means that ② most of the water already contained there most likely collected during the last ice age or earlier.
>
> … Ⓒ According to scientists, ① the aquifer fills with water little by little, showing that ② the remaining water must have come from the last ice age at the latest.

STEP 3 선택지들의 오답 여부를 재확인하여 정답 확정하기

오답에는 해당 문장의 핵심 정보가 왜곡되었거나 누락되어 있으므로 이를 다시 확인한다.

> Ⓐ Researchers claim that what fills the aquifer is the water from glaciers that melted quite a long time ago, and it is time to pump water into the aquifer again (✗).
> … 문장의 일부 핵심 정보가 왜곡되어 있음
>
> Ⓑ Geologists have realized that what is contained there may have arrived fairly recently (✗) due to the rate at which water filters through the ground.
> … 문장의 일부 핵심 정보가 왜곡되어 있음
>
> Ⓓ Geologists believe that the formation was created during the height of the last ice age because much of the moisture in the aquifer exists as ice and is released slowly (✗).
> … 문장의 일부 핵심 정보가 왜곡되어 있음
>
> 정답: Ⓒ According to scientists, the aquifer fills with water little by little, showing that the remaining water must have come from the last ice age at the latest.

Sample Question 1

TOEFL Reading

Population Growth in 18th Century Europe

The final factor that supported the surge in population was the growth of rural industry throughout Europe. In the cities, most industries like cloth production were managed by organizations called guilds that strictly regulated every stage of manufacturing. In the countryside, however, the people that farmed the land had long made their own clothing from local supplies of raw materials. As agriculture advanced, these rural poor also had increasing amounts of free time. Some merchants recognized the opportunity that such a large pool of skilled labor provided, and they began the putting-out system wherein they provided the farmers with raw materials for cloth and the tools needed to work with them, and the people produced finished material for a share of the profits. This provided the rural poor with a much needed source of income, particularly in the lean winter months when they could use the money to buy food and medicine. The influx of money also meant that young people could afford to marry and move out of their parents' homes. Since they had their children when they were younger, the children were more likely to survive.

Which of the sentences below best expresses the essential information in the highlighted sentence in the passage? *Incorrect* answer choices change the meaning in important ways or leave out essential information.

Ⓐ Merchants saw that they could utilize these skilled workers to produce cloth by giving them supplies and paying them with the money they made in the market.

Ⓑ Farmers produced finished cloth for a share of the profits that merchants made by selling their products.

Ⓒ Merchants began to purchase the cloth that farmers produced and sell it in markets to make a profit.

Ⓓ The merchants collected raw materials from the farmers and gave them finished cloth from the market in return.

18세기 유럽의 인구 증가

인구 급증을 뒷받침한 마지막 요소는 유럽 전역에 걸친 농촌산업 성장이었다. 도시에서는 직물 생산과 같은 대부분의 산업이 모든 제작 과정을 엄격하게 규제하는 길드라 불리는 조직에 의해 관리되었다. 그러나 지방에서는 농사를 짓던 사람들이 현지에서 공급되는 원자재로 오랫동안 직접 옷을 만들었다. 농업이 발전하자 지방의 빈곤계층은 갈수록 증가하는 여유 시간이 생겼다. 몇몇 상인들은 이렇게 대규모 숙련노동자 인력이 제공하는 기회를 알아보았고, 농부들에게 직물을 만들기 위해 필요한 원자재와 도구를 제공하고 사람들은 이익의 일부를 받는 대가로 완성물을 제공하는 선대제도를 시작했다. 이것은 지방의 빈곤계층에게 특히 수입이 적은 겨울철에 식량과 약을 구입하는 데 매우 필요한 수입원을 제공했다. 이런 돈의 유입은 젊은이들이 결혼하고 부모의 집에서 나올 수 있는 여유가 생긴다는 것을 뜻했다. 더 젊었을 때 아이를 낳기 때문에 아이들은 생존할 가능성이 더 높았다.

다음 중 지문의 음영 표시된 문장의 핵심 정보를 가장 잘 표현한 문장은 무엇인가? 오답은 의미를 크게 왜곡하거나 핵심 정보를 누락하고 있다.

Ⓐ 상인들은 이런 숙련 노동자들에게 재료를 주고 시장에서 자신들이 번 돈을 그들에게 지불함으로써 그들을 이용해 직물을 생산할 수 있다는 것을 알았다.

Ⓑ 농부들은 자신들의 생산품을 상인들이 판매하여 생기는 이익의 일부를 받는 대가로 완성된 직물을 생산했다.

Ⓒ 상인들은 농부들이 생산한 직물을 구입하고 돈을 벌기 위해 시장에서 그것을 팔기 시작했다.

Ⓓ 상인들은 농부들에게서 원자재를 모으고 그 대가로 시장의 완성된 직물을 그들에게 주었다.

Sample Question 2

TOEFL Reading

Economic Changes in Postclassical China

The improvement of transportation infrastructure in Postclassical China also encouraged domestic trade along the canal and the Yangtze River. The increased demand for products stimulated industrial production, which led to improved production techniques and finer quality products. The government soon consolidated industrial production under its direct control, and it established massive factories that employed thousands of workers. One was a textile factory that had more than 10,000 workers engaged in silk manufacturing. Due to improved methods for iron and steel production, China's output skyrocketed. ==The majority of the metal was produced in government-owned arsenals that employed over 100,000 workers, who used the metal to manufacture weapons and armor, and the remainder was used for tools and utensils that were sold throughout China.== Innovations in ceramics allowed craftsmen to create porcelain that was lighter, thinner, and more beautiful, and large factories were also built for its production. Other innovations of the time had enduring effects on the world, including movable-type printing, gunpowder, and a magnetic compass for sailing.

Which of the sentences below best expresses the essential information in the highlighted sentence in the passage? *Incorrect* answer choices change the meaning in important ways or leave out essential information.

Ⓐ Only what was left over from producing weaponry was devoted to manufacturing tools and utensils that were traded throughout the land.

Ⓑ Out of the ten thousand laborers who worked in government-owned plants, the majority produced weapons, while the rest produced nonmilitary equipment.

Ⓒ Most of the metal was produced in government-owned facilities which employed thousands of workers to transform it into weapons and armor.

Ⓓ The same government-owned plant which produced metal also hired laborers to manufacture tools and utensils that were traded throughout China.

고전 시대 이후 중국의 경제 변화

고전 시대 이후 중국의 운송 기반 시설 개선은 운하와 양자강을 따라 국내 무역을 촉진했다. 상품에 대한 수요 증가는 산업 생산을 활성화시켰고 이것은 개선된 생산 기술과 양질의 상품으로 이어졌다. 정부는 곧이어 산업 생산을 통합해 직할 통제 아래 두었고 수천 명의 직원을 고용하는 거대한 공장들을 세웠다. 그중 하나는 비단 제조에 1만 명 이상의 직원을 투입한 직물 공장이었다. 철과 강철 생산 방법의 개선으로 인해 중국의 생산량은 급등했다. ==금속의 대부분은 10만 명이 넘는 직원을 고용한 정부 소유의 무기고에서 생산됐고 그들은 금속을 사용해서 무기와 갑옷을 제작했다. 그리고 나머지는 중국 전역에 판매된 도구와 기구에 사용됐다.== 도예에 있어서의 혁신은 공예가들이 더 가볍고 더 얇고 더 아름다운 자기를 만들 수 있게 해주었고 그 생산을 위해 큰 공장들이 지어졌다. 가동 활자판, 화약, 그리고 항해에 사용되는 자기 나침반을 포함한 당대의 다른 혁신들은 세계에 지속적인 영향을 끼쳤다.

다음 중 지문의 음영 표시된 문장의 핵심 정보를 가장 잘 표현한 문장은 무엇인가? 오답은 의미를 크게 왜곡하거나 핵심 정보를 누락하고 있다.

Ⓐ 무기를 생산하는 것에서 남은 것만이 전국적으로 거래된 도구와 기구를 제작하는 데 사용됐다.

Ⓑ 정부 소유 공장에서 일한 노동자 1만 명 중에서 대다수는 무기를 생산했고 나머지는 비군사적인 용품을 생산했다.

Ⓒ 대부분의 금속은 수천 명의 노동자를 고용하여 그것을 무기와 갑옷으로 생산하는 정부 소유 시설에서 생산됐다.

Ⓓ 금속을 생산한 동일한 정부 소유 공장은 중국 전역에서 거래된 도구와 기구를 제작하기 위해 노동자들을 고용했다.

PAGODA TOEFL

Actual Test

READING

02 Fact / Negative Fact

- 사실/틀린 정보 찾기(Fact/Negative Fact) 문제는 지문에 제시된 세부 정보에 관해 묻는 문제로, Fact 문제는 선택지 중에서 지문의 내용과 일치하는 것을, Negative Fact 문제는 지문의 내용과 일치하지 않거나 지문에 언급되지 않은 것을 고르는 문제이다.
- 출제 빈도가 가장 높은 유형으로 지문당 1~4개의 문제가 출제되며, 질문이 출제된 단락의 번호가 문제와 함께 제시된다.
- 정답은 일반적으로 지문의 내용 중 핵심 정보는 넣되 주변 정보는 빼는 방식으로 패러프레이즈된다.

문제 유형

Fact

- According to paragraph X, which of the following is true of Y?
  X단락에 따르면, 다음 중 Y에 대해 사실인 것은 무엇인가?
- In paragraph X, the author states that
  X단락에서 글쓴이가 제시하는 것은?
- According to paragraph X, why/what/how Y?
  X단락에 따르면, 왜/무엇이/어떻게 Y인가?

Negative Fact

- All of the following are mentioned in paragraph X EXCEPT
  다음 중 X단락에서 언급되지 않은 것은?
- According to the passage, which of the following is NOT true of X?
  지문에 따르면, 다음 중 X에 대해 사실이 아닌 것은 무엇인가?

문제 풀이 전략

- 지문을 빠르게 훑어 읽으면서 문제의 키워드를 신속하게 찾을 수 있어야 한다. 이때, 고유명사, 숫자, 이름, 지명 등을 이용하면 좀 더 효율적이다.
- 지문에서 핵심어 포함 문장과 그 앞뒤 문장들을 꼼꼼히 살펴보면서 선택지와 비교한다.
- Fact와 Negative Fact 문제의 선택지에는 지문의 내용이 모두 패러프레이즈되어 있으므로 유의한다. 패러프레이징에 익숙해지려면 동의어 및 같은 의미를 나타내는 서로 다른 표현들을 잘 알고 있어야 한다.

피해야 할 오답 유형

- Fact: 지문에서 전혀 언급되지 않은 내용의 선택지, 지문에서 언급된 내용과 다른 선택지
- Negative Fact: 지문에서 언급된 내용이 패러프레이즈되어 있는 선택지

핵심 유형 공략

TOEFL Reading

Flying Fish

Flying fish can be found in every ocean, but they typically prefer tropical areas. To begin a flight, the fish will rapidly swing its tail to gain speed. This pushes the fish up out of the water where it will extend its long wing-like fins. It will adjust the fins to lift its body above the water and then glide on the wind. Their flights are usually about 50 meters long. However, by putting only their tail in the water and moving it to maintain speed, they can travel up to 400 meters. They can move at speeds around 70 kilometers per hour while swimming. They can glide up to 6 meters above the water, which often lands them on the decks of boats. This flight is a tactic they evolved to avoid their many predators which include dolphins, marlin, tuna, and squid.

All of the following are mentioned in the passage about the flying method of the fish EXCEPT

Ⓐ they use their tail to gain the driving force for jumping.
Ⓑ they can fly up to 50 meters high and stay in the air for 400 meters.
Ⓒ they use their fins like a bird's wings to ride on the wind.
Ⓓ they can fly far longer with their tail moving in the water.

날치

날치는 모든 바다에서 발견될 수 있지만, 전형적으로 열대 지역을 선호한다. 비행을 시작하기 위해 이 물고기는 속도를 내려고 빠르게 꼬리를 흔든다. 이것은 이 물고기를 물 밖으로 밀어내고 물고기는 긴 날개 같은 지느러미를 뻗는다. 그것은 지느러미를 조절하여 몸을 물 위로 들어올린 다음 바람을 타고 활공한다. 그들의 비행은 보통 약 50미터에 달한다. 하지만 꼬리만 물에 넣고 속도를 유지하기 위해 움직이면 최대 400미터까지 이동할 수 있다. 그들은 수영하는 동안 시속 70킬로미터의 속도로 움직일 수 있다. 그들은 물 위로 6미터까지 활공할 수 있는데, 이로 인해 종종 보트 갑판에 내려앉는다. 이 비행은 돌고래, 청새치, 참치, 오징어를 포함한 많은 포식자들을 피하기 위해 진화한 전술이다.

다음 중 이 물고기의 비행 방법에 대해 지문에서 언급되지 않은 것은?

Ⓐ 점프하는 추진력을 얻기 위해 꼬리를 사용한다.
Ⓑ 최대 50미터 높이까지 날 수 있고 400미터까지 공중에 머물 수 있다.
Ⓒ 바람을 타기 위해 지느러미를 새의 날개처럼 사용한다.
Ⓓ 꼬리를 물속에서 움직이면서 훨씬 더 오래 날 수 있다.

STEP 1 질문의 요지와 핵심어 파악하기

질문을 읽고 난 후, Fact/Negative Fact 중 무엇을 묻는 문제인지와 질문의 핵심어를 파악한다.

STEP 2 지문에서 핵심어 주변 정보 확인하기

지문을 빠르게 훑어 읽으며 질문의 핵심어나 관련 내용을 찾아 앞뒤 문장의 세부 정보를 확인한다.

STEP 3 지문 내의 세부 정보와 선택지 대조해 보기

Negative Fact의 답은 지문에 아예 등장하지 않은 내용이거나, 지문에 언급된 사실을 약간만 왜곡해서 패러프레이즈한 내용일 수 있다.

> Their flights are usually about 50 meters long. However, by putting only their tail in the water and moving it to maintain speed, they can travel up to 400 meters.
>
> → 날치는 보통 50미터 거리를 날지만, 꼬리만 물속에 넣은 상태로 움직이면 최대 400미터까지 이동할 수 있다고 했으므로 선택지 Ⓑ의 '400미터까지 공중에 머물 수 있다'와 일부 일치하지 않음
>
> 정답: Ⓑ they can fly up to 50 meters high and stay in the air for 400 meters.

Sample Question 1

TOEFL Reading

Pyramids and the Golden Ratio

Mathematical influence on art is evident when you look at the Great Pyramids. This complex of pyramids was commissioned by Egyptian Pharaoh Khufu and completed in 2,560 BCE. Since the 19th century, pyramidologists have noted that the golden ratio is present in the design of these ancient monuments. Specifically, they point out that the length of the base edges of the Khufu Pyramid range from 755 to 756 feet, the height of the structure is 481.4 feet, and the slant height of the perpendicular bisector of the face of the pyramid is 612 feet. The ratio of the slant height to half its base length is 1.619, which is less than 1% shy of the golden ratio. This also indicates that half of the cross-section of Khufu's pyramid is actually a Kepler triangle. Of course, these findings resulted in debate between the world's most prominent pyramidologists. One faction claims that the evidence shows that the golden ratio was purposely made a part of the pyramid design while the other faction states that the golden ratio's presence is merely a coincidence.

According to the passage, which of the following is NOT true of the golden ratio of the Great Pyramids?

Ⓐ The Great Pyramid is one example which shows a close relationship between math and art.

Ⓑ Some scholars who study pyramids believe the presence of the golden ratio had a direct effect on the pyramids.

Ⓒ The difference between the golden ratio and the calculated proportions of Khufu's pyramid is more than 1%.

Ⓓ The existence of the golden ratio in the pyramid design still remains controversial among many renowned researchers.

피라미드와 황금 비율

대 피라미드를 보면 수학이 예술에 미친 영향을 분명히 알 수 있다. 이 피라미드 단지는 이집트 파라오 쿠푸가 의뢰하였으며 기원전 2,560년에 완공되었다. 19세기 이래로 피라미드 연구학자들은 이런 기념비적인 고대 건축물들의 설계에 황금 비율이 존재한다고 언급했다. 구체적으로 학자들은 쿠푸 피라미드 하단 모서리 길이는 755~756피트(약 230미터), 높이는 481.4피트(약 147미터), 정면의 수직 이등분선인 경사면 높이는 612피트(약 187미터)라고 언급한다. 하단 길이의 절반에 대한 경사면 높이의 비율은 1.619이며, 이것은 황금 비율에서 1퍼센트가 부족한 것이다. 이는 또한 쿠푸 피라미드 횡단면의 절반이 실제로 케플러의 삼각형이라는 것을 나타낸다. 물론 이런 연구 결과는 세계에서 가장 저명한 피라미드 연구학자들 사이의 논쟁을 야기했다. 한 당파는 이것이 황금 비율이 피라미드 설계에 의도적으로 적용되었다는 증거라고 주장하는 반면 다른 당파는 황금 비율의 존재는 그저 우연의 일치일 뿐이라고 말한다.

지문에 따르면, 다음 중 대 피라미드의 황금 비율에 대해 사실이 아닌 것은 무엇인가?

Ⓐ 대 피라미드는 수학과 예술의 밀접한 관계를 보여주는 한 가지 예이다.

Ⓑ 피라미드를 연구하는 일부 학자들은 황금 비율의 존재가 피라미드에 직접적인 영향을 주었다고 믿는다.

Ⓒ 황금 비율과 계산된 쿠푸 피라미드 비율과의 오차는 1퍼센트 이상이다.

Ⓓ 피라미드 설계에 있는 황금 비율의 존재는 명성 있는 많은 연구자들 사이에서 아직도 논란이 되고 있다.

Sample Question 2

TOEFL Reading

Citizen's Arrest

In the event of a crime, the person or persons committing an illegal act may be arrested by someone who is not a sworn law enforcement officer. This is known as a citizen's arrest. This right is afforded to common citizens in many countries. The practice of allowing citizens to make arrests dates back to medieval English common law. In medieval England, the sheriff encouraged ordinary citizens to help catch criminals. However, making a citizen's arrest can actually lead to trouble for the person carrying it out. The citizen making an arrest could be exposing him or herself to the possibility of a lawsuit or serious criminal charges if an innocent person is arrested or if the suspect's civil rights are violated in some way. Some of the possible charges against the citizen making an arrest could include kidnapping, impersonating a police officer, and wrongful arrest. This may be the reason why stories of citizen's arrests actually taking place are uncommon.

According to the passage, those who make a citizen's arrest could be in trouble when

Ⓐ they arbitrarily apprehend criminals without the permission of authorities.

Ⓑ they are not officially designated citizens who have the right to exert governmental power.

Ⓒ they abduct a suspect, represent themselves as a police officer, or arrest an innocent person.

Ⓓ they don't take appropriate actions to place serious criminals under arrest.

시민 체포

범죄가 발생하면 불법 행위를 저지른 사람 또는 사람들은 정식 임명된 사법 기관 공무원이 아닌 사람에 의해 체포될 수 있다. 이것은 시민 체포라고 알려져 있다. 이런 권리는 많은 나라에서 일반 시민들에게 주어진다. 시민들이 체포를 할 수 있도록 허용하는 이 관행은 중세 영국의 관습법으로 거슬러 올라간다. 중세 영국에서는 주 장관이 일반 시민들에게 법을 어기는 자들을 잡도록 장려했다. 그러나 시민에 의한 범인 체포는 실제로 체포를 수행하는 사람을 곤경에 처하게 할 수 있다. 죄 없는 사람이 체포되거나 용의자의 인권이 어떤 식으로든 침해되었을 경우, 체포를 수행하는 시민은 소송이나 심각한 형사 기소를 당할 가능성에 스스로를 노출할 수 있다. 체포를 수행하는 시민을 상대로 있을 수 있는 기소 중에는 납치, 경찰 사칭, 부당 체포가 있다. 이것이 시민 체포가 실제로 일어났다는 이야기가 흔치 않은 이유일 것이다.

지문에 따르면, 시민 체포를 하는 사람이 곤경에 처하게 되는 때는?

Ⓐ 당국의 허가 없이 독단적으로 범죄자를 체포하는 때이다.

Ⓑ 공권력을 행사할 권리를 가지고 있는 공식 지정 시민이 아닐 때이다.

Ⓒ 용의자를 납치하거나 경찰을 사칭하거나 무고한 사람을 체포하는 때이다.

Ⓓ 중범죄자를 체포하기 위한 적절한 조치를 취하지 않은 때이다.

PAGODA TOEFL
Actual Test
READING

03 Vocabulary

- 어휘(Vocabulary) 문제는 주어진 어휘의 동의어(Synonym)를 묻는 문제이다.
- 지문당 1~2개의 문제가 출제되며, 해당 단어나 구는 지문에 음영으로 표시된다.

📖 문제 유형

- The word "X" in paragraph Y is closest in meaning to
  Y단락의 단어 "X"와 의미상 가장 가까운 것은?

- The phrase "X" in paragraph Y is closest in meaning to
  Y단락의 구 "X"와 의미상 가장 가까운 것은?

💡 문제 풀이 전략

- 빈출 어휘의 다양한 동의어와 관련 표현을 익혀두는 것이 좋다.
- 질문과 선택지에 등장하는 어휘의 다양한 의미를 고려해야 한다.
- TOEFL에서는 성, 수, 격의 일치 여부로 답을 고를 수 없음을 알아둔다.
- 해당 어휘의 앞뒤 문장에 동의어나 반의어의 단서가 있는지 찾아본다.
- 해당 어휘를 포함한 문장의 문맥을 살펴 가능한 답의 범위를 좁힌다.
- 가능한 선택지를 문장에 넣어 보고 문맥이 자연스럽게 연결되는지 확인한다.

🚨 피해야 할 오답 유형

- 지문의 내용과 관련이 있는 어휘
- 문장 속에서 무난하게 해석되는 어휘

핵심 유형 공략

TOEFL Reading   REVIEW   HELP   BACK   NEXT

(…) This technology incorporates the cable and pulley system of an elevator and the metal tracks and wheels of a railway train. (…)

The word "incorporates" in paragraph 1 is closest in meaning to
Ⓐ persuades   Ⓑ combines
Ⓒ restrains   Ⓓ determines

(…) 이 기술은 엘리베이터의 케이블과 도르래 시스템에 철도 열차의 철로와 바퀴를 결합한 것이다. (…)

1단락의 단어 "incorporates(결합하다)"와 의미상 가장 가까운 것은?
Ⓐ 설득하다   Ⓑ 결합하다
Ⓒ 억제하다   Ⓓ 결정하다

STEP 1 어휘력 활용하기

평소 어휘력이 풍부하다면 문제의 어휘를 보고 선택지에서 바로 동의어를 고를 수 있다.

incorporate: 포함하다, 결합하다 (≒ integrate, include, contain, take in)

STEP 2 문맥에서 단서 찾기

해당 어휘를 모른다면 앞뒤 문맥을 살펴보고 단서를 찾아 선택지에서 오답을 소거한다.

This technology incorporates ① the cable and pulley system of an elevator and ② the metal tracks and wheels of a railway train.
Ⓐ persuades   Ⓑ combines   Ⓒ restrains   Ⓓ determines
→ 이 기술이 ①과 ②를 incorporates한다고 했으므로, Ⓐ persuades(설득하다), Ⓒ restrains(억제하다)는 문맥에 어울리지 않으므로 소거한다.

STEP 3 문장에 대입해 보기

오답 소거 후에 남은 선택지들을 문장에 대입해 보고 가장 적절한 것을 정답으로 고른다.

This technology combines / determines the cable and pulley system of an elevator and the metal tracks and wheels of a railway train.
→ 이 기술은 엘리베이터의 케이블과 도르래 시스템에 철도 열차의 철로와 바퀴를 결합한 것이다 / 결정한 것이다.
정답: Ⓑ combines

Sample Question 1

TOEFL Reading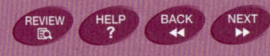

Spamming

Perhaps the largest annoyance to be found when connected to modern communication systems is "spam." Those who send spam are called "spammers," while the act of sending spam is known as "spamming." Spamming is basically defined as an abuse of electronic messaging systems in which unsolicited bulk messages are sent indiscriminately to a large number of recipients. The most widely recognized form of spam is e-mail spam, but the term is also applied to similar abuses of other forms of communication. Advertisers find spamming to be an effective strategy due to both the low cost and lack of regulation. The lack of regulation has made it difficult to hold spammers accountable for their mass mailings. Since it is cheaper and easier to reach more people, the number of spam messages has skyrocketed. However, the costs of spam on the public, such as lost productivity in the workplace and cases of fraud, have made spam the target of new legislation in many countries.

The word "accountable" in the passage is closest in meaning to

Ⓐ defendable
Ⓑ acceptable
Ⓒ responsible
Ⓓ manageable

스패밍(스팸 메일 보내기)

아마도 현대 통신 시스템과 관련하여 가장 성가신 것으로 생각되는 것은 '스팸(메일)'일 것이다. 스팸 메일을 보내는 사람들은 '스패머'라고 불리며 스팸 메일을 보내는 행동은 '스패밍'이라고 알려져 있다. 스패밍은 기본적으로 원하지 않는 대규모의 메시지를 무차별적으로 많은 수신자들에게 보내서 전자 메시지 시스템을 남용하는 것으로 정의된다. 가장 널리 알려진 형태의 스팸은 이메일 스팸이지만, 스팸이라는 용어는 다른 종류의 통신 수단을 비슷하게 남용한 경우에도 또한 적용된다. 광고주들은 스팸 메일을 보내는 것이 비용이 저렴하고 규제가 적기 때문에 효과적인 전략이라고 생각한다. 규제의 부족으로 인해 스팸 메일을 보내는 사람들에게 대량 메일에 대한 책임을 지게 하기가 어려워졌다. 더 많은 사람들에게 연락하는 것이 더 저렴하고 더 쉽기 때문에 스팸 메시지의 수는 급증했다. 그러나 직장에서의 생산성 저하와 사기 사건과 같이 스팸이 대중에게 치르게 하는 비용으로 인해 많은 국가에서 스팸 메일을 새로운 법안의 대상으로 삼고 있다.

지문의 단어 "accountable(책임을 지는)"과 의미상 가장 가까운 것은?

Ⓐ 방어할 수 있는
Ⓑ 받아들일 수 있는
Ⓒ 책임이 있는
Ⓓ 관리할 수 있는

Sample Question 2

TOEFL Reading

The Bombing of Hiroshima

In 1945, the United States made the decision to drop an atomic bomb and hopefully end World War II once and for all with a devastating strike upon their enemy, Japan. On August 6th of that year, a U.S. B-29 bomber flew through clear skies until it was approximately 10,000 meters above the Japanese city of Hiroshima. Once in position, the crew opened the craft's bomb bay doors and released a single bomb. At 8:15 A.M., only forty-three seconds after the bomb's release, two large pieces of uranium collided within the casing of the descending weapon. The explosion that resulted scorched the earth beneath in a matter of seconds, and an estimated 12 square kilometers of Hiroshima was effectively obliterated. The entire world was amazed, yet horrified, that a single bomb was capable of such destruction. The United States Military was deliberate in choosing Hiroshima for a target. The city had factories supplying Japan's military machine as well as serving as an inland port for their military missions into Korea, China, and Southeast Asia. In addition, as headquarters for Japan's Second Army, the city housed approximately 43,000 military personnel, 20,000 forced laborers and roughly 280,000 civilians.

The phrase "once and for all" in the passage is closest in meaning to

Ⓐ immediately
Ⓑ conclusively
Ⓒ permanently
Ⓓ indefinitely

히로시마의 폭격

1945년 미국은 적국 일본에 원자 폭탄을 투하하기로 결정했으며 파괴적인 공격으로 제2차 세계 대전을 완전히 끝내길 바랐다. 그해 8월 6일에 미국의 B-29 폭격기는 맑은 하늘을 날아 일본 히로시마의 약 1만 미터 상공에 이르렀다. 위치를 잡자마자 전투기 조종사는 전투기의 포문을 열고 폭탄 한 발을 투하했다. 폭탄 투하 후 단 43초 만인 오전 8시 15분에 낙하하는 무기의 외피 내부에서 두 개의 큰 우라늄 덩어리가 충돌했다. 그 결과로 인한 폭발이 몇 초 사이에 아래에 있는 땅을 불태웠고, 히로시마의 약 12제곱 킬로미터가 사실상 흔적도 없이 사라졌다. 전 세계는 폭탄 하나가 그런 파괴력을 가지고 있다는 것에 놀랐고 공포에 휩싸였다. 미군은 의도적으로 히로시마를 목표로 선택했다. 히로시마는 한국, 중국과 동남아로 군사 행동을 하기 위한 내륙 기지 역할을 해오고 있었을 뿐만 아니라 일본군에 장비를 공급하는 공장을 가지고 있었다. 또한 히로시마는 일본의 제2부대 본부로서 약 4만 3천 명의 군인들과 2만 명의 강제 노역자들, 그리고 약 28만 명의 민간인들이 거주하고 있었다.

지문의 구 "once and for all(완전히)"과 의미상 가장 가까운 것은?

Ⓐ 즉시
Ⓑ 확실히
Ⓒ 영원히
Ⓓ 무기한으로

04 Reference

- 지시어(Reference) 문제는 주어진 지시어가 지문 내에서 가리키는 대상이 무엇인지를 찾는 문제로, 해당 지시어나 구는 지문에 음영으로 표시된다.
- 지문당 1개의 문제가 출제되거나, 아예 출제되지 않을 때도 있다.

📖 문제 유형

- The word "X" in paragraph Y refers to   Y단락의 단어 "X"가 가리키는 것은
- The phrase "X" in paragraph Y refers to   Y단락의 구 "X"가 가리키는 것은

💡 문제 풀이 전략

- 지시 대상은 주로 지시어보다 먼저 언급되지만, 간혹 지시어가 먼저 나오는 경우도 있으므로 주의한다.
- 다양한 지시어의 성격과 쓰임을 미리 알아두면 지시 대상을 신속하게 찾을 수 있다. 지시 대상은 단어, 구, 절, 혹은 문장 전체가 될 수도 있다.
- 선택지에는 모두 성, 수, 격이 일치하는 단어가 등장하기 때문에 성, 수, 격의 일치 여부로는 정답의 범위를 좁힐 수 없다는 점을 염두에 둔다.
- 문맥을 보고 정답을 바로 고를 수 없는 경우에는 선택지를 하나씩 대입해 보며 오답을 소거한다.

지시어의 종류	지시어의 쓰임
인칭대명사	it, its [단수]	they, their, them [복수]
지시대명사/형용사	this, that [+단수명사]	these, those [+복수명사] the former 전자, the latter 후자
지시부사	there [장소], then [시간]
부정대명사/형용사	all 모두, none 아무도, several 몇몇, some 일부, others 다른 사람들/것들, both 둘 다, one 하나(의), another 또 다른 하나(의), neither (둘 중) 어느 것도 아닌, either (둘 중) 어느 하나(의)
관계대명사	who, which, that

피해야 할 오답 유형

- 지시어와 너무 멀리 떨어져 있는 대상
- 가까이에 있는 단어이지만 문맥에 맞지 않는 대상
- 지시어 이전에 전혀 언급되지 않은 대상

핵심 유형 공략

TOEFL Reading

Pointillism

In the 1880s, Georges Seurat and Paul Signac developed a new style of painting. With most painting styles, artists blend colors and then brush them onto the canvas using strokes to create shape and texture. However, in their new technique, small distinct dots of pure color are placed in patterns. The viewers must use their eyes and minds to blend the colors into a more complete image.

The word "them" in the passage refers to

Ⓐ styles
Ⓑ artists
Ⓒ colors
Ⓓ strokes

점선주의

1880년대에 조르주 쇠라와 폴 시냐크는 새로운 화풍을 개발했다. 대부분의 화풍에서는 형태와 질감을 나타내기 위해 화가가 색을 혼합한 후에 그것들을 붓질하여 화폭에 칠한다. 하지만 그들의 새로운 기법의 경우 순색의 작고 뚜렷한 점들을 일정한 무늬로 배치한다. 그림을 보는 사람들은 그들의 눈과 마음을 이용해 색을 섞어서 보다 완전한 그림으로 만들어야 한다.

지문의 단어 "them(그것들)"이 가리키는 것은?

Ⓐ 화풍들
Ⓑ 화가들
Ⓒ 색깔들
Ⓓ 붓질들

> **STEP 1** 지시어 포함 문장과 앞뒤 문장 살펴보기

지시어가 포함된 문장과 그 주변의 문장을 살펴보며 선택지에 제시된 대상들을 확인한다.

> In the 1880s, Georges Seurat and Paul Signac developed a new style of painting. With most painting Ⓐ styles, Ⓑ artists blend Ⓒ colors and then brush them onto the canvas using Ⓓ strokes to create shape and texture. However, in their new technique, small distinct dots of pure color are placed in patterns.

> **STEP 2** 선택지에서 문맥에 맞지 않는 대상 소거하기

정답을 바로 고를 수 없다면 앞뒤 문맥을 살펴보고 단서를 찾아 선택지에서 오답을 소거한다. '그것들을 화폭에 칠한다'는 것으로 보아 Ⓑ artists(화가), Ⓓ strokes(붓질)는 문맥에 어울리지 않으므로 소거한다.

> **STEP 3** 정답 후보인 선택지를 해당 문장에 대입해 보기

확실한 오답을 소거한 후에 남은 선택지들을 해당 문장에 대입해 보고 최종 정답을 고른다.

> With most painting Ⓐ styles, Ⓑ artists blend Ⓒ colors and then brush styles / colors onto the canvas using Ⓓ strokes to create shape and texture.
> 대부분의 화풍에서는 형태와 질감을 나타내기 위해 화가가 색을 혼합한 후에 화풍 / 색을 붓질하여 화폭에 칠한다.
>
> 정답: Ⓒ colors

Sample Question 1

TOEFL Reading

Max Weber's Sociological Influence

German sociologist and political economist Maximilian Karl Emil "Max" Weber had a major influence on social theory and social research. Weber's major works, released just before the turn of the 20th century, dealt with the rationalization and disenchantment that he associated with the rise of the capitalist system and the age of modernity that accompanied it. Weber, along with others like Georg Simmel, was a central figure in the establishment of methodological anti-positivism. Anti-positivism presented sociology as a discipline in which one must study social action through resolutely subjective means. Of his works, Weber is most famous for his thesis on economic sociology: *The Protestant Ethic and the Spirit of Capitalism*. In this thesis, he argued that the Protestantism particular to the people of the Western Hemisphere (Europe) was a key player in the rise of capitalism, bureaucracy, and the rational-legal nation-state. He argued against the ideas of Karl Marx and Friedrich Engels, which he felt were overly materialistic interpretations of the development of capitalism. Instead, he emphasized the cultural influences firmly embedded in religion.

The word "it" in the passage refers to

Ⓐ theory
Ⓑ century
Ⓒ rise
Ⓓ age

막스 베버의 사회학적 영향

독일 사회학자이자 정치 경제학자인 막시밀리안 칼 에밀 '막스' 베버는 사회 이론과 사회 연구에 중요한 영향을 미쳤다. 20세기로 접어들기 바로 전에 발표된 베버의 대표작들은 합리화와 각성을 다루었는데 그는 그것을 자본주의 체제의 대두와 그것을 동반한 현대 시대와 연관지었다. 베버는 게오르그 짐멜과 같은 다른 이들과 함께 방법론적 반실증주의를 확립한 중심 인물이었다. 반실증주의는 사회학을 확실히 주관적인 수단을 통해 사회적 행위를 연구해야 하는 지식 분야로 소개했다. 그의 작품들 중에서 베버는 〈프로테스탄트 윤리와 자본주의 정신〉이라는 경제 사회학 논문으로 가장 유명하다. 이 논문에서 그는 서반구(유럽) 사람들에게 각별한 프로테스탄트주의가 자본주의, 관료 제도, 그리고 합리적이며 합법적인 민족 국가의 발흥에 중요한 역할을 했다고 주장했다. 그는 칼 마르크스와 프리드리히 엥겔스의 사상에 반대론을 펼쳤는데, 그는 이 사상들이 자본주의 발달에 대한 지나친 유물론적인 해석이라고 생각했다. 대신에 그는 종교에 단단히 뿌리 박힌 문화적 영향을 강조했다.

지문의 단어 "it(그것)"이 가리키는 것은?

Ⓐ 이론
Ⓑ 세기
Ⓒ 대두
Ⓓ 시대

Sample Question 2

TOEFL Reading

Earth's Atmosphere

Most people know that Earth is the third planet from the Sun, a medium-sized star. The Earth is approximately 4.5 billion years old, and it has been constantly changing during that time. However, few people realize that the Earth is now on its third atmosphere. The first atmosphere was helium and hydrogen, but it dissipated early on because the planet was so hot. As the planet cooled, volcanic eruptions produced a second atmosphere of steam and carbon dioxide. The water vapor from the steam condensed and formed the oceans that cover most of the planet. Around three billion years ago, bacteria evolved to consume carbon dioxide and excrete oxygen, while other bacteria released nitrogen. The concentration of these gases slowly increased, and organisms that could not adapt to **them** died out. The Earth's atmosphere is as violent as the land beneath it. At any moment, there are around 1,500 electrical storms in progress, and eleven lightning bolts strike the land each second. A tornado tears across the surface every six hours, and a giant cyclonic storm moves over the oceans at least once a week.

The word "**them**" in the passage refers to

Ⓐ oceans
Ⓑ bacteria
Ⓒ gases
Ⓓ organisms

지구의 대기

대부분의 사람들은 지구가 태양으로부터 세 번째에 있는 행성이고 중간 크기의 별이라는 것을 알고 있다. 지구는 대략 45억 살이며 그 세월 동안 끊임없이 변해왔다. 하지만 지구가 현재 세 번째 대기 상에 있다는 것을 아는 사람은 거의 없다. 첫 번째 대기는 헬륨과 수소였지만, 지구가 너무 뜨거웠기 때문에 일찍 소멸되었다. 지구가 식자 화산 폭발이 증기와 이산화탄소로 이루어진 두 번째 대기를 만들어 냈다. 그 증기에서 나온 수증기가 응결하여 지구 대부분을 덮고 있는 대양을 형성했다. 약 30억 년 전, 박테리아들이 진화하여 이산화탄소를 마시고 산소를 배출하게 되었으며 한편 다른 박테리아들은 질소를 배출했다. 이러한 기체들의 농도는 서서히 증가했고, 그것들에 적응할 수 없었던 생물들은 멸종되었다. 지구의 대기는 그 아래에 있는 대지만큼이나 격렬하다. 매 순간 약 1,500여 건의 뇌우가 일어나고 있으며, 초당 11번의 번개가 땅에 떨어진다. 6시간마다 토네이도가 표면을 가르고, 적어도 일주일에 한 번씩은 거대한 저기압성 폭풍이 대양 위를 이동한다.

지문의 단어 "**them**(그것들)"이 가리키는 것은?

Ⓐ 대양들
Ⓑ 박테리아들
Ⓒ 기체들
Ⓓ 생물들

PAGODA TOEFL
Actual Test
READING

05 Rhetorical Purpose

- 의도 파악(Rhetorical Purpose) 문제는 글쓴이가 지문에서 특정 어구나 설명 방식을 사용한 의도 및 역할을 묻는 문제이다.
- 질문에 그대로 언급된 특정 어구는 지문에 음영 표시되어 있으며, 전체적인 설명 방식을 묻는 질문에는 지문의 단락 번호가 표시된다.
- 지문당 1개의 문제가 출제되거나, 아예 출제되지 않을 때도 있다.

📖 문제 유형

- Why does the author mention "X" in paragraph Y?
  Y단락에서 글쓴이가 "X"를 언급하는 이유는 무엇인가?
- What is the purpose of paragraph X? X단락의 목적은 무엇인가?
- The author mentions "X" in order to 글쓴이가 "X"를 언급하는 이유는?
- In paragraph X, the author mentions "Y" to X단락에서 글쓴이가 "Y"를 언급하는 이유는?

💡 문제 풀이 전략

- 문제에서 묻고 있는 특정 어구, 즉 키워드를 지문에서 신속하게 찾아 그 주변에서 관련 단서를 파악하는 것이 중요하다.
- 지문의 전체 구조나 개별 문장의 의미보다는 키워드와 해당 단락 사이의 논리 전개 방식에 초점을 맞춰야 한다.
- 글쓴이의 의도와 키워드의 역할에 관한 다양한 표현들을 알아두면 지문과 보기를 비교할 때 도움이 된다.

설명/예시	to illustrate | to explain | to describe | to clarify | to list | to exemplify | to give an example of
비교/대조	to compare | to contrast
강조/부연	to emphasize | to highlight | to further develop the idea
주장/제안	to suggest | to support | to argue | to present | to propose
증명/입증	to demonstrate | to show | to prove | to give a reason for
반박/반론	to contradict | to repute

피해야 할 오답 유형

- 글쓴이의 의도 및 설명 방식 면에서는 맞는 것처럼 보이지만, 지문의 세부 정보와 다른 내용이 담긴 선택지

핵심 유형 공략

TOEFL Reading

Monetary Value

When bank notes were first introduced, they were greeted with disdain by many people. They trusted coins made of gold and silver and believed that paper money was worthless. Even today, people still say that money isn't worth the paper it's printed on. However, the opposite is becoming true for coins. Due to rising prices for silver, copper, zinc and other metals commonly used to make coins, they are becoming more expensive than their stated value. Many countries have sought cheaper alternatives like aluminum while other countries have chosen to phase out some coins altogether. For example, the Canadian government will soon stop making pennies. The coin is worth one cent, but they cost 1.6 cents to manufacture. The discontinuation of the penny is expected to save the Canadian government 11 million Canadian dollars a year. To compensate for this, retailers will increase or decrease prices to the nearest five cents.

The author mentions "the opposite is becoming true for coins" in the passage in order to

Ⓐ demonstrate that coins have fewer problems than paper money.

Ⓑ clarify a principle to determine the face value of metal coins.

Ⓒ contradict the idea that coins are preferred over bills.

Ⓓ suggest that the value of coins has declined due to the market.

통화 가치

지폐가 처음 도입되었을 때, 많은 사람들이 그것들을 멸시했다. 그들은 금과 은으로 만들어진 주화를 신뢰했고 지폐는 가치가 없다고 믿었다. 심지어 오늘날에도 사람들은 여전히 돈이 인쇄된 종이만큼의 가치가 없다고 말한다. 그러나 주화의 경우 그 반대 현상이 나타나고 있다. 일반적으로 주화를 만들 때 사용되는 은, 구리, 아연과 다른 금속의 가격 상승으로 인해 그것들은 명시된 가치보다 더욱 비싸지고 있다. 많은 나라들이 알루미늄과 같은 더 저렴한 대안을 모색하는 한편 다른 나라들은 일부 주화를 단계적으로 폐지하기로 결정했다. 예를 들어, 캐나다 정부는 곧 페니 발행을 중단할 것이다. 이 동전은 1센트의 가치가 있지만 제조하는 데 1.6센트가 든다. 페니의 단종으로 캐나다 정부는 연간 1,100만 캐나다 달러를 절약할 수 있을 것으로 예상된다. 이를 보완하기 위해 소매업체들은 가격을 가장 근접한 5센트로 올리거나 내릴 것이다.

지문에서 글쓴이가 "주화의 경우 그 반대 현상이 나타나고 있다"고 언급하는 이유는?

Ⓐ 주화가 지폐보다 문제가 더 적다는 것을 증명하기 위해

Ⓑ 금속 주화의 액면가를 결정하는 원칙을 명확히 하기 위해

Ⓒ 주화가 지폐보다 선호된다는 생각에 반박하기 위해

Ⓓ 시장으로 인해 주화의 가치가 하락했음을 시사하기 위해

STEP 1 　지문에서 질문 대상인 특정 어구 찾기

질문에서 묻고 있는 대상을 지문에서 신속하게 찾아 해당 어구 앞뒤의 문장들을 살펴본다.

> 질문　The author mentions "the opposite is becoming true for coins" in the passage
>
> 지문　They trusted coins made of gold and silver and believed that paper money was worthless (…) However, the opposite is becoming true for coins. Due to rising prices for silver, copper, zinc and other metals commonly used to make coins, they are becoming more expensive than their stated value. (…)

STEP 2 　지문에서 글쓴이의 의도 및 설명 방식 파악하기

질문 대상 주변에 있는 정보들을 참고해 글쓴이가 해당 어구를 사용한 의도를 파악해 본다.

> 지문　They trusted coins made of gold and silver and believed that paper money was worthless (…) However, the opposite is becoming true for coins. Due to rising prices for silver, copper, zinc and other metals commonly used to make coins, they are becoming more expensive than their stated value. (…)
>
> 설명 방식(의도)　반박/반론
> 세부 정보　과거에는 지폐보다 주화가 선호되었지만, 오늘날에는 이와 반대가 되었다.

STEP 3 　지문의 설명 방식과 세부 정보를 선택지와 대조하기

지문에서 파악한 설명 방식 및 전달하고자 하는 내용을 선택지에 있는 정보와 비교, 대조한다.

> 설명 방식(의도)　반박/반론
> 세부 정보　화폐 선호도 – 과거: 주화〉지폐 ⇒ 현재: 주화〈지폐
>
> Ⓐ **demonstrate** [증명] that coins have fewer problems than paper money. (주화의 문제가 더 적음)
> Ⓑ **clarify** [설명] a principle to determine the face value of metal coins. (주화 액면가 결정 원칙)
> Ⓒ **contradict the idea** [반박] that coins are preferred over bills. (선호도: 주화〉지폐)
> Ⓓ **suggest** [주장] that the value of coins has declined due to the market. (주화의 가치↓)
>
> 그런 다음, 이 두 가지 조건을 모두 만족하는 보기를 고른다.
> ① 지문에서 키워드가 하는 역할을 정확히 제시한 보기
> ② 지문에서 파악한 키워드 관련 세부 정보를 담고 있는 보기
>
> 정답: Ⓒ contradict the idea that coins are preferred over bills.

Sample Question 1

TOEFL Reading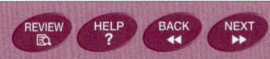

UNESCO – Preservation of Art Forms and Traditions

The United Nations Educational, Scientific and Cultural Organization (UNESCO) is better known for its work protecting world monuments and natural wonders, but in 2003, the organization started a list to promote the preservation of art forms and other traditions in the face of globalization. The aim of the list is to recognize particular elements of living cultural heritage, such as language and rituals, in order to protect and ensure the continuation of cultural diversity and to foster a sense of community. For a tradition to be recognized on the list, it must be deemed functional in the spread of knowledge of intangible heritage, and protective measures need to be taken in order to promote the continuation of this process. Most recently in 2010, the art of French gastronomy, traditional Mexican cuisine, the Mediterranean diet, and art forms like the Peking opera, Flamenco, and Gagok, among others, have been added to the list. The acupuncture and moxibustion of traditional Chinese medicine were also nominated to join the list.

The author mentions "acupuncture and moxibustion" in order to

Ⓐ highlight major tasks of UNESCO including festivals and rituals.

Ⓑ introduce assets awaiting designation on UNESCO's list.

Ⓒ show the increasing diversification of UNESCO's field of interest.

Ⓓ classify the broadened activities of UNESCO.

유네스코 – 예술 형식과 전통의 보존

국제연합교육과학문화기구(유네스코)는 세계적인 기념물들과 자연의 경관들을 보호하는 업무로 더 잘 알려져 있지만, 2003년에 이 기구는 세계화에 직면하여 예술 형식과 그외 다른 전통의 보존을 장려하기 위해 목록을 만들기 시작했다. 이 목록의 목적은 언어와 의례와 같이 살아 있는 문화유산을 구성하는 구체적인 요소들을 공인하는 것인데, 이는 문화적 다양성이 지속되도록 보호하고 지키며 공동체 의식을 강화하기 위한 것이다. 어떠한 전통이 이 목록에 오르기 위해서는 무형 유산에 대한 지식 확산에 도움이 된다고 여겨져야 하고, 이 과정의 지속을 촉진하기 위해 보호 조치가 취해져야 한다. 가장 최근인 2010년에는 프랑스식 미식법, 멕시코의 전통 요리법, 지중해식 식습관, 그리고 경극, 플라멩코와 가곡과 같은 예술 형식들이 목록에 추가되었다. 전통 한의학의 침술과 뜸질도 이 목록에 오르도록 추천되었다.

글쓴이가 "침술과 뜸질"을 언급한 이유는?

Ⓐ 축제와 의례들을 포함해 유네스코의 주요 임무를 강조하기 위해

Ⓑ 유네스코 목록에 지정되기를 기다리는 유산들을 소개하기 위해

Ⓒ 유네스코의 관심 분야가 점점 다양해짐을 보여주기 위해

Ⓓ 유네스코의 확장된 활동을 분류하기 위해

Sample Question 2

TOEFL Reading

Censorship

Censorship usually strikes a sour note for most people in democratic societies, but it sometimes has its place. For instance, censorship is carried out during wartime with the purpose of preventing the release of information that might prove useful to the enemy. This typically involves keeping information concerning times and locations secret. At other times, the information may only be delayed in its release until it is of no use to the enemy. The reason why censorship is not considered as immoral during wartime as it is during peacetime is because the underlying circumstances have changed. The issue shifts from personal liberty to personal safety. During World Wars I and II, the personal letters of British soldiers were censored. At that time, censorship was an incredibly time-consuming process, for the process consisted of commanding officers going through their own men's letters with a black marker and crossing out anything their men wrote that could possibly compromise the security of any ongoing operations. Many slogans were created to remind the population about censorship. "Loose lips sink ships" was one of the most famous of these slogans.

Why does the author use "Loose lips sink ships" as an example of a slogan?

(A) To reveal characteristics of censorship mostly related to physical expressions

(B) To accentuate the significance of censorship during the wars of the past

(C) To assert that censorship can't be justified even in case of emergency

(D) To introduce popular proverbs which disagree with censorship

검열

검열은 보통 민주주의 사회에서 대부분의 사람들에게 불쾌한 인상을 주지만, 가끔 검열이 자리할 곳이 있다. 예를 들면, 검열은 전시에 적에게 유용할 수도 있는 정보의 유출을 방지하려는 목적으로 실시된다. 이는 일반적으로 시간과 장소에 관한 정보를 기밀로 유지하는 것과 관련이 있었다. 다른 때는 적에게 그 정보가 쓸모 없어질 때까지 정보의 유출이 그저 지연될지도 모른다. 검열이 전시에는 평화로운 시기에 여겨지는 것만큼 비도덕적이라고 여겨지지 않는 이유는 근본적인 상황이 변했기 때문이다. 이 쟁점은 개인의 자유에서 개인의 안전으로 옮겨진다. 제1, 2차 세계 대전 동안 영국 군인들의 사적인 편지는 검열을 받았다. 그 당시 검열은 엄청나게 시간이 걸리는 과정이었다. 왜냐하면 이 과정에서 부대 지휘관들이 검은색 펜을 들고 부하들의 편지를 검토하다 그들이 쓴 것 중 현재 진행되고 있는 작전의 보안을 위태롭게 할 수 있는 모든 내용에 선을 그어 지웠기 때문이다. 사람들에게 검열에 대해 상기시키기 위해 많은 표어들이 만들어졌다. "가벼운 입은 배를 가라앉힌다"는 그 표어들 중에서 가장 유명했던 것 중 하나이다.

글쓴이가 "가벼운 입은 배를 가라앉힌다"를 표어의 예로 든 이유는 무엇인가?

(A) 주로 신체 표현과 관련된 검열의 특징들을 나타내기 위해

(B) 과거 전시에서의 검열의 중요성을 강조하기 위해

(C) 비상시에도 검열이 정당화될 수 없음을 주장하기 위해

(D) 검열에 반대하는 유명한 속담을 소개하기 위해

PAGODA TOEFL
Actual Test
READING

06 Inference

- 추론(Inference) 문제는 지문의 내용을 근거로 하여 명시되어 있지 않은 함축적 내용을 추론해 내는 문제로, 논리적인 인과 관계에 근거하여 합리적인 결론을 도출해 내야 한다.
- 질문에 infer 혹은 imply라는 동사가 직접 언급되므로 문제 유형을 파악할 수 있다.
- 지문당 1~2개의 문제가 출제되거나, 아예 출제되지 않을 때도 있다.

📖 문제 유형

- According to paragraph X, what can be inferred about Y?
  X단락에 따르면, Y에 대해 추론할 수 있는 것은 무엇인가?
- It can be inferred from paragraph X that X단락에서 추론할 수 있는 것은?
- Which of the following can be inferred about X? 다음 중 X에 대해 추론할 수 있는 것은 무엇인가?
- Based on the information in paragraph X, what can be inferred about Y?
  X단락의 정보에 근거하여, Y에 대해 추론할 수 있는 것은 무엇인가?
- The author of the passage implies that 지문의 글쓴이가 암시하는 것은?
- What is X believed to indicate? X는 무엇을 가리킨다고 여겨지는가?

💡 문제 풀이 전략

- 주관적인 생각이나 상식에 의한 판단을 피하고, 항상 지문에 주어진 객관적 정보에만 근거하여 정답을 고르도록 한다.
- 지문 내용에 근거하여 추론하되 단순히 지문에 나와 있는 단어나 내용이 담긴 선택지를 정답으로 고르지 않도록 주의한다.
- 추론의 단서가 단락 전체에 광범위하게 분포되어 있는 경우에는 선택지를 먼저 읽고 해당 내용을 지문에서 확인하여 오답을 소거해 나가면서 정답의 범위를 좁히도록 한다.
- 추론 근거는 해당 문장이나 단락 내에 있기도 하지만 지문 전체에 분포되어 있기도 한다.

🚨 피해야 할 오답 유형

- 지문의 내용과 관련이 없는 선택지
- 지문에 추론 근거가 없는 배경 지식에 관한 선택지
- 논리적 비약이 심하거나 지나친 일반화의 오류를 범한 선택지

핵심 유형 공략

TOEFL Reading

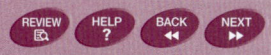

Polaris

Polaris, also known as Alpha Ursae Minoris or the North Star, is a bright star, though not the brightest, located 434 light-years away from Earth. From Earth, however, it is positioned almost straight above Earth's North Pole. For this reason, while other stars appear to move in a circle in the sky due to Earth's rotation, Polaris seems to stay in the same place from anywhere it can be seen on Earth. This unique characteristic allowed sailors of the past to figure out which way was north, approximately where they were on the ocean, and in which direction they were moving. In fact, when lost, scientists have argued that it is safer to rely on Polaris than a compass. Nevertheless, when Egyptians built the pyramids 5,000 years ago, Thuban, in the constellation Draco the Dragon, was the North Star. In fact, the earliest document that refers to Polaris as the North Star was written after the birth of Christ. This is because the place in the sky the North Pole points at changes slowly over time due to small differences in Earth's rotation and Polaris's position.

It can be inferred from the passage that

Ⓐ compasses easily malfunction at sea.
Ⓑ Polaris will not always be the North Star.
Ⓒ Earth's rotation has influenced Polaris.
Ⓓ other stars actually move in a circle.

폴라리스

알파 우르새 미노리스 또는 북극성으로도 알려진 폴라리스는 지구에서 434광년 떨어진 곳에 위치해 있으며, 비록 가장 밝지는 않지만 밝은 별이다. 하지만 지구에서 봤을 때 그것은 지구 북극의 거의 바로 위에 위치해 있다. 이런 이유로, 지구의 자전 때문에 다른 별들이 하늘에서 원을 그리며 움직이는 것처럼 보이는 반면 폴라리스는 지구상에서 볼 수 있는 어느 곳에서도 같은 장소에 머물러 있는 것처럼 보인다. 이 독특한 특성은 옛날 선원들이 어느 쪽이 북쪽인지, 그들이 대략 바다 위 어디에 있는지, 그리고 어느 방향으로 움직이고 있는지 알아낼 수 있게 해주었다. 실제로 과학자들은 길을 잃었을 때 나침반보다 폴라리스에 의지하는 것이 더 안전하다고 주장해 왔다. 그럼에도 불구하고, 이집트인들이 5천 년 전에 피라미드를 지었을 때에는 용자리인 드라코 별자리에서 투반이 북극성이었다. 사실 폴라리스를 북극성이라고 지칭하는 가장 초기의 문서는 그리스도의 탄생 후에 쓰여졌다. 하늘에서 북극이 가리키는 지점이 지구의 자전과 폴라리스 위치의 작은 차이 때문에 시간이 지남에 따라 천천히 바뀌기 때문이다.

지문에서 추론할 수 있는 것은?

Ⓐ 나침반은 바다에서 쉽게 오작동한다.
Ⓑ 폴라리스가 언제나 북극성이지는 않을 것이다.
Ⓒ 지구의 자전이 폴라리스에 영향을 끼쳤다.
Ⓓ 다른 별들은 실제로 원을 그리며 움직인다.

STEP 1   지문에서 질문 대상(핵심어) 찾기

질문의 핵심어 혹은 질문의 선택지에 등장하는 대상들을 지문 안에서 찾는다.

> (...) For this reason, while ⓓ other stars appear to move in a circle in the sky due to Earth's rotation, Polaris seems to stay in the same place from anywhere it can be seen on Earth. (...) In fact, when lost, scientists have argued that it is safer to rely on Polaris than a ⓐ compass. Nevertheless, when Egyptians built the pyramids 5,000 years ago, Thuban, in the constellation Draco the Dragon, was ⓑ the North Star. (...) This is because the place in the sky the North Pole points at changes slowly over time due to small differences in ⓒ Earth's rotation and Polaris's position.

STEP 2   질문 대상의 주변에서 추론의 근거 파악하기

질문 대상이 언급된 문장과 그 주변에서 추론의 근거가 될 만한 내용을 파악한다.

> (...) For this reason, while ⓓ other stars appear to move in a circle in the sky due to Earth's rotation, Polaris seems to stay in the same place from anywhere it can be seen on Earth. (...) In fact, when lost, scientists have argued that it is safer to rely on Polaris than a ⓐ compass. Nevertheless, when Egyptians built the pyramids 5,000 years ago, Thuban, in the constellation Draco the Dragon, was ⓑ the North Star. (...) This is because the place in the sky the North Pole points at changes slowly over time due to small differences in ⓒ Earth's rotation and Polaris's position.
>
> ⓐ 과학자들은 길을 잃었을 때 나침반(compass)보다 폴라리스에 의지하는 것이 더 안전하다고 주장해 왔다.
> ⓑ 5천 년 전에는 용자리인 드라코 별자리에서 투반이 북극성(the North Star)이었다.
> ⓒ 지구의 자전과 폴라리스의 위치(Earth's rotation & Polaris's position)에 작은 차이가 생기기 때문에 시간이 지나면서 북극이 가리키는 지점이 천천히 바뀐다.
> ⓓ 다른 별들(other stars)은 하늘에서 원을 그리며 움직이는 것처럼 보인다.

STEP 3   지문 내용을 근거로 추론할 수 있는 선택지 고르기

지문에서 찾은 추론의 근거 문장에서 함축된 의미를 파악하고, 이를 선택지와 비교해 본다.

> ⓐ compasses easily malfunction at sea. → 길을 잃었을 때 나침반보다 폴라리스에 의지하는 것이 더 안전하다는 주장이 있으나, 바다에서 나침반 고장이 잦다는 의미는 아님 (X)
> ⓑ Polaris will not always be the North Star.
>   → 5천 년 전에는 다른 별이 북극성이었으므로 미래에 폴라리스가 북극성이 아니게 될 가능성 있음 (O)
> ⓒ Earth's rotation has influenced Polaris.
>   → 지구의 자전 때문에 북극의 지점이 변하는 것이지 폴라리스에 영향을 주는 것은 아님 (X)
> ⓓ other stars actually move in a circle.
>   → '다른 별들이 원을 그리며 움직이는 것처럼 보인다'고 했으므로 실제로 움직이는 것은 아님 (X)
>
> 정답: ⓑ Polaris will not always be the North Star.

Sample Question 1

TOEFL Reading

Newton's Law of Gravitation

Physicists enjoy examining phenomena in order to show that a relationship can be found if they are only examined closely enough. This search for unification between phenomena has been going on for centuries. In 1665, Isaac Newton, a young man, who was only 23 at the time, made a fundamental contribution to physics when he showed that the force that holds the Moon in its orbit is the very same force that makes an apple fall. This is taken so much for granted now that it is difficult for us to imagine the past view that the motions of earthbound bodies and heavenly bodies were different kinds of motion and were governed by different sets of laws. Newton concluded that not only does the Earth attract an apple and the Moon, but that each object in the universe attracts every other object. This thought takes a little time to get used to because the familiar attraction of the Earth for earthbound bodies is so great that it overshadows the attractions that these same earthbound bodies have for each other.

It can be inferred from the passage that Isaac Newton

Ⓐ studied astronomy while he was at university.

Ⓑ proposed that some objects repel each other.

Ⓒ believed that celestial objects behave differently.

Ⓓ encountered strong opposition to his theory.

뉴턴의 만유인력 법칙

물리학자들은 현상들을 충분히 면밀하게 조사하면 관련성이 발견될 수 있다는 것을 보여주기 위해 그것들에 대한 연구를 즐긴다. 현상 간의 통합을 위한 이런 연구는 수 세기 동안 지속되어 왔다. 1665년 당시 겨우 스물세 살이었던 젊은 청년 아이작 뉴턴은 달이 궤도를 돌게 하는 힘과 사과를 떨어지게 만드는 힘이 동일하다는 사실을 보여주며 물리학에 핵심적인 공헌을 했다. 이는 현재 매우 당연하게 받아들여져서, 우리는 땅에 있는 물체와 하늘에 있는 물체의 움직임이 다른 종류의 움직임이며 다른 법칙에 의해 지배된다는 과거의 시각을 상상하기 어렵다. 뉴턴은 지구가 사과와 달을 끌어당길 뿐만 아니라, 우주에 있는 물체 하나하나가 외부에 있는 모든 물체를 끌어당긴다는 결론을 내렸다. 이 개념에 익숙해지는 데에는 약간의 시간이 걸리는데, 그 이유는 지구가 땅 위에 있는 물체들을 끌어당기는 우리에게 익숙한 인력이 너무 커서 지상의 이 물체들끼리 서로를 끌어당기는 인력을 무색하게 만들기 때문이다.

지문에서 아이작 뉴턴에 대해 추론할 수 있는 것은?

Ⓐ 대학에서 천문학을 공부했다

Ⓑ 몇몇 물체가 서로를 밀어낸다고 제안했다

Ⓒ 천체(天體)가 다르게 움직인다고 믿었다

Ⓓ 그의 이론에 대한 강한 반박에 부딪혔다

Sample Question 2

TOEFL Reading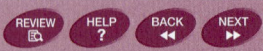

Somali Pirates

Though we live in a progressive age, Somalia's 1,880-mile coastline is currently crawling with pirates. This is a serious problem for the Somali people given that the country is dependent on food aid from other nations, which arrives mostly by ship. The pirates are organized and work in teams. The pirates even have a spokesman. The pirates attack everything from yachts to oil tankers and usually demand millions of dollars in ransom for the ships and their crews. 2010 was one of the worst years on record, with more than 50 ships attacked, 25 hijacked, and at least 14 being held by pirates. Somali waters are now considered the most dangerous in the world. The Somali pirates are typically former fishermen who have turned to the more lucrative work of patrolling the seas with binoculars, rifles, and rocket-propelled grenades. They travel in light speedboats deployed from a mother ship and have attacked tankers as far as 300 miles from the coast. Somali officials say the number of pirates is increasing. With more than 1,000 gunmen at their disposal, they have evolved into a sophisticated, organized crime ring headquartered along the rocky shores of northern Somalia.

It can be inferred from the passage that Somali pirates

Ⓐ put their countrymen in danger as well as ships and crews of other countries.

Ⓑ run training camps and purchase political influence with ransom money.

Ⓒ gather thousands of applicants mostly consisting of former fishermen for their training.

Ⓓ are forced to dispose of their arms by the government as their numbers are increasing.

소말리아 해적

우리는 진보의 시대에 살고 있지만, 1,880마일에 이르는 소말리아의 해안선은 지금도 해적들로 들끓고 있다. 소말리아가 다른 나라로부터의 식량 원조에 의존하고 있으며 그 대부분이 배편으로 온다는 점에서 이는 소말리아 사람들에게 심각한 문제이다. 해적들은 조직화되어 있으며 팀으로 일한다. 해적들에게는 심지어 대변인도 있다. 해적들은 요트부터 유조선에 이르기까지 모든 것을 공격하며 배나 선원의 몸값으로 보통 수백만 달러를 요구한다. 2010년은 기록상 최악의 해 중 하나였는데, 그 해에는 50척 이상의 배가 공격을 당했고, 25척이 납치되었으며, 최소 14척이 해적들에게 억류되었다. 소말리아의 바다는 현재 세계에서 가장 위험한 곳으로 간주되고 있다. 소말리아 해적들은 쌍안경, 소총, 로켓 추진 유탄을 들고 바다를 순찰하는 좀 더 돈벌이가 되는 일로 전향한 전직 어부들인 경우가 일반적이다. 그들은 모선에 배치된 경쾌속정을 타고 이동하며 연안에서 300마일이나 떨어진 곳에 있는 유조선들을 공격한 적도 있다. 소말리아 정부 관계자들은 해적들의 수가 증가하고 있다고 말한다. 언제든 현장에 투입할 수 있는 1천여 명의 무장 병력을 거느리고 있는 그들은 소말리아 북부의 암석 해안에 본거지를 둔 정교하고 조직화된 범죄단으로 진화했다.

지문에서 소말리아 해적에 대해 추론할 수 있는 것은?

Ⓐ 다른 국가의 배와 선원들뿐만 아니라 자기 나라 사람들까지 위험에 처하게 한다.

Ⓑ 몸값으로 받은 돈으로 훈련 캠프를 운영하고 정치적 영향력을 얻는다.

Ⓒ 훈련을 위해 주로 전직 어부로 구성된 수천 명의 지원자들을 모집한다.

Ⓓ 숫자가 늘어남에 따라 정부로부터 무기를 처분하라는 압력을 받는다.

PAGODA TOEFL

Actual Test

READING

07 Insertion

- 문장 삽입(Insertion) 문제는 글 전체의 논리적 흐름에 맞도록 주어진 문장을 적절한 위치에 삽입하는 문제로, 지문에 주어진 문장이 삽입될 수 있는 후보 네 곳이 박스[■]로 표시되어 있다.
- 지문당 1개의 문제가 출제되며, 항상 끝에서 두 번째 문제(9번)로 출제된다.

📖 문제 유형

Look at the four squares [■] that indicate where the following sentence could be added to the passage. 지문에 다음 문장이 들어갈 수 있는 위치를 나타내는 네 개의 사각형[■]을 확인하시오.
---------------------------------- [삽입 문장] ----------------------------------
Where would the sentence best fit? 이 문장이 들어가기에 가장 적합한 곳은?

💡 문제 풀이 전략

- 지문 전체를 빠르게 훑어 읽으면서 신속하게 삽입 문장과 주위 문장 간의 연결 관계를 파악하도록 한다.
- 삽입 문장이나 지문에서 단서를 파악하기 어려운 경우, 총 4개의 [■]에 문장을 차례대로 넣어서 살펴본다.
- 삽입 문장은 앞뒤 문장과의 관계가 유기적이어야 하며, 단락 전체 혹은 지문 전체의 논리적인 흐름에서도 벗어나지 않아야 한다.
- 삽입 문장에서 지시어, 연결어, the+명사, 반복어구, 유사어구 등의 단서를 찾는다.

지시어	it, they, this, these, that, those, one, some, both, the former, the latter
연결어	[예시] for example, for instance [부연] in addition, furthermore, in other words, also, besides, similarly [대조] but, however, in contrast, on the contrary, meanwhile, on the other hand [인과] therefore, so, as a result, because of, thus, due to, consequently, in conclusion
반복어구	삽입 문장의 중심 소재, 앞뒤 문장의 대응 표현

🚨 피해야 할 오답 유형

- 삽입 문장에 나온 단어들이 언급된 문장 주변의 위치
- 앞뒤 문장과는 연결되지만 전체 단락의 흐름을 저해하는 위치
- 문장을 삽입했을 때 크게 어색하지는 않지만 연결성이 부족한 위치

핵심 유형 공략

TOEFL Reading

Swirling Waters

A whirlpool is a swirling body of water created when two opposing currents meet. Very few of them have the power to be truly dangerous, although some of the largest ones are quite dangerous to swimmers and small boats. [■A] The strong rotating current may exhaust swimmers enough to drown them or damage boats. [■B] These accounts usually have whirlpools that not only rotate, but also pull downwards, swallowing ships. When this suction does happen in nature, it is caused by a crack opening in the ocean floor. The suction is created by water pouring down into the newly opened space and is a one-time occurrence. [■C] Regularly occurring whirlpools are caused by powerful currents that flow through narrow, shallow straits, and some appear at the bases of waterfalls. The larger ones are usually referred to as maelstroms. The most powerful whirlpool can reach speeds of nearly 28 kilometers per hour. [■D] It is located near the Lofoten Islands of Norway, and it was the first to be referred to as a maelstrom. This is actually a Dutch term that translates as "grinding current."

Look at the four squares [■] that indicate where the following sentence could be added to the passage.

However, the power of whirlpools is often exaggerated, especially in fiction but also in historical records.

Where would the sentence best fit?

Click on a square [■] to add the sentence to the passage.

소용돌이치는 물

소용돌이는 두 개의 상반된 해류가 만났을 때 생성되는 빙빙 도는 수역이다. 극소수만 정말로 위험을 끼칠 수 있는 위력을 가지고 있지만, 가장 큰 것들 중 일부는 수영하는 사람들과 작은 배에 꽤 위험하다. [■A] 강한 회전 해류는 수영하는 사람들을 익사할 만큼 지치게 만들거나 배에 피해를 입힐 수 있다. [■B] 보통 이러한 경우에는 회전을 할 뿐만 아니라 아래로 끌어당겨 배를 삼키는 소용돌이가 존재한다. 이러한 흡입이 자연에서 일어나는 경우는 해저의 균열 구멍에 의해 발생하는 것이다. 이 흡입은 새로 열린 공간에 물이 쏟아져 내리면서 만들어지는 것으로 일회성 현상이다. [■C] 규칙적으로 발생하는 소용돌이는 좁고 얕은 해협을 통과해 흐르는 강력한 물살에 의해 발생하며, 일부는 폭포 아래 부분에 나타난다. 큰 것들은 보통 마엘스트롬이라고 불린다. 가장 강력한 소용돌이는 거의 시속 28킬로미터 속도에 다다를 수 있다. [■D] 그것은 노르웨이의 로포텐 제도 근처에 위치해 있으며, 최초로 마엘스트롬이라고 일컬어졌다. 이것은 사실 '갈아넣는 해류'로 번역되는 네덜란드어 단어이다.

지문에 다음 문장이 들어갈 수 있는 위치를 나타내는 네 개의 사각형[■]을 확인하시오.

하지만 소용돌이의 위력은 흔히 과장되곤 하는데, 소설에서 특히 그렇지만 역사 기록에서도 그러하다.

이 문장이 들어가기에 가장 적합한 곳은?

STEP 1   주어진 삽입 문장을 읽으며 단서 파악하기

삽입 문장을 읽으며 문장의 성격과 단서를 파악하여 해당 단락 내에서의 위치를 가늠해 본다.

삽입 문장	However, the power of whirlpools is often exaggerated, especially in fiction but also in historical records. (소용돌이의 위력은 흔히 과장됨)
문장의 성격	반론/부연/예시 (주장이나 판단의 문장 뒤에 나오는 성격)
문장 내 단서	However [연결어: 역접]

→ '소용돌이의 위력이 강력함'을 주장하거나 판단하는 문장 뒤에 위치할 가능성이 높음

STEP 2   해당 단락에서 삽입 문장과의 연결 고리 찾기

네 개의 사각형[■] 주변 문장에서 삽입 문장 내 단서와 이어지는 연결 고리를 찾는다.

삽입 문장	However (역접의 연결어), the power of whirlpools is often exaggerated, especially in fiction but also in historical records. (소용돌이의 위력은 흔히 과장됨)
지문	Very few of them have the power to be truly dangerous ... small boats. [■A] The strong rotating current may exhaust swimmers enough to drown them or damage boats. (인명과 재산을 앗아가는 소용돌이의 위험성) [■B] These accounts (가리키는 대상: fiction & historical records) usually have whirlpools that not only rotate, but also pull downwards, swallowing ships. (...) The suction is created by water pouring down into the newly opened space and is a one-time occurrence. [■C] Regularly occurring whirlpools are caused by powerful currents (...) The most powerful whirlpool can reach speeds of nearly 28 kilometers per hour. [■D] It is located near the Lofoten Islands of Norway, (...)

STEP 3   정답 위치에 삽입하여 문맥을 통해 최종 확인하기

여러 단서를 토대로 고른 위치에 문장을 삽입해 보고 해석과 문맥을 통해 최종적으로 확인한다.

The strong rotating current may exhaust swimmers enough to drown them or damage boats. [■B] However, the power of whirlpools is often exaggerated, especially in fiction but also in historical records. These accounts usually have whirlpools that not only rotate, but also pull downwards, swallowing ships.

정답: [■B]

Sample Question 1

TOEFL Reading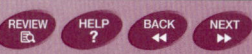

A Nation of Immigrants

One of the most common statements that appear in speeches made by election day hopefuls is, "We are a nation of immigrants." By uttering these words, the politician is trying to appeal to one of the few things that nearly all Americans, besides the Native Americans, have in common. The fact that the vast majority of Americans are immigrants or the descendants of immigrants helps to define the characteristics of the American people. And it also explains part of what is extraordinary in the relatively short history of the United States of America. [■A] Though Americans lack some traditions that exist in these other countries, there is the common experience of emigrating from another country. [■B] Many Americans, now and throughout the country's history, live under the belief that they are agents of destiny, meant to settle in and build up America. [■C] Herman Melville, the American author of *Moby Dick*, expressed this same sentiment in a different way: "Our blood is as the flood of the Amazon, made up of a thousand noble currents all pouring into one." [■D]

Look at the four squares [■] that indicate where the following sentence could be added to the passage.

Americans cannot refer to their ancient soil or their founding race like the citizens of other homogenous countries.

Where would the sentence best fit?

Click on a square [■] to add the sentence to the passage.

이민자들의 국가

당선을 꿈꾸는 선거 후보자들이 하는 연설에서 나오는 가장 흔한 말 중 하나는 "우리는 이민자들의 국가입니다"라는 것이다. 이러한 말을 함으로써, 그 정치가는 북미 원주민을 제외한 거의 모든 미국인들에게 해당되는 몇 안 되는 공통점들 중 하나에 호소하려고 하는 것이다. 대다수의 미국인들이 이민자이거나 이민자의 후손이라는 사실은 미국인들의 특징을 규정하는 데 도움이 된다. 그리고 이는 또한 비교적 짧은 미합중국 역사에서 특이한 점을 일부 설명해 준다. [■A] 미국인들은 다른 단일 민족 국가들의 시민들처럼 그들의 고대 영토 또는 건국 민족에 대해 말하지 못한다. 미국인들에게는 다른 국가들에 존재하는 일부 전통이 없지만, 다른 나라에서 이민을 왔다는 공통된 경험이 있다. [■B] 많은 미국인들은 지금이나 역사적으로나 자신이 미국에 정착하여 미국을 세우도록 정해진 숙명을 타고난 사람들이라는 믿음으로 살고 있다. [■C] 〈모비딕〉을 쓴 미국 작가 허먼 멜빌은 이와 같은 감정을 다른 방식으로 표현했다. "우리의 피는 모두가 한 곳으로 흘러들어 가는 천 개의 고귀한 지류로 이루어진 아마존 강의 물결과 같다." [■D]

지문에 다음 문장이 들어갈 수 있는 위치를 나타내는 네 개의 사각형[■]을 확인하시오.

미국인들은 다른 단일 민족 국가들의 시민들처럼 그들의 고대 영토 또는 건국 민족에 대해 말하지 못한다.

이 문장이 들어가기에 가장 적합한 곳은? [■A]

Sample Question 2

TOEFL Reading

Environmental Value

All economic systems depend upon the products, services, and functions provided by the ecosystem, and they would collapse without it. [■A] In a sense, this means that its value is infinite, but that does not mean that it is incalculable. [■B] The value of ecosystem services like waste assimilation can and must be calculated. [■C] This takes a significant toll on the ecosystem, but companies are rarely held accountable for the impact that they have. [■D] When a company sets a price for its product, it uses what is called full cost pricing. This calculation includes the direct costs like materials, time, and labor used in manufacturing the item plus the costs of research and development and an extra amount so that the manufacturer can make a profit. This calculation must be expanded to include the direct and indirect costs that production has on the environment so that the money can be used to help renewable resources recover and to protect non-renewable resources from total depletion.

Look at the four squares [■] that indicate where the following sentence could be added to the passage.

The environment receives huge amounts of waste from various stages in production, and it processes what it can, but the rest remains as pollution.

Where would the sentence best fit?

Click on a square [■] to add the sentence to the passage.

환경 가치

모든 경제 체계는 생태계에 의해 제공되는 상품, 서비스와 기능에 의존하며 그것이 없으면 무너질 것이다. [■A] 어떤 면에서 이는 그것의 가치가 무한이라는 것을 뜻하지만 계산할 수 없다는 의미는 아니다. [■B] 폐기물 정화 같은 생태계 서비스의 가치는 계산될 수 있으며 반드시 계산되어야 한다. [■C] 환경은 생산의 여러 단계에서 대량의 폐기물을 받아내며, 그것이 처리할 수 있는 것은 그렇게 하지만 나머지는 오염으로 남게 된다. 이는 생태계에 큰 피해를 입히지만 기업들은 자신이 끼치는 영향을 거의 책임지지 않는다. [■D] 기업은 상품의 가격을 정할 때 전부원가 가격책정이라는 것을 사용한다. 이 계산법에는 그 제품을 제조하는 데 사용된 재료, 시간, 노동력과 같은 직접비용에 연구개발 비용과 제조사가 이윤을 낼 수 있게 추가적인 금액을 더한 것이 포함된다. 이 계산법은 재생가능 자원이 회복되는 것과 재생불가능 자원을 완전 고갈로부터 보호하는 것을 지원하는 데 돈이 사용될 수 있도록 생산이 환경에 끼치는 직간접적인 비용을 포함하는 것으로 확장되어야 한다.

지문에 다음 문장이 들어갈 수 있는 위치를 나타내는 네 개의 사각형[■]을 확인하시오.

환경은 생산의 여러 단계에서 대량의 폐기물을 받아내며, 그것이 처리할 수 있는 것은 그렇게 하지만 나머지는 오염으로 남게 된다.

이 문장이 들어가기에 가장 적합한 곳은? [■C]

**PAGODA TOEFL
Actual Test
READING**

08 Summary

- 요약(Summary) 문제는 주어진 도입 문장(Introductory sentence)을 읽고 6개의 선택지 중에서 지문의 핵심 내용을 담고 있는 3개의 선택지를 골라 요약문을 완성하는 문제이다.
- Drag-n-Drop 유형으로, 선택지를 골라 순서에 상관없이 요약표의 [•] 옆에 끌어다 놓으면 된다.
- 지문의 마지막 문제(10번)로 나오며 Category Chart 유형과 번갈아 가며 0~1개의 문제가 출제된다. 다만 Category Chart 문제보다 Summary 문제의 출제 비율이 훨씬 더 높다.
- 정답 3개를 모두 맞혔을 경우 2점이며, 이를 기준으로 오답 1개당 1점씩 감점된다.

📖 문제 유형

Directions: An introductory sentence for a brief summary of the passage is provided below. Complete the summary by selecting the THREE answer choices that express the most important ideas in the passage. Some sentences do not belong in the summary because they express ideas that are not presented in the passage or are minor ideas in the passage. ***This question is worth 2 points.***

지시문: 지문을 간략하게 요약한 글의 첫 문장이 아래 제시되어 있다. 지문의 가장 중요한 내용을 표현하는 세 개의 선택지를 골라 요약문을 완성하시오. 일부 문장들은 지문에 제시되지 않았거나 지문의 지엽적인 내용을 나타내기 때문에 요약문에 포함되지 않는다. *이 문제의 배점은 2점이다.*

-------------------------------- [도입 문장] --------------------------------

-
-
-

Answer Choices

Ⓐ ------------------------------ Ⓓ ------------------------------
Ⓑ ------------------------------ Ⓔ ------------------------------
Ⓒ ------------------------------ Ⓕ ------------------------------

Drag your answer choices to the spaces where they belong.
To remove an answer choice, click on it. To review the passage, click on **View Text**.

선택한 답안을 맞는 곳에 끌어다 넣으시오.
선택한 답안을 삭제하려면, 답안에 대고 클릭하시오. 지문을 다시 보려면 지문 보기를 클릭하시오

💡 문제 풀이 전략

- 지문 내용을 요약, 재구성하는 유형이므로 지문을 읽으며 노트 정리하는 습관을 들인다.
- 글의 중심 내용(major idea)과 부가 정보(minor idea)를 구분하는 연습을 해 두는 것이 좋다.
- 주어진 도입문과 노트 정리를 활용하면 지문을 다시 읽지 않아도 오답을 소거할 수 있어 시간을 단축할 수 있다.

🚨 피해야 할 오답 유형

- 지문에 언급되지 않았거나 지문과 다른 내용이 담긴 선택지
- 지문에 언급된 내용 중 부가적인 정보(minor idea)가 담긴 선택지

📖 핵심 유형 공략

STEP 1 단락별로 핵심 내용 정리하기

주어진 도입 문장을 읽고 6개의 선택지 중에서 중심 내용과 부가 정보를 구분한다. 시간 단축을 위해 처음 지문을 읽을 때 단락별 핵심 내용을 노트에 정리해 둔다.

노트 정리 예시	진공 활동
	단락 1. 동물들의 행동은 학습이 아닌 유전적 영향의 결과
	단락 2. 진공 활동은 경험이나 정상적 자극 없이 하는 유전적 행동
	단락 3. 사육 동물들은 불가능한 상황에서도 야생 동물들의 습성을 모방

STEP 2 예상 오답 소거하기

노트 정리한 내용을 참고하여 지문에 언급되지 않은 선택지를 예상 오답으로 소거한다. 지문에 언급된 내용일지라도 부가 정보를 담고 있는 선택지는 예상 오답으로 소거한다. 노트에 정리해 놓은 단락별 요지와 가장 가까운 내용의 선택지 3개를 골라 표를 완성한다.

STEP 3 남은 선택지가 도입문을 뒷받침하는지 확인하기

위의 두 단계를 통해 정답을 확정하기 어려운 경우에는 지문을 다시 빠르게 훑어 읽으면서 관련 내용을 확인한다. 예상 오답을 소거하고 남은 선택지들이 도입 문장을 뒷받침하는 문장인지 확인하여 정답을 확정한다.

Sample Question 1

TOEFL Reading

Divinization and the Roman Catholic Church

In the Catholic Church, divinization is the belief that people can be made divine or holy through the performance of particular religious rituals called sacraments. The practice of rituals is present in many religions, but perhaps it is most strongly associated with Catholics. This vital tenet of the Catholic religion is most strongly manifested through the taking of Holy Communion (Eucharist). The majority of Christian faiths also practice this ritual, but since they almost exclusively stemmed from the Catholic Church, any distinctions in how they partake of the Eucharist are minor. The essential nature of this ceremony is the belief that by reenacting the events of Christ's Last Supper with his disciples members of the church are also able to affirm themselves as loyal followers. At his final meal, Christ blessed the bread and the wine, calling them his body and blood, and the disciples ate and drank them, thereby taking some of his holiness into themselves. This gift, as the most authoritative of Catholic theologians Saint Thomas Aquinas wrote, "surpasses every capability of created nature, since it is nothing short of a partaking of the Divine Nature, which exceeds every other nature."

Directions: An introductory sentence for a brief summary of the passage is provided below. Complete the summary by selecting the THREE answer choices that express the most important ideas in the passage. Some sentences do not belong in the summary because they express ideas that are not presented in the passage or are minor ideas in the passage. ***This question is worth 2 points.***

Divinization can be realized through the ceremony of Holy Communion in the Catholic Church.

-
-
-

Answer Choices

(A) It was Saint Thomas Aquinas that emphasized the importance of divinization and Holy Communion.
(B) Believers reproduce the sacred event of partaking of Christ's body and blood when performing Communion.
(C) Followers believe they can testify their loyalty to Christ by imitating the Last Supper.
(D) Christ's disciples ate and drank the sacred bread and wine to spread the holiness of Christ.
(E) The core of Catholicism is well represented in the process of taking Communion.
(F) The procedures of Holy Communion are quite different in other Christian religions.

Drag your answer choices to the spaces where they belong.
To remove an answer choice, click on it. To review the passage, click on **View Text**.

신성화와 로마 가톨릭 교회

가톨릭 교회에서 신성화는 성례라 불리는 특별한 종교 의식을 수행함으로써 사람이 신성해지거나 성스러워질 수 있다는 믿음이다. 의식의 실행은 많은 종교에서 찾아볼 수 있지만, 아마도 가톨릭교도와 가장 강하게 연관되어 있을 것이다. 가톨릭교의 필수 교리는 성찬식(성체 성사)에 참여함으로써 가장 강하게 드러난다. 대다수의 기독교 신앙에서도 이 의식을 행하지만, 그 신앙들이 거의 가톨릭 교회에서만 파생된 것이기 때문에 성체를 모시는 방법에 대한 차이는 작다. 이 의식의 중요한 본질은 그리스도가 최후의 만찬에서 그의 제자들과 함께 했던 일들을 재연함으로써 교회의 신자들도 스스로를 충실한 신앙인들이라고 주장할 수 있다는 믿음이다. 마지막 만찬에서 그리스도는 빵과 포도주를 그의 몸과 피라고 부르며 축성했고, 제자들은 그것들을 먹고 마심으로써 그리스도의 신성함을 받아들였다. 가톨릭 신학자들 중에서 최고 권위자인 성 토마스 아퀴나스는 이 선물이 "창조된 본성의 어떤 능력보다도 뛰어난데, 이는 다른 모든 본성을 능가하는 신성을 나누는 것이나 다름없기 때문이다"라고 기록했다.

지시문: 지문을 간략하게 요약한 글의 첫 문장이 아래에 제시되어 있다. 지문의 가장 중요한 내용을 표현하는 세 개의 선택지를 골라 요약문을 완성하시오. 일부 문장들은 지문에 제시되지 않았거나 지문의 지엽적인 내용을 나타내기 때문에 요약문에 포함되지 않는다. *이 문제의 배점은 2점이다.*

신성화는 가톨릭 교회의 성찬식 의식을 통해 이루어질 수 있다.

- Ⓑ 신도들은 성찬식을 거행할 때 그리스도의 몸과 피를 먹고마시는 신성한 사건을 재현한다.
- Ⓒ 신도들은 최후의 만찬을 모방함으로써, 그리스도에 대한 자신들의 충성을 증명할 수 있다고 믿는다.
- Ⓔ 가톨릭교의 핵심은 성찬식에 참여하는 과정을 통해 잘 나타난다.

Ⓐ 신성화와 성찬식의 중요성을 강조한 것은 성 토마스 아퀴나스였다.
Ⓓ 그리스도의 제자들은 그리스도의 거룩함을 전파하기 위해 성스러운 빵과 포도주를 먹고 마셨다.
Ⓕ 성찬식 절차가 다른 기독교에서는 상당히 다르다.

Sample Question 2

TOEFL Reading

The Politician Illusion

In a sense, politics has always been something of a dishonest game. Voters in democratic societies insist upon their belief in a higher order. They cling to this politico-religion that promises a better life and passionately defend the illusion that the men and women that choose to lead them are of a finer nature than themselves. Traditionally, the successful politician maintains this illusion. To succeed today, a politician must exploit this illusion to the fullest extent, especially if he wishes to be president. In 1967, an advisor to President Richard Nixon wrote in a memorandum, "Potential presidents are measured against an ideal that's a combination of leading man, God, father, hero, pope, king, with maybe a touch of the avenging Furies thrown in." This same advisor, perhaps aware that Nixon qualified only as "father," discussed improvements that would have to be made, not upon Nixon himself, but upon the image of him which was perceived by the voters.

Directions: An introductory sentence for a brief summary of the passage is provided below. Complete the summary by selecting the THREE answer choices that express the most important ideas in the passage. Some sentences do not belong in the summary because they express ideas that are not presented in the passage or are minor ideas in the passage. ***This question is worth 2 points.***

Politics in democratic societies rely on the illusory hopes of the public.

-
-
-

Answer Choices

Ⓐ Nowadays, political candidates need to maximize this illusion to win an election, especially for a presidential election.
Ⓑ The admirable reflections on politicians are composed of figures such as leader, God, father, hero, pope, and king.
Ⓒ This fantasy is usually due to the belief that politicians are men of more commendable qualities.
Ⓓ According to a political consultant, successful politicians should possess all kinds of ideal images created by the public.
Ⓔ Richard Nixon could not meet the needs of the general public at the moment of his presidential election.
Ⓕ It is deceitful and vulgar for statesmen to make use of their fake fantasies in order to gain popularity.

Drag your answer choices to the spaces where they belong.
To remove an answer choice, click on it. To review the passage, click on **View Text**.

정치가의 환상

어떤 면에서 정치는 항상 일종의 부정적인 게임 같은 것이다. 민주주의 사회의 유권자들은 더 고차원적으로 자신들의 소신을 주장한다. 유권자들은 더 나은 삶을 약속하는 정치 종교에 의존하고 그들이 지도자로 선택한 남녀가 그들 자신보다 더 훌륭한 본성을 지니고 있을 것이라는 환상을 열렬히 옹호한다. 전통적으로, 성공한 정치가는 이런 환상을 유지한다. 오늘날 정치가가 성공하기 위해서는, 특히 대통령이 되고자 한다면 이러한 환상을 충분히 이용해야 한다. 1967년에 리처드 닉슨 대통령의 한 고문은 비망록에 다음과 같이 적었다. "대통령 후보자들은 지도자, 하나님, 아버지, 영웅, 교황과 왕을 합쳐 놓은 것에다가 복수의 세 여신까지 살짝 가미한 이상형과 비교하여 평가된다." 아마도 닉슨이 '아버지'로서의 자질밖에 없다는 것을 간파했던 그 고문은 닉슨 본인이 아니라 유권자들에게 인지되는 그의 이미지에 대해 이루어져야 할 개선점을 논한 것이었다.

지시문: 지문을 간략하게 요약한 글의 첫 문장이 아래 제시되어 있다. 지문의 가장 중요한 내용을 표현하는 세 개의 선택지를 골라 요약문을 완성하시오. 일부 문장들은 지문에 제시되지 않았거나 지문의 지엽적인 내용을 나타내기 때문에 요약문에 포함되지 않는다. *이 문제의 배점은 2점이다.*

민주주의 사회에서 정치는 대중들의 환상에 기반한 희망에 의존한다.

- Ⓐ 오늘날 정치 후보자들은 선거, 특히 대통령 선거에서 이기기 위해 이러한 환상을 극대화할 필요가 있다.
- Ⓒ 이러한 환상은 보통 정치가들이 더 훌륭한 성품을 지닌 사람들이라는 믿음에서 비롯된다.
- Ⓓ 한 정치 고문에 따르면, 성공한 정치가들은 대중들이 만들어낸 이상적인 모든 이미지를 지니고 있어야 한다.

Ⓑ 정치가들에게 투영되는 존경할 만한 모습은 지도자, 하나님, 아버지, 영웅, 교황, 왕 등의 인물로 이루어져 있다.

Ⓔ 리처드 닉슨은 대통령 선거 시기에 일반 대중의 요구를 충족시킬 수 없었다.

Ⓕ 정치가들이 인기를 얻기 위해 가짜 환상을 이용하는 것은 기만적이고 천박하다.

09 Category Chart

- 분류(Category Chart) 문제는 주어진 7개/9개의 선택지 중에서 5개/7개를 골라 지문에서 비교, 대조되고 있는 각각의 범주(category)에 분류해 넣는 문제이다.
- Drag-n-Drop 유형으로, 선택지를 골라 순서에 상관없이 표의 [•] 옆에 끌어다 놓으면 된다.
- 지문의 마지막 문제(10번)로 나오며 Summary 유형과 번갈아 가며 0~1개의 문제가 출제된다. 다만 Summary 유형에 비해 출제 빈도가 현저히 낮다.
- 선택지가 7개일 경우에는 정답 5개 기준으로 3점 만점, 선택지가 9개일 경우에는 정답 7개 기준으로 4점 만점이며, 오답 1개당 1점씩 감점된다.

문제 유형

Directions: Complete the table by matching the sentences below. Select the appropriate sentences from the answer choices and match them to the category to which they relate. TWO of the answer choices will NOT be used. **This question is worth 3 points.**

지시문: 아래 문장들을 알맞게 넣어 표를 완성하시오. 선택지에서 적절한 문장을 골라 관계 있는 범주에 연결하시오. 선택지 중 두 개는 정답이 될 수 없다. *이 문제의 배점은 3점이다.*

Answer Choices	Category 1
Ⓐ -------------------------------	•
Ⓑ -------------------------------	•
Ⓒ -------------------------------	•
Ⓓ -------------------------------	**Category 2**
Ⓔ -------------------------------	•
Ⓕ -------------------------------	•
Ⓖ -------------------------------	

Drag your answer choices to the spaces where they belong.
To remove an answer choice, click on it. To review the passage, click on **View Text**.

💡 문제 풀이 전략

- 노트 정리가 반드시 필요한 유형이므로, 지문의 제목이나 문제 유형을 미리 확인 후 지문 내용을 범주별로 정리해 두도록 한다.
- 노트 정리를 하기 전에 표에 어떤 범주가 제시되어 있는지 먼저 확인하는 것이 좋다.
- 비교, 대조 지문의 전개 방식(AB-AB방식/AA-BB방식)을 파악해 두면 노트 정리에 도움이 된다.
- 각 항목에 해당되는 정보를 고를 때, 이 선택지들이 지문 내용을 재진술하고 있음에 유의한다.

🚨 피해야 할 오답 유형

- 지문에 언급되지 않았거나 지문과 다른 내용이 담긴 선택지
- 단순히 지문에 쓰인 단어나 표현으로 이루어져 있는 선택지
- 지문과 화제는 같지만 두 범주의 정보가 혼재되어 있는 선택지
- 비교, 대조되는 두 개의 범주 중에 어디에도 해당되지 않는 선택지

📖 핵심 유형 공략

STEP 1 지문을 읽으며 항목별로 노트 정리하기

노트 정리 예시	Synthetic Diamonds	Simulated Diamonds
	1. identical physical properties to natural gems but are made in a lab 2. jewelers have difficulty determining them 3. more perfect than natural stones (fewer flaws) 4. using the HPHT technique	1. look like other genuine stones 2. use the mineral (cubic zirconium) 3. simple examination → it is false

STEP 2 노트의 항목과 선택지를 비교하여 범주표 완성하기

노트에 정리하지 못한 내용은 View Text 버튼을 눌러 지문에서 다시 확인한다.

STEP 3 남은 선택지 2개의 오답 여부를 재확인하여 정답 확정하기

지문에 언급되지 않았거나 지문의 내용과 다른 선택지는 오답 처리하여 정답을 확정한다.

Sample Question

TOEFL Reading

Bees in Agriculture

The bees utilized in agriculture have traditionally been honeybees because they pollinate farmers' crops and produce a substantial amount of honey. Honeybees live in large colonies that contain thousands of individuals, which means that they can cover large areas. They also communicate by dancing to tell their hive mates where a food source can be found. However, honeybees are not necessarily the best choice for pollinating certain crops. Honeybees are very sensitive to weather conditions, and they are only active during the daytime. Honeybees cannot tolerate temperatures below 10 degrees Celsius, and even light drizzle will make honeybees stay in their hives. Bumblebees, on the other hand, are able to handle a wider range of weather and light conditions. They can easily absorb heat even from weak sunlight, and their thicker body hair conserves warmth much better. They can also generate their own heat internally by vibrating their flight muscles. This technique is very similar to the shivering that mammals employ. They can also fly in much stronger wind conditions, and they are not deterred by light rain. Bumblebee tongues are longer than those of honeybees, so they can reach nectar in flowers that honeybees cannot. Bumblebees also visit flowers that do not offer nectar in order to collect pollen.

Directions: Complete the table by matching the sentences below. Select the appropriate sentences from the answer choices and match them to the category to which they relate. TWO of the answer choices will NOT be used. *This question is worth 3 points.*

Answer Choices	Honeybees
(A) Able to fly when there is precipitation (B) Share locations of food sources with other bees (C) Use shivering to maintain body temperature (D) More active during daytime than in twilight (E) Transport pollen to other insects (F) Visit flowers that do not offer nectar (G) Live in large colonies	• • •
	Bumblebees
	• •

Drag your answer choices to the spaces where they belong.
To remove an answer choice, click on it. To review the passage, click on **View Text**.

농업에서의 벌들

농업에 이용된 벌들은 전통적으로 꿀벌이었는데 그 이유는 이들이 농부들의 작물을 수분해 주고 많은 양의 꿀을 만들어 내기 때문이다. 꿀벌은 수천 마리의 벌들이 포함되어 있는 큰 집단으로 사는데, 이것이 이들이 큰 구역을 아우를 수 있다는 뜻이다. 이들은 또한 식량원을 찾을 수 있는 곳을 벌집 식구들에게 알리기 위해 춤으로 소통을 한다. 그러나 꿀벌은 특정 작물을 수분하기에 반드시 최적의 선택지인 것은 아니다. 꿀벌은 날씨 조건에 매우 예민하며 낮에만 활동한다. 꿀벌은 섭씨 10도 이하의 기온을 견디지 못하며 가벼운 이슬비만 내려도 벌집 안에 머문다. 반면 호박벌은 더 다양한 날씨와 빛 조건에 대응할 수 있다. 심지어 약한 햇빛으로부터 열기를 흡수할 수 있으며, 이들의 더 두꺼운 털은 온기를 훨씬 더 잘 보존하게 해 준다. 또한 비행 근육을 진동하게 하여 내부적으로 스스로의 열기를 생산할 수 있다. 이 기술은 포유류가 이용하는 몸의 떨림과 아주 비슷하다. 호박벌은 또한 훨씬 더 강한 바람 조건에서도 날 수 있으며 약한 비 때문에 행동을 그만두지 않는다. 호박벌의 혀는 꿀벌의 혀보다 더 길어서 꿀벌이 닿지 못하는 꽃 내부의 꿀에도 닿을 수 있다. 또한 호박벌은 꽃가루를 모으기 위해 꿀을 제공하지 않는 꽃에도 찾아간다.

지시문: 아래 문장들을 알맞게 넣어 표를 완성하시오. 선택지에서 적절한 문장을 골라 관계 있는 범주에 연결하시오. 선택지 중 두 개는 정답이 될 수 없다. *이 문제의 배점은 3점이다.*

선택지	꿀벌
Ⓐ 강수가 있을 때 날 수 있다 Ⓑ 다른 벌들과 식량원의 위치를 공유한다 Ⓒ 떨림을 이용해 몸의 온도를 유지한다 Ⓓ 해 질 녘보다 낮에 더 활발하다 Ⓔ 꽃가루를 다른 곤충들에게 옮긴다 Ⓕ 꿀을 제공하지 않는 꽃들을 찾아간다 Ⓖ 큰 집단으로 서식한다	• Ⓑ • Ⓓ • Ⓖ
	호박벌
	• Ⓐ • Ⓕ

PART 02
Actual Tests

Actual Test 01

Actual Test 02

Actual Test 03

Actual Test 04

Actual Test 05

Actual Test 06

Actual Test 07

Actual Test 01

TOEFL Reading

Reading Section Directions

This section measures your ability to understand academic passages in English.

You will have 36 minutes to read and answer the questions 2 passages.

Most questions are worth 1 point but the last question in each set is worth more than 1 point. The directions indicate how many points you may receive.

Within each screen, you can go to the next question by clicking **Next**. You may skip questions and go back to them later. If you want to return to previous questions, click on **Back**.

You can click on **Review** at any time and the review screen will show you which questions you have answered and which you have not answered. From this review screen, you may go directly to any questions you have already seen in the Reading section.

You may now begin the Reading section.

Click on **Continue** to go on.

Passage 1

Flightless Birds

1 ➡ Birds that currently live or used to live on many continents have lost the ability to fly at various points in their evolutionary histories. Such evolution seems paradoxical, since flight is a trait that so many animals from different classes have developed wholly independently. Indeed, convergent evolution would seem to argue against the whole idea of losing such an advanced ability. [■A] However, evolution is not about achieving advanced traits, but rather about developing the traits that are necessary to survive in a given habitat. [■B] Therefore, birds that have lost this ability must have done so because flight did not give them an advantage in their habitat. [■C] A group of large, flightless birds called ratites no longer needed to fly because they did not need to migrate for food or warmth, or because they had no predators from which they needed to escape. [■D] They developed larger bodies supported by strong legs and laid larger eggs.

2 ➡ Many flightless bird species are classified into the ratite group due to the many physical features they share. These birds include the ostriches of Africa, rheas of South America, and the emus and cassowaries of Australia, all of which are very large birds with extremely small wings, long legs and long necks. Other extinct species that are placed in this group are the moa of New Zealand and the elephant bird of Madagascar, which disappeared in the last few thousand years, most likely because of human activity. Although flightless birds all possess vestigial wings, their breast bones lack the ridge that flight muscles attach to in flying bird species. These birds have totally abandoned flight and rely upon their powerful legs for movement and defense.

3 ➡ The largest of the flightless birds went extinct millions of years ago, but they were truly impressive specimens. When the dinosaurs

---

1. The word "paradoxical" in paragraph 1 is closest in meaning to
   Ⓐ inevitable
   Ⓑ contradictory
   Ⓒ arbitrary
   Ⓓ mundane

2. Which of the following is NOT mentioned in paragraph 1?
   Ⓐ What convergent evolution is
   Ⓑ What caused some birds to be flightless
   Ⓒ How flightless birds survived
   Ⓓ How evolutionary changes in birds took place

3. According to paragraph 2, all of the following are common physical features of ratites EXCEPT
   Ⓐ long necks
   Ⓑ long legs
   Ⓒ vestigial wings
   Ⓓ ridge-shaped chest bones

disappeared, niches in many habitats were vacated, and birds were often the animals that filled them before mammals took their place. This resulted in some truly giant birds that replaced both large herbivores and predators. One example of this is *Titanis walleri*, which was a member of the Phorusrhacidae family of the Americas also known as "terror birds." This hunter stood at 2.5 meters tall and would have weighed around 150 kilograms. It had powerful legs it used to hunt its prey, both for chasing the animals and knocking them to the ground. It also had a massive, hooked beak that was well-suited to tearing flesh. Another ancient bird called the Diatryma was included in the same group, but scientists now believe it was a large herbivore. Although it was of similar size and had a powerful beak, recent data shows that its diet consisted primarily of tough plant matter. For this reason, it would have needed a large caecum, an organ used to digest such a diet, which would have made flight difficult.

4 ➡ The wide distribution of ratite species has long puzzled scientists. For many decades, the most popular theory was that they descended from a common flightless ancestor. The continents that they live on, Africa, Australia and South America, were once connected into one landmass called Gondwana that split apart about 180 million years ago. This would have isolated the animals and allowed them to evolve independently. However, geologic evidence shows that the supercontinent of Gondwana broke apart far too long ago for that to be the case. A recent genetic survey of ratite species supports the more likely theory that the flightless giants evolved from a common ancestor that could fly. Members of this species spread across the world to the already divided continents, and then lost their ability to fly.

5 ➡ However, members of the ratite family are not exclusively large. The kiwi of New Zealand and the tinamou of South America are ratites with stout, robust bodies despite their diminutive

4. Which of the following can be inferred about terror birds from paragraph 3?
   Ⓐ *Titanis walleri* was the largest land predator in the Western Hemisphere when it lived.
   Ⓑ They were ultimately unable to compete with mammalian predators.
   Ⓒ They lived alongside the dinosaurs and competed with them for food.
   Ⓓ They were not as fast and agile as birds that hunt while flying.

5. Why does the author mention "Diatryma" in paragraph 3?
   Ⓐ To cast doubt on its being classified as a "terror bird"
   Ⓑ To explain why "terror birds" had large digestive organs
   Ⓒ To draw a line between a giant bird and a large herbivore
   Ⓓ To introduce a bird that was mistakenly categorized

6. In paragraph 4, which of the following is NOT mentioned about Gondwana?
   Ⓐ It was an ancient supercontinent that broke up about 180 million years ago.
   Ⓑ It incorporated the current continents of Africa, Australia, and South America.
   Ⓒ It started to split when magma from below the Earth's crust began pushing upward.
   Ⓓ Its breakup is believed to have isolated the animals living on it.

TOEFL Reading

size. Still, they have another important trait that they share with other ratites: very large eggs. It makes sense for the ostrich to lay the biggest egg as the largest bird in the world, but the kiwi actually lays the largest egg relative to its own body size, and the ostrich egg is the smallest in comparison to the size of the adult bird. It remains unclear why kiwis lay such large eggs, but there are two possibilities. Either kiwis have always been small and their eggs have grown, or kiwis used to be much larger, and their eggs have not shrunk very much. Either way, a large egg provides definite survival advantages for kiwi chicks. They hatch with an extra supply of yolk that they can live off of for over two weeks, which means they are born pretty much ready to run. This makes it possible for them to better evade flying predators, so it might be worth carrying such outsized eggs.

7. According to paragraph 5, what advantage do huge eggs bring to the kiwi?

   (A) Their large size prevents predators from eating them easily.
   (B) They give kiwi chicks a competitive edge over flying birds.
   (C) The chicks do not need to be fed after they hatch.
   (D) A female can only lay one egg at a time, which requires less energy.

8. Which of the sentences below best expresses the essential information in the highlighted sentence in the passage? *Incorrect* answer choices change the meaning in important ways or leave out essential information.

   (A) The ostrich has the largest egg compared to the body of the adult bird, while the kiwi has the smallest compared to its body.
   (B) Although it is a much smaller bird, the kiwi actually lays larger eggs than the ostrich does.
   (C) Since it is the largest bird in the world, it is not surprising that the ostrich lays the largest egg, but the kiwi actually lays a very large egg as well.
   (D) The ostrich actually has the smallest egg compared to the adult's body although it is the largest bird, whereas the kiwi has the largest egg compared to its body.

9. Look at the four squares [■] that indicate where the following sentence could be added to the passage.

Flight became an unnecessary expenditure of energy, so their bodies gradually lost the structures that were needed for flying.

Where would the sentence best fit?

Click on a square [■] to add the sentence to the passage.

10. **Directions:** An introductory sentence for a brief summary of the passage is provided below. Complete the summary by selecting the THREE answer choices that express the most important ideas in the passage. Some sentences do not belong in the summary because they express ideas that are not presented in the passage or are minor ideas in the passage.
This question is worth 2 points.

Many species of birds like the ratites have lost the ability to fly as they adapted to the habitats in which they live.

-
-
-

Answer Choices

(A) Many of the early flightless birds evolved to fill niches that had been left vacant by the dinosaurs when they went extinct.
(B) *Titanis walleri* was the largest of the "terror birds" at 2.5 meters tall.
(C) Scientists originally thought that ratites were flightless when the continents separated, but they have since learned that their ancestors must have flown across the oceans.
(D) Ratite species live in Australia, Africa, and South America today.
(E) Some scientists believe that the ancestors of modern kiwis must have been much larger than their descendants.
(F) The smallest ratite species is the kiwi, which lays disproportionally large eggs.

Drag your answer choices to the spaces where they belong.
To remove an answer choice, click on it. To review the passage, click on **View Text**.

Groundwater

1 ➡ Water, the lifeblood of our planet, exists not only in visible bodies like rivers and lakes but also in hidden reserves beneath the Earth's surface—groundwater. Porous rock formations, such as sandstone and limestone, serve as one type of natural reservoir, harboring vast quantities of groundwater within their interconnected pore spaces. Known as aquifers, these formations vary in permeability and depth, influencing their capacity to store and transmit water. Unconfined aquifers, closer to the surface and replenished by rainfall, are vital for sustaining wells and springs. [■A] In contrast, confined aquifers, situated between impermeable layers, store significant volumes of pressurized water, serving as essential sources for irrigation, industry, and municipal supply. [■B]

2 ➡ Considering this, understanding the geological and absorptive characteristics of these formations is crucial for predicting groundwater behavior and optimizing water resource management strategies. [■C] For instance, sandstone, with its high porosity and permeability, can store substantial volumes of water and facilitate rapid groundwater flow. [■D] Conversely, limestone, characterized by interconnected networks of fractures and cavities, acts as a highly productive aquifer, albeit with variations in permeability due to differing degrees of karstification. Hence, there is always the need for accurate surveying of an area's geology in order to ensure that water is managed efficiently.

3 ➡ Soil, often referred to as Earth's skin, also plays a pivotal role in regulating water distribution and replenishing groundwater reservoirs. When precipitation infiltrates the soil, it is absorbed and retained within the soil matrix, forming soil moisture. The water-holding capacity of soil is influenced by various factors,

1. The word "harboring" in paragraph 1 is closest in meaning to
   Ⓐ retaining
   Ⓑ bearing
   Ⓒ protecting
   Ⓓ possessing

2. According to paragraph 2, what can be inferred about limestone?
   Ⓐ Groundwater flow through limestone is typically slower than what is seen in sandstone.
   Ⓑ Limestone tends to be a much more productive aquifer than sandstone because of its diminished porosity.
   Ⓒ Its network of chambers and pockets makes limestone an abundant source of groundwater.
   Ⓓ Limestone's significantly higher levels of karstification render it more permeable than sandstone.

3. The word "infiltrates" in paragraph 3 is closest in meaning to
   Ⓐ pressures
   Ⓑ penetrates
   Ⓒ purifies
   Ⓓ pervades

TOEFL Reading

including texture, structure, organic matter content, and land management practices. Soils rich in organic matter demonstrate superior water retention capabilities, fostering microbial activity and enhancing groundwater recharge.

4 ➡ Agricultural practices significantly impact soil moisture dynamics and groundwater recharge rates. Conventional tillage practices can disrupt soil structure, increase surface runoff, and reduce infiltration, thereby hindering groundwater recharge. In contrast, conservation practices such as cover cropping, reduced tillage, and agroforestry can enhance soil health, promote infiltration, and mitigate runoff, ultimately replenishing groundwater reservoirs and sustaining water availability during dry periods. For instance, the concept of "managed aquifer recharge" (MAR) involves intentionally augmenting natural groundwater replenishment processes. MAR techniques include the injection of excess surface water or treated wastewater into aquifers, the construction of recharge basins and infiltration galleries, and the implementation of land use practices that enhance infiltration. By strategically managing soil moisture and promoting groundwater recharge, municipalities can alleviate water scarcity concerns and enhance the resilience of water supply systems.

5 ➡ Another critical source of groundwater is wetlands, encompassing a diverse array of ecosystems such as marshes, swamps, and bogs. They are invaluable natural assets due to their multifaceted roles in water storage, purification, and habitat provision. These waterlogged landscapes function as natural sponges, absorbing excess water during high flow periods and slowly releasing it during dry spells, thereby mitigating floods and droughts. Moreover, wetlands serve as highly effective filtration systems, trapping sediments, nutrients, and pollutants, thereby improving water quality before it reaches downstream ecosystems. The hydrology of wetlands is intricately linked to groundwater dynamics, with wetlands

4. According to paragraph 4, how do managed aquifer recharge (MAR) practices positively impact soil's groundwater storage function?

Ⓐ The implementation of land use practices enhances soil runoff quality.
Ⓑ MAR is often used in conjunction with agroforestry and cover cropping to maintain reservoir health.
Ⓒ Infiltration galleries are constructed to increase the permeability of soil.
Ⓓ The practice of inserting surface water into aquifers helps keep soil aquifers sustainable.

5. According to paragraph 5, how do wetlands regulate water levels in their areas?

Ⓐ Water level regulation serves a critical role in the maintenance of wetland ecosystems and their unique plant life.
Ⓑ The diversity of wetland sediment creates the perfect setting for effective reservoir activity and regulation.
Ⓒ Wetlands clean water in reservoirs by trapping impurities and other foreign bodies.
Ⓓ Wetlands are able to take in surplus water, which is later gradually discharged in periods of drought.

6. What can be inferred about wetland plant and animal life in paragraph 5?

Ⓐ Wetland conditions create unique habitats that have led to the emergence of several amphibious species.
Ⓑ Many of the plants and animals that inhabit wetlands cannot be found in any other part of the world.
Ⓒ Shallow groundwater tables create unusual conditions that have forced plants to adapt to saturated topographies.

often serving as critical recharge areas for adjacent aquifers. The presence of shallow groundwater tables within wetland ecosystems sustains unique plant communities adapted to waterlogged conditions and provides essential habitat for a diverse array of aquatic and terrestrial species. Furthermore, wetlands act as carbon sinks, sequestering organic matter and reducing greenhouse gas emissions, thereby contributing to climate change mitigation efforts.

6 ➡ Finally, permafrost, perennially frozen ground found in polar and subpolar regions, represents a unique and significant component of the Earth's cryosphere. Permafrost regions store vast reserves of frozen water within their icy matrix, making them essential components of the global hydrological cycle. However, with rising temperatures due to climate change, permafrost degradation has accelerated, leading to the release of stored water and alterations in hydrological processes. In addition, thawing permafrost results in land subsidence, increased runoff, and changes in groundwater flow patterns, posing significant challenges for infrastructure, ecosystems, and indigenous communities in northern regions. Furthermore, the release of greenhouse gasses trapped within permafrost, particularly methane and carbon dioxide, exacerbates global warming, creating a feedback loop that further accelerates permafrost thaw and climate change impacts.

7 ➡ Understanding the dynamics of permafrost and its interactions with groundwater systems is essential for predicting and mitigating the impacts of climate change on water resources in polar and subpolar regions. Integrated research efforts combining field observations, remote sensing, and numerical modeling can enhance our understanding of permafrost hydrology and inform adaptation strategies to mitigate the impacts of permafrost thaw on water resources, infrastructure, and ecosystems.

D Some of the wetland animal species have learned to adapt to intermittent periods of flooding and dry spells.

7. Why does the author mention indigenous communities in paragraph 6?

   A to point out global warming's effects on permafrost zones and their inhabitants
   B to bring to attention a population that is affected by changes in permafrost
   C as a call to action to address climate change
   D to add to a list of ways thawing permafrost impacts polar and subpolar regions

8. Which of the following best expresses the essential information in the highlighted sentence? Incorrect answer choices change the meaning in important ways or leave out essential information.

   A Scientists are combining field observations, remote sensing, and numerical modeling to better inform the public so that new adaptation strategies can create a more sustainable future for permafrost biomes.
   B The success of permafrost thaw mitigation strategies will depend on the quality of the integrated research and modeling currently being carried out.
   C Mitigating permafrost thaw reduces its impact on water resources, infrastructure, and ecosystem, which will be possible through enhanced understanding via a cohesive effort of field research, remote sensing, and numerical modeling.
   D Fully grasping permafrost hydrology and creating more effective adaptation strategies through an integrated approach to research can help minimize the effects of permafrost thaw.

TOEFL Reading

9. Look at the four squares [■] that indicate where the following sentence could be added to the passage.

   The porosity and permeability of these rocks determine the rate at which water can flow through them, with well-connected pore spaces facilitating rapid recharge and extraction.

   Where would the sentence best fit?

   Click on a square [■] to add the sentence to the passage.

10. **Directions:** An introductory sentence for a brief summary of the passage is provided below. Complete the summary by selecting the THREE answer choices that express the most important ideas in the passage. Some sentences do not belong in the summary because they express ideas that are not presented in the passage or minor ideas in the passage. *This question is worth 2 points.*

    One of the most important sources of freshwater on the planet, groundwater can be found in various types of topographical landscapes, with each type presenting its own unique capabilities in holding groundwater.

    -
    -
    -

    Answer Choices

    (A) Aquifers are able to hold substantial amounts of groundwater, although the absorptive qualities of the aquifer depends on the level of porosity inherent to the different rock formations found in the aquifer.

    (B) Limestone and sandstone are excellent examples of the differing levels of permeability found in aquifers, since the two feature differing levels of karstification.

    (C) Soil is also an important source of groundwater, as it absorbs precipitation, albeit at various levels depending on the makeup of the soil.

    (D) Although agricultural practices sometimes diminish soil's capacity as a reservoir, various strategies, such as the implementation of the concept of MAR, have shown the potential to counter some of the impacts of agricultural activity on the soil.

    (E) Wetlands are a unique source of groundwater and have many critical functions, including acting as a carbon sink, creating conditions for unique wildlife, and absorbing excess water.

    (F) Permafrost is another distinct component in Earth's groundwater resources, in which polar and subpolar climates result in the conditions for the ground to retain frozen water.

    Drag your answer choices to the spaces where they belong.
    To remove an answer choice, click on it. To review the passage, click on **View Text**.

Actual Test 02

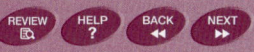

TOEFL Reading

Reading Section Directions

This section measures your ability to understand academic passages in English.

You will have 36 minutes to read and answer the questions 2 passages.

Most questions are worth 1 point but the last question in each set is worth more than 1 point. The directions indicate how many points you may receive.

Within each screen, you can go to the next question by clicking **Next**. You may skip questions and go back to them later. If you want to return to previous questions, click on **Back**.

You can click on **Review** at any time and the review screen will show you which questions you have answered and which you have not answered. From this review screen, you may go directly to any questions you have already seen in the Reading section.

You may now begin the Reading section.

Click on **Continue** to go on.

Passage 1

TOEFL Reading

The Fall of the Mayan Civilization

1 ➡ The Mayan civilization that once covered much of modern day Guatemala and Southern Mexico was inarguably one of the greatest civilizations ever to exist in Pre-Columbian America. Their settlements date back to around 2,000 BCE, and some existed until the Spanish conquest of the region. They are known for their monumental step-pyramids, stonemasonry, understanding of astronomy and mathematics, and a fully developed hieroglyphic writing system. Their civilization reached its peak during what is called its Classical Period, extending from 250 CE to around 900 CE, when their cities reached their highest state of development. However, their flourishing society suffered a catastrophic collapse at this time from which they never fully recovered. Many theories have been suggested to explain such a sudden decline, including natural disasters, war, and plague. While these may have contributed to the overall decline, the root cause appears to have been an interconnected series of events involving agriculture, conflict, and climate change.

2 ➡ In the Classical Period, the Maya experienced rapid expansion and their population reached into the millions. Most of their large religious and political complexes were built during this time, and their civilization developed into a large politically and economically interconnected society comprised of many small kingdoms and empires. By the 8th century, populations surrounding the central lowlands had reached new peaks of size and density. This was also the area that held the most political influence. Their growing aristocracy, who enjoyed luxuries and the best food, are believed to have expanded rapidly. The outlying kingdoms served as the primary centers for trade, and they brought in goods from throughout Mesoamerica. While relationships with their neighbors were not always peaceful,

1. Based on paragraph 1, what can be inferred about the Mayan civilization?
   Ⓐ Nobody truly knows how the Mayan civilization collapsed.
   Ⓑ The golden age of the Mayan civilization began with the ending of the Classical Period.
   Ⓒ Most of the Mayan population lived in cities.
   Ⓓ The Mayan civilization eventually recovered from the Spanish conquest.

2. According to paragraph 2, which of the following is NOT true of the Classical Period?
   Ⓐ It was a period of constant warfare with their neighbors.
   Ⓑ It was a period during which the number of aristocrats grew.
   Ⓒ It was a period of flourishing trade.
   Ⓓ It was a period during which many buildings were constructed.

and warfare did indeed occur, they were generally friendly. The greatest danger to the Maya, although they were probably oblivious to the fact, came from within.

3 ➡ Early in the Classical Period, from about 440 to 660 CE, the area the Maya lived in experienced significantly higher rainfall than it had in the past. This extended wetter period allowed them to expand their agriculture and produce unprecedented amounts of food. The food surplus allowed the population to grow, and fueled the civilization's rapid expansion. The Maya used permanent farms and raised terraces for cultivation, and their usual method of crop rotation involved fallow cycles, leaving the land uncultivated in order to allow it to recover. However, the increased rainfall would have meant that the minerals and nutrients in the soil of their farms would be replenished more quickly by the mountain runoff, and the temptation to shorten fallow cycles must have been nearly irresistible in a climate that fostered such growth. In addition, the Maya began cutting down expanses of rainforest to clear land for farming and to provide lumber and firewood, reducing the amount of groundcover. Since they raised little livestock, they were also rapidly depleting the area of the animals they relied on for meat. The Maya were overtaxing the carrying capacity of their environment, but they would not realize this until it was too late.

4 ➡ As their civilization continued to expand throughout the 8th and 9th centuries, the advantageous rainfall began to lessen. As this trend continued, pressures began to grow within Mayan society. The large urban centers with their aristocratic populations were a huge drain on agriculture, so as the output decreased, they had to compensate by importing food. This transferred the burden out onto the surrounding communities, which increased competition and conflict between cities and regions. As the societal and economic divide between the peasants and the aristocrats widened further,

3. Which of the sentences below best expresses the essential information in the highlighted sentence in the passage? *Incorrect* answer choices change the meaning in important ways or leave out essential information.

   Ⓐ The increased rainfall quickly diminished the minerals and nutrients in the soil, so it was hard for them to shorten their fallow cycles.
   Ⓑ The farmers resisted the temptation to shorten fallow cycles because the increased rainfall fostered growth on the farms where minerals and nutrients were replenished.
   Ⓒ The farmers probably wanted to shorten rest periods because the increased rainfall replenished their farms and made it easier to grow crops.
   Ⓓ The farmers began to use shorter rest periods for their farms because the soil was washed away by water coming from the surrounding countryside.

4. According to paragraph 3, what is one possible cause for the increase in population?

   Ⓐ Significantly higher rainfall
   Ⓑ Shorter fallow cycle
   Ⓒ Reduced expanses of rainforest
   Ⓓ Increased food production

5. What is the main purpose of paragraph 4?

   Ⓐ To demonstrate the negative effects of reckless expansion
   Ⓑ To discuss the effects of rainfall on competition between large urban centers
   Ⓒ To explain what began the downfall of the Mayan civilization
   Ⓓ To highlight the social divide between peasants and aristocrats

TOEFL Reading

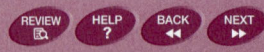

the lower classes began to revolt against the established order, and food shortages only worsened the situation. Their whole society was teetering on the brink of an abyss.

5 ➡ Then around 1,000 CE, the already faltering civilization was struck by a true disaster: a prolonged drought struck the southern regions. [■A] The drought was a symptom of a global shift in climate that seriously affected other areas in the world, but for the Mayan civilization it was devastating. [■B] Their practice of clearing forest exacerbated the problem in two ways. The land that had been cleared was poor for farming, and the lack of trees disrupted the normal evaporation cycle. [■C] Internal warfare escalated as supplies dwindled, and eventually their whole system collapsed. [■D] The Mayan civilization was ultimately a victim of its own unchecked expansion. The drought did not completely destroy their culture as some of the city states in the north survived and continued to expand, but they too fell after the arrival of the Spanish.

6. According to paragraph 4, what was the likely result of importing food?
   Ⓐ It increased the number of aristocrats.
   Ⓑ The farmers began to revolt against the traders.
   Ⓒ It caused conflicts amongst those in large urban centers.
   Ⓓ The social divide between the upper class and lower class widened.

7. The word "exacerbated" in paragraph 5 is closest in meaning to
   Ⓐ evoked
   Ⓑ placated
   Ⓒ aggravated
   Ⓓ controlled

8. According to paragraph 5, why was the drought especially devastating for the Mayan civilization?
   Ⓐ It was a symptom of a global shift in climate.
   Ⓑ Deforestation worsened the drought.
   Ⓒ The Maya fought for water.
   Ⓓ It was a result of unchecked expansion.

TOEFL Reading

9. Look at the four squares [■] that indicate where the following sentence could be added to the passage.

   Therefore, when the drought reduced rainfall by 25 to 40%, their agricultural system became completely unsustainable.

   Where would the sentence best fit?

   Click on a square [■] to add the sentence to the passage.

10. **Directions:** An introductory sentence for a brief summary of the passage is provided below. Complete the summary by selecting the THREE answer choices that express the most important ideas in the passage. Some sentences do not belong in the summary because they express ideas that are not presented in the passage or are minor ideas in the passage.
    This question is worth 2 points.

    While there are many theories that attempt to explain the fall of the Mayan civilization, there seems to have been several interlinked factors that led to the sudden decline of one of the greatest civilizations ever to exist in Pre-Columbian America.

    -
    -
    -

    Answer Choices

    Ⓐ The Maya reached the peak of their civilization by the 9th century CE.
    Ⓑ The widening gap and deepening conflict between the aristocrats worsened the economic situation.
    Ⓒ With less rainfall, the farms were not able to produce enough food, resulting in food shortages that applied critical pressure to Mayan society.
    Ⓓ The drought was the final straw for the weakened Mayan society, completely collapsing their already dysfunctional agricultural system.
    Ⓔ The prolonged drought forced the Maya to import food from surrounding communities.
    Ⓕ Relying heavily on increased rainfall, the Maya overtaxed the natural resources of the land.

    Drag your answer choices to the spaces where they belong.
    To remove an answer choice, click on it. To review the passage, click on **View Text**.

Altruism in Meerkats

1 ➡ Meerkats are small members of the mongoose family that live in the Kalahari and Namib Deserts of southern Africa. Scientists have studied them for centuries due to their complex societal structure and their altruism, which they practice to a level not often seen in nature. Meerkats breed cooperatively, which means that a group will consist of a dominant breeding pair and up to 40 male and female assistants who do not breed. These assistants spend most of their time taking care of the young by feeding them, training them, and protecting them from danger. As a social predator, it is not unusual that meerkats should do these things as a group, but the extent they carry this behavior to is remarkable.

2 ➡ Meerkats are primarily insectivores, but they will also eat small reptiles, mammals, fungi, and occasionally birds. The majority of the group will usually go out to gather food together, leaving a few to guard the young. Once the pack locates prey, it is difficult for that animal to escape as meerkats are extremely fast and excellent diggers. [■A] Surprisingly, one of their preferred prey animals is scorpions. [■B] While many members of the mongoose family are immune to various snake and insect venoms, it is unclear how much immunity meerkats possess, but this does not deter them. [■C] When a meerkat pounces on a scorpion, the arachnid often has no time to prepare a strike, and the meerkat circumvents any attack by swiftly biting off the scorpion's stinger. [■D] The meerkat can then devour the disarmed creature at its leisure, or use it as a teaching tool for the young.

3 ➡ Young meerkats feed on milk like any other mammal as infants, but that milk is not always produced by their mother. If the mother is away hunting, other females will actually lactate to feed the infant young. Once they are weaned, however, they must be taught to forage with the

1. According to paragraph 1, what sets apart the meerkats from other animals?
   Ⓐ They are one of the few mammal species that breed cooperatively.
   Ⓑ They are a popular subject of study for scientists.
   Ⓒ They are the smallest member of the mongoose family.
   Ⓓ They are altruistic to an extent rarely observed.

2. Which of the sentences below best expresses the essential information in the highlighted sentence in the passage? *Incorrect* answer choices change the meaning in important ways or leave out essential information.
   Ⓐ Because many members of the mongoose family hold immunity to various venoms, meerkats do not fear venomous animals.
   Ⓑ Unlike with other members of the mongoose family, we don't know how much immunity meerkats possess, but this isn't an obstacle for the meerkats.
   Ⓒ Compared to many members of the mongoose family which have immunity to various venoms, meerkats are not aware if they possess immunity.
   Ⓓ While it is unclear how much immunity meerkats possess, other members of the mongoose family are weak against most venoms, and this discourages them.

TOEFL Reading

adults. To teach them how to hunt dangerous prey like scorpions or centipedes, the adults will start with dead and disarmed prey. Once the young learn how to eat solid food, they will give them prey that has been disarmed but remains very much alive. After they get used to killing their own food, the adults will then show them how to remove the stinger. At that point, it becomes the young animals' turn, and they either succeed or receive a painful and potentially fatal wound. Apart from this kind of training, the adults normally go to great lengths to protect all of the members of their clan.

4 ➡ While most of the clan goes foraging or tends to the young, a few animals will find a place to act as a sentry, either by standing on their hind legs on high ground or by climbing up into a nearby bush, but this also makes them visible to predators. If a sentry spots danger, it will bark, and the entire clan will flee to the nearest burrows. Some researchers have claimed that since the sentries often are the first animals to run, it shows that this behavior may not be entirely altruistic. However, the first animal to reemerge is usually the same sentry animal, and it will continue to give warning barks until it has confirmed that the surface is safe. This behavior is truly selfless, because the animal is not only exposing itself to potential danger, but also announcing its presence to any nearby predators with its barking.

5 ➡ When the clan is unable to avoid a threat in this way, they exhibit further altruistic behavior. If they are threatened in a group, the adults will bunch together and attack the creature en masse in an action called mobbing. This behavior is meant to scare away the predator by making the group appear to be a single larger animal. This is not always effective against snakes, and sometimes individuals get bitten. When there is danger, the babysitter will quickly usher the young underground, but this is not always possible. When there is no safe place to hide, she will gather the young into a group and

3. The word "circumvents" in paragraph 2 is closest in meaning to
   (A) overcomes
   (B) eradicates
   (C) preserves
   (D) avoids

4. What is the purpose of paragraph 3 as it relates to paragraph 2?
   (A) To describe the training young meerkats go through to participate in hunting mentioned in paragraph 2
   (B) To provide an example of how young meerkats develop the immunity to venoms mentioned in paragraph 2
   (C) To explain why meerkats prefer to hunt dangerous prey as mentioned in paragraph 2
   (D) To differentiate the feeding practices of young meerkats from those of adults as discussed in paragraph 2

5. According to paragraph 4, what is the reasoning against regarding sentry behavior as altruistic?
   (A) Sentries are the first to enter their burrows.
   (B) Sentries do not participate in high-risk duties such as hunting dangerous prey.
   (C) Sentries give false warnings to steal food.
   (D) Sentries are safe from predator attacks.

6. Based on paragraph 4, what can be inferred about meerkats?
   (A) Meerkats are quite vulnerable to predator attacks.
   (B) Meerkats have poor vision.
   (C) Meerkats takes turns acting as sentries.
   (D) Meerkats dig many burrows in their territory.

then lie on top of them. Ideally, this will keep them from attracting attention, but it may result in the female sacrificing herself for the lives of the young.

7. The word "usher" in paragraph 5 is closest in meaning to
   A) move
   B) lead
   C) carry
   D) push

8. Which of the following is NOT mentioned in the passage about meerkats?
   A) Defensive mechanisms
   B) Foraging behavior
   C) Domestication by humans
   D) Breeding habits

TOEFL Reading

9. Look at the four squares [■] that indicate where the following sentence could be added to the passage.

   Then, it uses sand to wash away any venom that may remain on the scorpion's exoskeleton.

   Where would the sentence best fit?

   Click on a square [■] to add the sentence to the passage.

10. **Directions:** An introductory sentence for a brief summary of the passage is provided below. Complete the summary by selecting the THREE answer choices that express the most important ideas in the passage. Some sentences do not belong in the summary because they express ideas that are not presented in the passage or are minor ideas in the passage. **This question is worth 2 points.**

    Meerkats, one of the mostly widely studied mammals living in southern Africa, are well known for their exceptionally altruistic behavior.

    -
    -
    -

    Answer Choices

    (A) Male and female assistants in a group do not breed until the dominant pair permits them to.
    (B) When sentries spot a predator, they issue a series of distinct barks until the danger has passed.
    (C) When meerkats are attacked by predators, they display altruistic behavior by mobbing the predator and placing the safety of their young first.
    (D) Every adult member of the group plays a role in feeding, training, and protecting the young, even though they are not their own offspring.
    (E) The training for foraging and hunting for food is done in a multi-step process.
    (F) Meerkats bite off the scorpion's stinger first to ensure that the arachnid does not strike them with its venom.

    Drag your answer choices to the spaces where they belong.
    To remove an answer choice, click on it. To review the passage, click on **View Text**.

Actual Test 03

정답 및 해석 | P. 26

TOEFL Reading

Reading Section Directions

This section measures your ability to understand academic passages in English.

You will have 36 minutes to read and answer the questions 2 passages.

Most questions are worth 1 point but the last question in each set is worth more than 1 point. The directions indicate how many points you may receive.

Within each screen, you can go to the next question by clicking **Next**. You may skip questions and go back to them later. If you want to return to previous questions, click on **Back**.

You can click on **Review** at any time and the review screen will show you which questions you have answered and which you have not answered. From this review screen, you may go directly to any questions you have already seen in the Reading section.

You may now begin the Reading section.

Click on **Continue** to go on.

Passage 1

Deep Sea Biology

1 ➡ After centuries of exploration, scientists have revealed that life exists nearly everywhere on the surface of the Earth. This includes the deepest trenches in the ocean. However, proof of such life remained elusive for a long time because we lacked the technology to reach such depths. Therefore, many hypotheses that supposed that life could not survive there arose. These ideas were logical and convinced many experts that the reason that specimens could not be collected was because they did not exist. However, as evidence of organisms from the depths mounted, many of these ideas were proven wrong. One of the most famous mistaken theories about deep sea biology was created by Edward Forbes.

2 ➡ Edward Forbes was a naturalist and marine biologist from the Isle of Man who had a short but prolific career. He is best known for his time spent upon the HMS Beacon in the Aegean Sea on its survey voyage and the theory on oceanic life that he developed there. Using a dredging rig, he conducted a study of ocean life at varying depths, and came to the conclusion that life did not exist below 300 fathoms (1 fathom is about 2 meters). This belief became known as the azoic hypothesis and was widely accepted by the scientific community until it was disproven by later expeditions of discovery.

3 ➡ Forbes was invited to take part in the expedition by the commander of the ship, Captain Thomas Graves, in 1841. The majority of the trip was spent in the Greek Islands and Asia Minor, where Forbes devoted his time on land to botany. At sea, however, he was constantly dredging, completing at least 150 dredges at depths from 1 fathom to 130 fathoms. His goal was to catalogue how depth, pressure and the geology of the seafloor affected the sizes and types of organisms present. Unsurprisingly, his dredges proved that organisms became smaller

---

1. The word "elusive" in paragraph 1 is closest in meaning to
   - Ⓐ undefined
   - Ⓑ apparent
   - Ⓒ complicated
   - Ⓓ recognizable

2. Which of the sentences below best expresses the essential information in the highlighted sentence in the passage? *Incorrect* answer choices change the meaning in important ways or leave out essential information.
   - Ⓐ After conducting expeditions of discovery, the scientific community was found to be wrong about the azoic hypothesis.
   - Ⓑ The discoveries and expeditions made by the scientific community helped to disprove the azoic hypothesis.
   - Ⓒ The azoic hypothesis had been considered as true until it was proven to be erroneous by later discoveries.
   - Ⓓ It was the scientific community that revealed the error of the azoic hypothesis, which had been widely accepted before.

3. According to paragraph 2, which of the following can be inferred about Edward Forbes?
   - Ⓐ As an experienced biologist, he took part in the survey voyage of the HMS Beacon.
   - Ⓑ During the survey in the Aegean Sea, he developed a theory about marine life.
   - Ⓒ He became a well-respected member of the scientific community.
   - Ⓓ He correctly concluded that there was no life in the deep sea.

and fewer in number the deeper he searched.

4 ➡ Based upon the specimens and data he recovered, Forbes divided the depths of the ocean into eight fairly distinct zones based upon the fauna present. However, due to the fact that he could only dredge up to a certain depth, he was forced to extrapolate what conditions were like deeper down. This led him to believe that the deepest ocean abysses were utterly devoid of life. He could not conceive how organisms could withstand the brutal pressure, cold and absolute darkness that would be present, and his dredges seemed to support his logic. So, he called this the azoic zone, which literally means "without life." His hypothesis was greeted with general support, and became a dominant theory until it was proven utterly wrong many years later.

5 ➡ The reasons for his mistaken hypothesis come down to particular details of his investigation: the device he used to collect samples and the location. The dredge Forbes used was actually quite poorly designed for its intended use. The opening on the front of the dredge was actually fairly small, meaning that more animals were deflected by it than were captured. To make matters worse, the net on the back of it that was intended to hold the specimens until they were brought to the surface had holes that were large enough for many smaller organisms to freely pass through. In addition, the Aegean Sea had considerably lower levels of fauna than other seas of comparable size and depth. Combined, these factors actually limited the amount of data he could collect.

6 ➡ Another popular but erroneous hypothesis was created by the French naturalist François Peron. Prior to Forbes's survey of the Aegean, Peron explored the depths of the Baltic Sea, paying particular attention to the temperatures he recorded. He correctly noted that the temperature of the water falls as you descend. Pressure also increases with depth, so he

4. According to paragraph 3, why did Forbes participate in the expedition?

   Ⓐ To collect a variety of botanical samples in the Greek Islands and Asia Minor
   Ⓑ To find evidence to support his hypothesis that organisms could not inhabit the deep sea
   Ⓒ To develop an effective dredging device with which to study the seabed ecosystem
   Ⓓ To research the effects of depth, pressure and the geology under the sea on organisms

5. According to paragraph 4, why did Forbes conclude that life did not exist in the deepest ocean?

   Ⓐ He thought the environment was too tough for organisms to survive.
   Ⓑ He was unable to discover anything when he reached a certain depth.
   Ⓒ He faced unexpected obstacles while dredging.
   Ⓓ He successfully classified the zones according to species diversity.

6. Why does the author mention "the device he used to collect samples and the location" in paragraph 5?

   Ⓐ To describe how poor the technology was in Forbes's time
   Ⓑ To point out what caused Forbes to draw an erroneous conclusion
   Ⓒ To explain how Forbes collected samples from the ocean
   Ⓓ To emphasize the difficulty Forbes experienced during his exploration

believed that the water at the ocean floor was so cold and dense that there must be ice at the bottom of the ocean. These ideas led him to also conclude that the deep sea was lifeless. Like Forbes, Peron's theory also received wide support, even though it later turned out to be false.

7 ➡ As technology advanced, subsequent exploration of the ocean's depths revealed just how flawed these ideas were. [■A] Improved dredging equipment allowed much more effective collection of specimens, and organisms were found at depths well below 300 fathoms. [■B] Forbes's theory that life could not exist below that mark was shattered by Charles Wyville Thomson in 1868 when he collected specimens from over 2,400 fathoms (4,389 meters). [■C] The Challenger expedition measured the Mariana Trench in 1875 and found that it was over 4,475 fathoms (8,184 meters) deep. [■D] Today, the trench is known to reach a maximum depth of 5,960 fathoms (10,900 meters), and life has been found even there.

7. All of the following are mentioned in paragraph 5 as reasons for Forbes's mistaken hypothesis EXCEPT

   Ⓐ the dredge was originally designed for use on the surface of the sea rather than in the deep sea.
   Ⓑ the device Forbes used had a small hole which made it difficult to capture animals.
   Ⓒ the net of the dredge did not function efficiently and failed to hold tiny organisms.
   Ⓓ the Aegean Sea had lower levels of life compared to other seas.

8. According to paragraph 6, all of the following are true about Peron's hypothesis EXCEPT

   Ⓐ Peron's hypothesis was similar to that of Forbes in that it was lifeless in the deep sea.
   Ⓑ Peron found that the temperature becomes lower with depth by recording temperatures in the Baltic Sea.
   Ⓒ Peron thought ice was present at the bottom of the ocean due to the low seawater temperature.
   Ⓓ Peron's hypothesis was correct in that the high pressure at the ocean floor makes it impossible for organisms to inhabit it.

TOEFL Reading

9. Look at the four squares [■] that indicate where the following sentence could be added to the passage.

   Scientists also discovered that the oceans were far deeper than they had ever imagined.

   Where would the sentence best fit?

   Click on a square [■] to add the sentence to the passage.

10. **Directions:** An introductory sentence for a brief summary of the passage is provided below. Complete the summary by selecting the THREE answer choices that express the most important ideas in the passage. Some sentences do not belong in the summary because they express ideas that are not presented in the passage or are minor ideas in the passage.
    This question is worth 2 points.

    Many hypotheses that have been presented to suggest that no life exists in the deepest ocean have since been disproven.

    -
    -
    -

    Answer Choices

    (A) Forbes divided the depths of the sea into eight regions based on the data he had collected and concluded it is lifeless in the abysmal depths of the ocean.
    (B) Forbes found that the size and number of organisms decrease as you descend deeper into the sea.
    (C) Forbes's theory had been generally supported in the contemporary scientific field before it was revealed to be wrong.
    (D) The defective device Forbes used for his research and environmental conditions in the Aegean Sea led Forbes to the incorrect conclusion.
    (E) Peron was the first to discover the link between the pressure and the temperature under the sea.
    (F) Peron also developed a hypothesis that no living things existed in the depths of the ocean because of the low temperature and high pressure there.

    Drag your answer choices to the spaces where they belong.
    To remove an answer choice, click on it. To review the passage, click on **View Text**.

New York City Urban Planning

1 ➡ Originally settled by the Dutch under the name of New Amsterdam, New York is one of the oldest planned cities in the United States. Like many early colonial cities, it began its existence as a fortification and was constructed along military guidelines. They eventually surrendered it to England, which in turn lost it when the United States achieved its independence. As the city expanded, a great deal of effort went into keeping the city organized. In fact, in 1811, the city council adopted a plan that divided up the mostly undeveloped northern portion of Manhattan Island and employed a strict grid pattern, regardless of terrain. However, due to the city's rampant growth, these measures often proved insufficient, and there were many serious problems involving health, sanitation and safety.

2 ➡ New York City has always been an important port city, but few anticipated the number of immigrants it would receive, and many buildings had to be rapidly constructed to accommodate the new arrivals. By 1800, the city's population had reached 30,000 people, most of whom lived in an area that only comprises a fraction of the modern city. Some historians estimate that New York's population increased at a rate of around 100 percent every ten years, which meant that even more people were forced to live in hastily constructed tenements. Such massive immigration and overcrowding inevitably created conditions that were perfect for infectious diseases to ravage the city. Epidemics of cholera, malaria, and typhoid swept through the population in the early 19th century, killing thousands in some of the worst outbreaks the country has ever seen. The demolition of many apartment buildings and the development of the northern part of the island served to alleviate the overcrowding, but these diseases would return again. One famous case was an outbreak of typhoid in the early 1900s. A woman whom the press labeled

1. The word "They" in paragraph 1 refers to
   Ⓐ the Dutch
   Ⓑ colonial cities
   Ⓒ guidelines
   Ⓓ the United States

2. The word "inevitably" in paragraph 2 is closest in meaning to
   Ⓐ relentlessly
   Ⓑ unavoidably
   Ⓒ perversely
   Ⓓ allegedly

3. Based on paragraph 2, what can be inferred about epidemics in New York City in the early 19th century?
   Ⓐ They caused many people to resettle on the northern part of the island.
   Ⓑ Immigration declined due to the unsanitary conditions.
   Ⓒ The authorities were unable to locate the sources of outbreaks.
   Ⓓ Population growth slowed because of massive outbreaks of disease.

TOEFL Reading

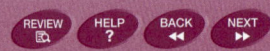

Typhoid Mary was a carrier of the disease who caused the deaths of over fifty people while working as a maid.

3 ➡ Along with overcrowding, New York also suffered from an inadequate sanitation system. All of the cabs and wagons that transported people and goods through the city streets were pulled by horses, and an estimated 200,000 of them were living there by the beginning of the 20th century. By necessity, most of these animals lived on the island of Manhattan, often in residential areas. [■A] These animals generated large amounts of waste that piled up throughout the city due to a lack of infrastructure. [■B] This waste made the streets reek in the summer, and it mixed with heavy snow in the winter, sometimes accumulating in frozen piles up to two meters high. [■C] Not only that, but the horses also were often overworked and otherwise mistreated to the extent that many of them died in the streets, where their bodies would remain since no one had the responsibility of cleaning them up. [■D] This situation was not remedied until 1909, when the Queensboro Bridge was opened to traffic. This allowed the waste to be transported over to rural Queens where it was used to fertilize farmland.

4 ➡ Waste from animals and humans led to an even more serious health problem: contaminated drinking water. Manhattan Island had never had a reliable water supply, with its brackish rivers forcing people to rely upon well water. Already insufficient, as the population grew, the aquifer those wells reached into became seriously polluted, which led to severe outbreaks of cholera. To cope with this problem, they had to look far outside of the city to find a viable source of water. The city undertook a large and complex project to bring fresh water from the Croton River to the island. Built between 1837 and 1842, the Old Croton Aqueduct brought water 66 kilometers to reservoirs in the city. Life in the city rapidly improved, but its growth did not slow down, and many additional aqueducts

4. According to paragraph 3, what was the main role of horses in New York?

   Ⓐ Pulling cabs and wagons
   Ⓑ Disposing of waste in residential areas
   Ⓒ Fertilizing farmland
   Ⓓ Clearing snow in the winter

5. Which of the sentences below best expresses the essential information in the highlighted sentence in the passage? *Incorrect* answer choices change the meaning in important ways or leave out essential information.

   Ⓐ The population was unable to filter the water from the polluted wells, leading to severe cholera outbreaks.
   Ⓑ The wells were used as sewers, polluting the aquifer and causing severe outbreaks of cholera amidst the growing population.
   Ⓒ The aquifer which the wells reached into, already insufficient with population growth, became polluted and led to increased disease.
   Ⓓ As the population grew, the wells could no longer reach the aquifer, which led to epidemics.

6. According to paragraph 4, what did the Old Croton Aqueduct achieve?

   Ⓐ It linked the Croton River to the Great Lakes.
   Ⓑ It provided an ample supply of clean water to the city.
   Ⓒ It paved the way for additional population growth.
   Ⓓ It improved the quality of life in the city.

have been built since.

5 ➡ As serious as the health and sanitation issues were, a serious safety issue went largely ignored until disaster struck. After years of construction, the Erie Canal opened, successfully linking the Hudson River to the Great Lakes in 1825. This shipping lane dramatically increased trade in New York, and warehouses sprang up throughout the financial district to accommodate the merchants' goods. Unfortunately, like most of the city's other buildings, these warehouses were made of wood, and a calamitous fire started in a warehouse on the bitterly cold and windy evening of December 16, 1835. Before its flames were finally put out, the Great Fire of New York razed southeastern Manhattan, destroying most of the buildings in Wall Street and the New York Stock Exchange. The builders had ignored the dangers of constructing so many wooden buildings in such close proximity, and the fire took full advantage of their oversight. Following the conflagration, city planners regulated the minimum distance between buildings and created newer, stricter fire prevention policies.

7. Why does the author mention "Great Fire of New York" in paragraph 5?

   Ⓐ To prove that fire has a more disastrous effect on society than poor sanitation
   Ⓑ To highlight the unexpected consequences of constructing the Erie Canal
   Ⓒ To point out an aspect of urban planning the city planners neglected
   Ⓓ To introduce the history of fire safety regulations in New York City

8. Which of the following is NOT mentioned in the passage as a source of misfortune in New York City?

   Ⓐ Massive immigration
   Ⓑ Poor sanitation system
   Ⓒ Lack of drinking water
   Ⓓ Wooden buildings

9. Look at the four squares [■] that indicate where the following sentence could be added to the passage.

Most often, waste was left in the middle of the street, as horse owners were far less likely to clean up after their horses if they were not on their own property.

Where would the sentence best fit?

Click on a square [■] to add the sentence to the passage.

10. **Directions:** An introductory sentence for a brief summary of the passage is provided below. Complete the summary by selecting the THREE answer choices that express the most important ideas in the passage. Some sentences do not belong in the summary because they express ideas that are not presented in the passage or are minor ideas in the passage.
This question is worth 2 points.

New York, one of the oldest planned cities in the United States, underwent significant trial and error in tackling problems such as public health, sanitation, and fire safety during its development.

-
-
-

Answer Choices

(A) The huge number of immigrants settling down in New York rapidly increased the city's population, resulting in overcrowding and epidemic outbreaks.
(B) The lack of a proper sanitation system or a reliable water supply resulted in outbreaks of cholera, prompting the city to transport clean water to the island.
(C) The horse owners did not clean up after their horses, and often left the remains of dead horses on the streets, providing a trigger for epidemic outbreaks.
(D) Frequent outbreaks of infectious diseases led the city to demolish apartment buildings, and it was effective at curbing the death tolls.
(E) After the fire in 1835, a greater awareness of fire safety led to stricter regulations about constructing buildings.
(F) The building of the Queensboro Bridge allowed the waste accumulated in Manhattan to be transported to Queens, where it was used as fertilizer.

Drag your answer choices to the spaces where they belong.
To remove an answer choice, click on it. To review the passage, click on **View Text**.

Actual Test 04

TOEFL Reading

Reading Section Directions

This section measures your ability to understand academic passages in English.

You will have 36 minutes to read and answer the questions 2 passages.

Most questions are worth 1 point but the last question in each set is worth more than 1 point. The directions indicate how many points you may receive.

Within each screen, you can go to the next question by clicking **Next**. You may skip questions and go back to them later. If you want to return to previous questions, click on **Back**.

You can click on **Review** at any time and the review screen will show you which questions you have answered and which you have not answered. From this review screen, you may go directly to any questions you have already seen in the Reading section.

You may now begin the Reading section.

Click on **Continue** to go on.

The Purpose of Extrafloral Nectar

1 ➡ Many flowering plants produce nectar as a way to attract insects that are beneficial to their life cycle. Most of them produce nectar from the sepal, a structure at the base of the inside of the flower. Any organism that wishes to feed on the nectar has to brush past the flower's reproductive structures, which deposit pollen on the organism that it then transports to another flower. However, many plant species produce nectar on other parts of the plant in what are referred to as extrafloral nectaries, which clearly must serve another purpose. Most of the empirical evidence that has been gathered shows that extrafloral nectaries are a defensive mechanism that attracts insects to protect the plant. As a reward, the insects may freely feed upon the nectar provided.

2 ➡ Nectar is a complex brew of many chemicals which are designed to attract and provide sustenance to other organisms. About 95% of all nectars is natural sugars, but many types contain amino acids. In fact, all of the twenty amino acids that naturally occur in proteins have been found in various nectars. Many of the other compounds present in nectar are designed to attract specific organisms by their scent. These are often volatiles that carry long distances on breezes. However, other chemicals present in some nectars actually discourage the organism from taking a second sip. For example, tobacco plants include some nicotine in their nectar, which is very bitter and less aromatic, meaning that the organism will eagerly feed once, but most likely move on soon afterward. This allows the plant to conserve its nectar, which most plants reabsorb after fertilization to use in seed production.

3 ➡ Unlike flowers, extrafloral nectaries produce nectar continuously, regardless of whether the plant has reproduced. This is due to the fact that they attract insects for an entirely

1. According to paragraph 1, what is the primary function of extrafloral nectar?
   Ⓐ It induces pollination.
   Ⓑ It provides nutrients to insects.
   Ⓒ It poisons organisms that feed on plants.
   Ⓓ It serves as a defense mechanism.

2. Which of the sentences below best expresses the essential information in the highlighted sentence in the passage? *Incorrect* answer choices change the meaning in important ways or leave out essential information.
   Ⓐ Insects will move on to other tobacco plants after feeding on the nectar of one tobacco plant because it includes a certain amount of nicotine in its nectar.
   Ⓑ Because insects feeding on the nectar of tobacco plants find it bitter, they move on after only feeding once.
   Ⓒ Some insects are attracted to the nicotine present in tobacco plants because it is bitter and less aromatic, so they do not move on to other plants after feeding.
   Ⓓ Because the nicotine in the nectar of tobacco plants is poisonous, insects will only feed eagerly on the nectar once before moving on.

different reason. Scientists have observed ladybird beetles, wasps, and particularly ants feeding on extrafloral nectar, and they all provide protection to the plant as well. Ladybird beetles are voracious predators that are very fond of eating aphids, which are a significant pest because they can reproduce asexually. Parasitic wasps will stun, remove, and lay eggs inside of caterpillars that consume leaves. Ants provide the most protection as they will attack and consume any insects that attack the plant and are also capable of discouraging larger herbivores from feeding on the plants.

4 ➡ Although such relationships may seem obvious today, they were not always so well understood. Initially, many scientists thought that extrafloral nectaries were purely excretory organs, including Charles Darwin. In fact, his disagreement with Federico Delpino about this led the latter to engage in some of the first serious study of the phenomenon. Many experts at the time argued that the structures were actually hydathodes. Hydathodes are a type of specialized plant tissue that is very similar to stomata. However, they are actually used to secrete excess water instead of regulating gas exchange. Delpino published a paper based on his observations in 1886 that contended that plants deliberately attract ants with this nectar to gain their protection.

5 ➡ [■A] Delpino's work later received support from the research of entomologist William Morton Wheeler and botanist Barbara Bentley. [■B] Based upon his own observations, Wheeler proposed in 1910 that not only did the ants feed on the nectar, but that the plants were actually dependent upon the ants for their survival. [■C] He observed that plants that produced extrafloral nectar were almost entirely unable to reproduce without ants present and often died. [■D]

6 ➡ In Bentley's experiment, she deliberately set out to determine whether plants genuinely benefited from ants and vice versa. She

3. Based on paragraph 2, it can be inferred that
    Ⓐ the chemical composition of nectar varies little from plant to plant.
    Ⓑ most plants do not want organisms to feed on their nectar indefinitely.
    Ⓒ nectars contain all the building blocks of proteins.
    Ⓓ flowers stop producing nectar after they have been fertilized.

4. All of the following are mentioned in paragraph 3 EXCEPT
    Ⓐ ants can defend against animals much larger than them.
    Ⓑ aphids, which reproduce asexually, are a significant pest.
    Ⓒ the purpose of extrafloral nectaries is different from those in flowers.
    Ⓓ parasitic wasps provide protection against caterpillar eggs.

5. The word "secrete" in paragraph 4 is closest in meaning to
    Ⓐ emit
    Ⓑ secure
    Ⓒ conclude
    Ⓓ absorb

6. What is the function of paragraph 6 as it relates to paragraph 5?
    Ⓐ To show similarities between the work of Wheeler and Bentley
    Ⓑ To provide support for Delpino's work
    Ⓒ To illustrate what Bentley's experiment was about
    Ⓓ To cast doubt on the validity of Bentley's experiment

compared plants living in a carefully controlled environment free of ants to others in an environment that contained them. She found that after the plants had reproduced, there was a marked difference in the number of viable seeds that they produced. The plants that were exposed to ants produced an average of 215 seeds, whereas the plants in the controlled environment produced a mere 45. The ants protected the flowers throughout their stages of development, thereby providing the plants with a better opportunity to reproduce.

7 ➡ As the research by Wheeler and Bentley shows, these organisms depend upon each other for their survival. The ants provide the plants with much needed protection, while the plants provide the ants with an easily digestible energy source and protection against their predators. Most insects have parasitic relationships with plants, wherein the plants suffer for the insect's benefit. However, the relationships between extrafloral nectarine plants and their protectors appear to be wholly beneficial to both species. This means that they have evolved to share a mutualistic form of symbiosis. When this occurred or how long it took to happen remains unclear, but their interaction is clearly observable.

7. According to paragraph 6, Bentley conducted the experiment by

   Ⓐ introducing different types of insects to each environment.
   Ⓑ delaying the stages of development of plants in one environment.
   Ⓒ controlling the number of plants in each environment.
   Ⓓ comparing plants in an ant-free environment to those in one with ants.

8. Based on paragraph 7, it can be inferred that

   Ⓐ extrafloral nectaries are a product of evolution.
   Ⓑ a positive symbiotic relationship between insects and plants is rare.
   Ⓒ over time, the ants developed enzymes that could easily digest the amino acids present in nectar.
   Ⓓ more careful observation is needed to fully understand the relationship between extrafloral nectarine plants and their predators.

TOEFL Reading

9. Look at the four squares [■] that indicate where the following sentence could be added to the passage.

   Barbara Bentley conducted an experiment in 1977 that added further support to the theory.

   Where would the sentence best fit?

   Click on a square [■] to add the sentence to the passage.

10. **Directions:** An introductory sentence for a brief summary of the passage is provided below. Complete the summary by selecting the THREE answer choices that express the most important ideas in the passage. Some sentences do not belong in the summary because they express ideas that are not presented in the passage or are minor ideas in the passage. ***This question is worth 2 points.***

    While nectar produced inside flowers attracts insects to help pollinate them, nectar produced on other parts of the plant attracts insects to protect the plant.

    -
    -
    -

    Answer Choices

    (A) Nectar, which is primarily composed of natural sugars, includes other chemical compounds that give off scents to attract insects.

    (B) Both hydathodes and stomata are types of specialized plant tissues, but hydathodes secrete excess water while stomata regulate gas exchange.

    (C) While many scientists mistakenly assumed that extrafloral nectaries were excretory organs, Delpino was right in his argument that extrafloral nectar attracts insects to gain their protection.

    (D) Bentley's experiment, which showed that plants produced more seeds when ants were present, revealed the symbiotic relationship between insects and plants with extrafloral nectaries.

    (E) In fact, plants exposed to ants produced an average of 215 seeds while those in an ant-free environment produced an average of 45 seeds.

    (F) Insects such as parasitic wasps and ants feed on extrafloral nectar, consume pests which attack the plant, and deter larger herbivores from feeding on the plant.

    Drag your answer choices to the spaces where they belong.
    To remove an answer choice, click on it. To review the passage, click on **View Text**.

Passage 2

TOEFL Reading

History of Theater

1 ➡ The cultural exchange between ancient Greece and Rome laid the groundwork for the development of Roman theater, with Greek tragedies exerting a profound influence on the evolution of Roman dramatic tradition. Greek tragedies served as a source of inspiration for Roman playwrights, who eagerly embraced and adapted these works for Roman audiences. The enduring themes and universal truths explored in Greek tragedies resonated deeply with Roman spectators, who were drawn to the moral dilemmas, human struggles, and cosmic forces depicted in these timeless narratives. Works by Greek tragedians such as Aeschylus, Sophocles, and Euripides were introduced to Roman audiences through translations and adaptations, offering them a glimpse into the cultural and intellectual world of ancient Greece.

2 ➡ The translation of Greek tragedies into Latin by Roman playwrights was a complex and nuanced process that involved more than just linguistic conversion. Roman dramatists, such as Ennius and Accius, meticulously adapted these ancient Greek works to suit the tastes and sensibilities of Roman audiences. While striving to retain the essential themes and dramatic elements of the original texts, they also incorporated elements of Roman language, culture, and mythology, ensuring that the translated plays spoke to their intended audience. Ultimately, Roman translators faced the challenge of bridging the cultural and contextual gap between ancient Greece and Rome. They were tasked with navigating the differences in social customs, religious beliefs, and political systems, seeking to make the translated tragedies relevant and accessible to Roman spectators.

3 ➡ As a result, many of the characters in Greek tragedies underwent transformations to better suit the sensibilities of Romans. For example, in

1. According to paragraph 1, Roman audiences enjoyed Greek tragedies because
   Ⓐ Romans related to many of the Greek tragedies' themes.
   Ⓑ both cultures shared nearly identical cultural values.
   Ⓒ Roman tragedies also focused on moral dilemmas and mythical narratives.
   Ⓓ translations were adapted to fit the preferences of Roman citizens.

2. The word "timeless" in paragraph 1 is closest in meaning to
   Ⓐ aging
   Ⓑ enduring
   Ⓒ continuous
   Ⓓ endless

3. Why does the author mention "Ennius and Accius" in paragraph 2?
   Ⓐ to emphasize the challenges Roman dramatists faced
   Ⓑ to list some of the tasks translating Greek dramas entailed
   Ⓒ to give an example of Roman dramatists involved in translation work
   Ⓓ to describe the work involved in translating Greek tragedies

4. The word "navigating" in paragraph 2 is closest in meaning to
   Ⓐ maneuvering
   Ⓑ steering
   Ⓒ redirecting
   Ⓓ defusing

TOEFL Reading

Seneca's rendition of "Medea," the character of Medea becomes a more complex and morally ambiguous figure than in the original play by Euripides, who originally depicted her as slightly more emotionally predictable. Seneca portrays Medea as a powerful and cunning woman driven by a mixture of love, revenge, and despair, making her motivations and actions more relatable to Roman spectators. Furthermore, characters in Roman tragedies often embodied the ideals of Roman virtue and piety, reflecting the moral and ethical values of Roman society. For instance, the character of Hercules became a favorite in Roman adaptations of Greek tragedies, appearing as a symbol of strength, heroism, and divine favor, embodying qualities that were highly esteemed in Roman culture.

4 ➡ Roman playwrights also transformed Greek tragedies by enriching them with additional dialogue and soliloquies, thus enhancing the dramatic impact and emotional depth of the plays. **By inserting new lines of dialogue and introspective monologues, playwrights provided insights into the inner thoughts and motivations of the characters, allowing audiences to connect more deeply with their struggles and dilemmas.** These additions often served to intensify the emotional tension and psychological complexity of the narratives, drawing viewers into the emotional turmoil of the characters' experiences. Through these creative embellishments, Roman playwrights breathed new life into Greek tragedies, infusing them with a sense of immediacy and emotional authenticity that Roman audiences could more readily relate to.

5 ➡ Roman reinterpretations of Greek tragedies reflected the political climate of Rome through their portrayal of power dynamics, political intrigue, and societal tensions. Roman playwrights often infused Greek narratives with elements drawn from contemporary Roman politics, allowing them to comment on the complexities of power and governance in their own society. For example, characters such

5. According to paragraph 3, which of the following was NOT a change that the character Medea underwent by Roman playwrights?

Ⓐ Seneca added additional emotional volatility to Medea's character.

Ⓑ Playwrights transformed her personality into a more formulaic mixture of emotions.

Ⓒ It became more difficult for viewers to interpret Medea's intentions.

Ⓓ Medea's virtue and allegiance became more questionable in the Roman version.

6. Which of the following best expresses the essential information in the highlighted sentence? Incorrect answer choices change the meaning in important ways or leave out essential information.

Ⓐ Playwrights employed various dramatic techniques, including the addition of dialogues and soliloquies, to enhance the emotional resonance of the characters' experiences, thus intensifying the audience's engagement with their trials and tribulations.

Ⓑ In order to increase the audience's relatability with the characters, the addition of introspective monologues and extra dialogue became a common technique among playwrights, which facilitated further understanding of the character's introspections and motivations.

Ⓒ One of the greatest challenges for Roman playwrights was to create an authentic connection between viewers and the characters, which was often achieved by providing insight into the characters' struggles and dilemmas through additional dialogue and introspective monologues.

as Creon or Agamemnon were reimagined as authoritarian rulers or ambitious politicians, grappling with issues of legitimacy, authority, and the abuse of power. [■A] These adaptations served as allegories for the political realities of Rome, where struggles for power, political rivalries, and the machinations of ambitious individuals were commonplace. [■B] Furthermore, Roman playwrights used Greek tragedies to explore themes of justice, law, and the responsibilities of leadership, reflecting the societal anxieties and moral dilemmas of their time. [■C] By reinterpreting Greek tragedies within the context of Roman society, playwrights engaged with pressing questions about the nature of governance, the role of the state, and the obligations of rulers towards their subjects. [■D] These demonstrate how Roman playwrights offered audiences a reflection of their own political realities, prompting them to contemplate the ethical complexities of power and authority in Roman society.

6 ➡ The Roman reinterpretations of Greek tragedies served as a critical juncture in the legacy of Greek tragedies. The works of Greek tragedians continue to be studied around the world. Moreover, the enduring influence of Greek tragedies is evident in the cultural and intellectual achievements of Western civilization, where the principles of tragedy and catharsis continue to inform and inspire artistic expression. However, many argue that Roman translations, adaptations, and reinterpretations further enriched the theatrical value of Greek tragedies, helping to continue a tradition of dramatic excellence.

Ⓓ Because the addition of dialogues and internal monologues offered audiences a glimpse into the inner workings of the character's conflicts, it also fostered a stronger emotional connection between the viewers and the characters' experiences.

7. What can be inferred about the Romans from paragraph 5?

Ⓐ Many Romans were familiar with Roman politics and the power struggles that were common to their governments.

Ⓑ Nearly all Roman rulers were despotic and authoritarian.

Ⓒ Many Romans were disgruntled with the state of Roman politics and often displayed their protests publicly.

Ⓓ Politics was an important component of Roman existential philosophy as it related to their sense of justice and societal function.

8. Look at the four squares [■] that indicate where the following sentence could be added to the passage.

Oedipus and Antigone were remade into tragic figures confronting the consequences of their decisions in a world fraught with political turmoil and moral ambiguity.

Where would the sentence best fit?

Click on a square [■] to add the sentence to the passage.

TOEFL Reading

9. The author mentions "tragedy and catharsis" in paragraph 6 in order to
    - Ⓐ demonstrate the significance of Greek tragedy's influence on Western culture.
    - Ⓑ argue Greek tragedy's significance is indebted to the work of Roman reinterpretations.
    - Ⓒ point out two crucial components common to nearly all Greek tragedies.
    - Ⓓ add to a list of cultural, political, and philosophical impacts Greece had on the West.

10. **Directions:** An introductory sentence for a brief summary of the passage is provided below. Complete the summary by selecting the THREE answer choices that express the most important ideas in the passage. Some sentences do not belong in the summary because they express ideas that are not presented in the passage or minor ideas in the passage. *This question is worth 2 points.*

    Roman playwrights modified Greek tragedies in order to make the characters and narratives more relatable to Roman audiences.

    - Ⓐ Greek tragedies dwelled on many themes and values that were already familiar to Roman audiences.
    - Ⓑ Translating the Greek works required Roman playwrights to infuse the original tragedies with elements of Roman mythology, culture, and society.
    - Ⓒ The character Medea was reinterpreted as a more morally ambiguous and emotionally capricious figure.
    - Ⓓ Roman values such as virtue, piety, and strength were added to or enhanced in characters to result in further contextualization.
    - Ⓔ The addition of soliloquies enabled more insight into the private thoughts of characters, allowing the audience to connect more with the character.
    - Ⓕ Political themes of power, justice, and law were also incorporated into Greek tragedies to reflect the Roman political culture and climate.

    Drag your answer choices to the spaces where they belong.
    To remove an answer choice, click on it. To review the passage, click on **View Text**.

Actual Test 05

TOEFL Reading

Reading Section Directions

This section measures your ability to understand academic passages in English.

You will have 36 minutes to read and answer the questions 2 passages.

Most questions are worth 1 point but the last question in each set is worth more than 1 point. The directions indicate how many points you may receive.

Within each screen, you can go to the next question by clicking **Next**. You may skip questions and go back to them later. If you want to return to previous questions, click on **Back**.

You can click on **Review** at any time and the review screen will show you which questions you have answered and which you have not answered. From this review screen, you may go directly to any questions you have already seen in the Reading section.

You may now begin the Reading section.

Click on **Continue** to go on.

Dwarfism in Timberline Vegetation

1 ➡ Dwarfism among timberline vegetation on mountains represents a unique adaptation to the extreme environmental conditions prevalent at high elevations. Dwarfism refers to the phenomenon whereby trees and other vegetation exhibit stunted growth forms at high elevations near the timberline. This adaptation is a response to the challenging environmental conditions prevalent at these altitudes, including low temperatures, high winds, and limited nutrient availability. Dwarfed individuals of tree species such as pine, spruce, and fir often have reduced stature, slower growth rates, and altered morphological characteristics compared to their counterparts at lower elevations.

2 ➡ One pivotal factor contributing to dwarfism is the short growing season characteristic of mountain environments, where prolonged periods of snow cover and low temperatures limit the window of opportunity for plant growth and development. This abbreviated growing season constrains the duration during which plants can photosynthesize and accumulate biomass, resulting in reduced overall plant size. Furthermore, the physiological processes of plants are significantly influenced by temperature, with low temperatures at high elevations inhibiting metabolic activity and slowing down growth rates. As a consequence, plants invest fewer resources in above-ground growth and allocate more towards essential physiological functions such as maintenance and reproduction. Moreover, the nutrient-poor soils prevalent at timberline impose limitations on plant growth, as shallow and rocky substrates restrict root development and nutrient uptake. Consequently, plants exhibit adaptations such as increased root-to-shoot ratios and enhanced nutrient-use efficiency to cope with nutrient scarcity.

3 ➡ Dwarfism among timberline vegetation on

---

1. The word "**prevalent**" in paragraph 1 is closest in meaning to
   Ⓐ rampant
   Ⓑ pervasive
   Ⓒ visible
   Ⓓ tolerable

2. According to paragraph 2, all of the following are factors that contribute to dwarfism EXCEPT
   Ⓐ seasonal effects on plant growth
   Ⓑ poor quality soil
   Ⓒ diversion of resources
   Ⓓ extreme temperature and elevation

3. Through paragraph 2, we can infer that
   Ⓐ the same dwarf plant at a lower elevation would have shorter roots.
   Ⓑ plants at higher elevations compete less for soil nutrients.
   Ⓒ extreme attempts at maximizing resources causes many plants at higher elevations to ultimately fail.
   Ⓓ dwarfed plants result from limited opportunities for growth.

4. According to paragraph 3, how do dwarfed plants influence their surroundings?
   Ⓐ They alter the microclimates of timberline habitats by raising net temperatures.
   Ⓑ They create the conditions for a large array of plants to proliferate in the area.
   Ⓒ They provide shelter for wildlife that would otherwise be highly vulnerable to predators.
   Ⓓ Their effects on soil quality and stability create habitats for animals.

mountains fosters a tapestry of microhabitats, nurturing an array of flora and fauna finely attuned to the harsh conditions of high elevations. Take, for instance, the dense mats of alpine dwarf willows (*Salix herbacea*) and cushion plants like the Arctic bearberry (*Arctostaphylos alpinus*). These diminutive plants create sheltered nooks amidst the rugged terrain, offering refuge for creatures such as the American pika (*Ochotona princeps*), which relies on the protection provided by such vegetation to weather the intense winds and temperature fluctuations of the alpine environment. Moreover, the intricate root systems of these dwarfed plants, enhance soil stability and nutrient availability. Additionally, the presence of stunted conifers in these zones creates vertical structure in the landscape, providing niches for species like the northern flying squirrel.

4 ➡ Plants exhibiting dwarfism at timberline have undergone intricate evolutionary processes resulting in a suite of specialized adaptations primarily focused on leaf morphology. One prominent adaptation involves the reduction in leaf size, a strategic adjustment aimed at conserving water in the arid, windy conditions. This not only decreases the surface area available for transpiration but also minimizes the risk of damage from desiccating winds. [■A] Furthermore, alterations in leaf structure optimize light capture and photosynthetic efficiency, crucial for sustaining growth and metabolism. [■B] These adaptations may include alterations in thickness and shape, and the presence of specialized structures such as hairs or wax coatings. [■C] The increased leaf thickness helps to reduce water loss and provides structural support, while alterations in shape and the presence of surface structures serve to maximize the efficiency of photosynthesis. [■D]

5 ➡ Dwarfism among timberline vegetation encompasses critical implications for the functioning and conservation of mountain ecosystems, serving as both sensitive indicators

5. The author mentions "intricate root systems" in paragraph 3 in order to

   Ⓐ illustrate a critical function of dwarfed plants in creating natural environments for birds.
   Ⓑ emphasize the underappreciated effects of dwarfed plants on their ecosystems.
   Ⓒ further explain the structure of dwarfed plants.
   Ⓓ give an example of how dwarfed plants create habitats for animals.

6. According to paragraph 4, how do smaller leaf sizes benefit dwarfed plants?

   Ⓐ They enable plants to survive dry conditions by increasing vaporization.
   Ⓑ Smaller leaf sizes reduce exposure to harmful forces such as strong winds.
   Ⓒ They enhance the plant's photosynthetic capabilities by capturing more sunlight.
   Ⓓ A reduction in leaf size leads to an increase in thickness, which in turn increases water conservation.

7. Look at the four squares [■] that indicate where the following sentence could be added to the passage.

   Additionally, some dwarfed species exhibit a phenomenon known as "sun-tracking" or "heliotropism," where leaves adjust their orientation throughout the day to optimize exposure to sunlight.

   Where would the sentence best fit?

   Click on a square [■] to add the sentence to the passage.

of environmental change and vital components of these fragile habitats. Due to their specialized adaptations and limited tolerance for environmental fluctuations, dwarfed individuals are particularly vulnerable to disturbances such as climate change, habitat fragmentation, and human activities. Shifts in temperature, precipitation patterns, and snowpack dynamics associated with climate change can directly impact the distribution and abundance of dwarfed vegetation, altering the composition and structure of timberline ecosystems. Habitat fragmentation, often caused by human infrastructure development and land-use practices, further exacerbates the vulnerability of dwarfed vegetation by isolating populations and reducing genetic connectivity, hindering their ability to adapt and persist in changing environments. Human activities such as logging, grazing, and recreational tourism can also degrade fragile timberline habitats, disrupting plant communities and ecological processes essential for ecosystem functioning. **Monitoring the distribution and abundance of dwarfed vegetation can provide valuable insights into the ecological impacts of these threats on mountain ecosystems, informing conservation strategies and management decisions aimed at preserving these unique and biodiverse habitats.** Of course, conserving intact timberline habitats is essential for maintaining the biodiversity and ecological integrity of mountain landscapes, ensuring the continued survival of dwarfed vegetation and the myriad species that depend on them for habitat and resources.

8. According to paragraph 5, dwarfed plants help scientists better understand the effects of changes in the environment because

   Ⓐ a surprising share of human activity is concentrated in timberline habitats.
   Ⓑ dwarfed plants have evolved to survive in such extreme, unique conditions.
   Ⓒ habitat fragmentation disrupts timberline ecosystem sustainability.
   Ⓓ environmental changes aggravate the already extreme conditions dwarfed plants have adapted to.

9. Which of the following best expresses the essential information in the highlighted sentence? Incorrect answer choices change the meaning in important ways or leave out essential information.

   Ⓐ Insight gained through monitoring dwarfed mountain plants provides crucial information on the effects of environmental changes, which in turn can inform conservation and preservation efforts.
   Ⓑ One way that dwarfed plants inform conservation and management strategies is by providing climatic data that reflect changes in the surrounding environments as well as the effects of human activity.
   Ⓒ By tracking the spread and density of stunted plant life, researchers gain valuable understanding of how environmental pressures affect mountain ecosystems.
   Ⓓ Scientists and governments alike have taken advantage of studies on timberline dwarfed plants to inform their conservation strategies and policies regarding these unusual and special habitats.

10. Directions: An introductory sentence for a brief summary of the passage is provided below. Complete the summary by selecting the THREE answer choices that express the most important ideas in the passage. Some sentences do not belong in the summary because they express ideas that are not presented in the passage or minor ideas in the passage. *This question is worth 2 points.*

Dwarfed plants in timberline habitats are exceptionally distinct in both their features as well as the benefits they provide.

- (A) Dwarfism in plants arises from several unique factors, including seasonal differences and comparatively less available resources.
- (B) These plants survive in harsh climates by diverting more resources to root growth and survival, as opposed to size and breadth.
- (C) Dwarfed plants provide habitats for wildlife in a variety of ways, such as through their influence on soil quality and vertical food distributions.
- (D) Changes in leaf size have enabled dwarfed plants to weather the windy, arid conditions common in timberline environments.
- (E) Dwarfism provides clues to experts on ways to prevent climate change and other human-induced changes on natural habitats.
- (F) Plants such as alpine willows create refuge for animals that need protection from the extreme weather.

Drag your answer choices to the spaces where they belong.
To remove an answer choice, click on it. To review the passage, click on **View Text**.

Agricultural Pest Control

1 ➡ Without the adoption and subsequent development of agriculture, human society would never have been able to develop to the extent that it has, nor could our population have grown so rapidly. In order to farm, humans deliberately disrupt natural ecosystems to create the best possible conditions for the crops they wish to grow. [■A] They remove large numbers of the native species, alter the distribution of water, and enrich the soil with fertilizers. In addition, most farms practice monoculture to a certain extent, which means that one section to all of their land is used to grow the same plants. [■B] Such massive disruption of nature often leads to the explosion of species that consume those plants. [■C] In order to control pest organisms, farmers typically use chemical or biological controls; however, a more moderate approach appears to be the most effective in the long run. [■D]

2 ➡ Chemical controls are the most widely used method for limiting pest populations today, but they have a surprisingly long past. Around 2,500 BCE, ancient Sumerians used elemental sulfur powder to discourage pests, and a text called the Rig Veda, which dates back to around 4,000 years ago, mentions the use of poisonous plants for similar purposes. By the Renaissance, toxic chemicals like mercury, lead, and arsenic were being widely used to kill pests. Although these chemicals are toxic to humans as well, they were also used in makeup and medicines. At the time, people believed that small doses of poison were good for one's health, and no doubt thought that using them on crops would have little effect on them.

3 ➡ Beginning in the 17th century, people began extracting chemicals from plants to use as pesticides: nicotine sulfide from tobacco, pyrethrum from chrysanthemum flowers, and rotenone from the roots of tropical plants. All

---

1. All of the following are mentioned in paragraph 2 about past pest control EXCEPT
   Ⓐ Sumerians used powdered sulfur to deter pests.
   Ⓑ farmers used toxins that made produce unsafe for consumption.
   Ⓒ ancient farmers were aware of plants that are toxic to pests.
   Ⓓ texts on agriculture have been written for over 4,000 years.

2. Which of the sentences below best expresses the essential information in the highlighted sentence in the passage? *Incorrect* answer choices change the meaning in important ways or leave out essential information.
   Ⓐ At that time, people thought using a little poison on crops was helpful for their health.
   Ⓑ At that time, people took small doses of poison for their health by using them on the crops that they grew.
   Ⓒ At that time, the poisons which people used on their crops were not very dangerous, so they took them for their health.
   Ⓓ At that time, people thought that using poisons would not affect crops seriously since they were thought to be beneficial when used in small quantities.

TOEFL Reading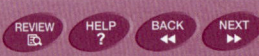

of these pesticides existed in nature, even the toxic elemental chemicals. However, in the early 20th century, synthesized chemicals became dominant. The first of these was DDT, which was initially used to control human parasites like mosquitoes and lice. Scientists soon learned to deliver DDT in any physical form, which led to its widespread use in agriculture. Since then, chemical pesticides have become the dominant control for agricultural pests, and their use has revealed many side effects of pest control.

4 ➡ Any attempt at controlling the population of a pest species entails the risk of affecting other species. Initially, this is caused by disrupting the predator-prey system. Even though local predators are unable to control the pest species, they may still depend upon them for food. However, chemical controls introduce additional problems. Firstly, the pesticides often kill organisms other than the intended pests, including their natural predators. Secondly, continuously exposing pests to chemicals will inevitably cause them to develop a resistance. Through natural immunity or repeated low level exposure, some will always survive to reproduce, and their population will rebound. Nearly every pesticide known to man has been used on mosquitoes, and they have always quickly adapted. Thirdly, pesticides spread into the surrounding environment, particularly through the water system. This can have far-reaching effects on organisms with no connection to the farms whatsoever, like birds that eat fish.

5 ➡ Thus, many farmers have decided to return to nature by introducing predatory species. Again, this is hardly a new idea as the Chinese are credited with deliberately introducing ant hives to their fruit orchards. After noticing that a particular species of ants attacked insects on their citrus trees, they began collecting and transplanting the ants' nests into their trees. Today, many farmers introduce spiders, wasps and other predatory animals to their fields. However, they must take great care with the

3. According to paragraph 3, all of the following are true about DDT EXCEPT
   (A) DDT replaced natural chemicals from plants that had been used to kill pests.
   (B) DDT was the first synthetic pesticide, and it came to be used widely in the 20th century.
   (C) DDT was originally synthesized to help agriculture by eliminating insects.
   (D) DDT was adapted to be available in various physical forms.

4. According to paragraph 4, how does intentional control of pest populations affect the food chain?
   (A) Pesticides make it unnecessary for natural predators to depend upon pests for food.
   (B) The use of pesticides may kill natural predators as well as pest species.
   (C) Pesticides affect the whole ecosystem by causing mutations in natural predators.
   (D) Pesticides often weaken the immunity of predators, allowing pests to thrive.

5. According to paragraph 5, the Chinese introduced ant hives to their orchards to
   (A) identify the organisms affecting their trees.
   (B) remove undesired plants from the rows of trees.
   (C) keep their citrus trees safe from fruit-damaging insects.
   (D) make their citrus trees more resistant to insects and disease.

organisms which they select. The introduction of any non-indigenous species can have serious unforeseen side effects. These organisms often have no natural predators in their new environment, so their population can grow unchecked. In addition, there is no guarantee that they will eat the correct organisms, or even remain in the desired area. This has occurred widely with the cane toad, which often fled farmers' fields due to insufficient ground cover. Since the toads are poisonous, they have had a disastrous impact on local predatory animals with no immunity to their toxin.

6 ➡ In order to avoid such problems and still maintain maximum possible crop yield, many experts recommend an approach called Integrated Pest Management (IPM). IPM involves many tactics, but it begins with determining the threat level to the crops. Merely sighting a possible pest is not sufficient cause to begin using pesticides. The situation should be carefully monitored until an identified pest becomes an economic threat to the farm. At that point, preventative measures like removing the affected plants, rotating crops, or selecting more resistant varieties of a plant are recommended. If these are ineffective, then introducing reliable predator species may be an option, but spraying of broad-spectrum pesticides should only be used as a last resort.

6. Why does the author mention the cane toad in paragraph 5?

   Ⓐ To give an example of a species with great adaptability
   Ⓑ To explain how to domesticate introduced species effectively
   Ⓒ To claim that any attempt to control a pest population is fruitless
   Ⓓ To show the danger of introducing foreign species indiscriminately

7. The word "tactics" in paragraph 6 is closest in meaning to

   Ⓐ alliances
   Ⓑ strategies
   Ⓒ standards
   Ⓓ advantages

8. What can be inferred about IPM from paragraph 6?

   Ⓐ It was designed to guarantee both ecological safety and productivity improvement.
   Ⓑ It aims to eradicate any kind of pest by introducing predator species.
   Ⓒ It puts the highest priority on environmental value and the protection of species.
   Ⓓ It was intended to expand agricultural fields and maximize crop yields.

9. Look at the four squares [■] that indicate where the following sentence could be added to the passage.

These species that endanger crops are labeled as pests.

Where would the sentence best fit?

Click on a square [■] to add the sentence to the passage.

10. **Directions:** An introductory sentence for a brief summary of the passage is provided below. Complete the summary by selecting the THREE answer choices that express the most important ideas in the passage. Some sentences do not belong in the summary because they express ideas that are not presented in the passage or are minor ideas in the passage.
This question is worth 2 points.

There have been various efforts to raise agricultural productivity by controlling pest organisms throughout human history.

-
-
-

Answer Choices

Ⓐ Thanks to the development of agriculture, mankind could flourish and build civilizations.
Ⓑ In the past, a variety of chemicals from nature were generally used as pesticides.
Ⓒ To avoid the adverse effects of chemical pesticides on the ecosystem, some farmers began to make use of the predator-prey system.
Ⓓ Before the advent of DDT, people had mainly depended upon specific predator species to discourage pests.
Ⓔ These days, the introduction of non-indigenous species is recommended for pest eradication since it has few side effects.
Ⓕ IPM is an approach which requires care for the balance between economic values and the ecosystem.

Drag your answer choices to the spaces where they belong.
To remove an answer choice, click on it. To review the passage, click on **View Text**.

Actual Test 06

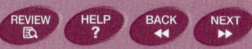

TOEFL Reading

Reading Section Directions

This section measures your ability to understand academic passages in English.

You will have 36 minutes to read and answer the questions 2 passages.

Most questions are worth 1 point but the last question in each set is worth more than 1 point. The directions indicate how many points you may receive.

Within each screen, you can go to the next question by clicking **Next**. You may skip questions and go back to them later. If you want to return to previous questions, click on **Back**.

You can click on **Review** at any time and the review screen will show you which questions you have answered and which you have not answered. From this review screen, you may go directly to any questions you have already seen in the Reading section.

You may now begin the Reading section.

Click on **Continue** to go on.

TOEFL Reading

The Development of Islamic Bookmaking

1 ➡ Bookmaking flourished in the Middle East between the 9th and 15th centuries. Islamic books from this period were finely hand-crafted with luxurious materials and had detailed and artistically wrought covers and interior illustrations. This flowering of literary artistry was the result of two major events in the Muslim world. The first was the development of an official language with a codified alphabet and an accepted writing style. The second was the importation of paper-making technology, which allowed books to be produced on a vaster scale. These books were one of the main venues for artistic expression in the Arab world, and they employed not only calligraphers and painters, but also leather and paper makers and professional binders. This bookmaking industry was financially supported by princes and caliphs and lasted until printing presses were imported.

2 ➡ Islamic bookmaking extends back to the beginning of the religion it supports. According to the teachings of Islam, the Quran was imparted to the Prophet Muhammad by the archangel Gabriel between 610 and 632 CE, and he in turn translated the word of Allah into his own native Arabic. At first, his followers memorized his words and verbally relayed them to others, but this method of spreading the word was inconvenient, and worse yet, unreliable. In order to faithfully repeat his words, his assistants began writing down the Quran on any available material. These were eventually collected together, but a problem emerged: there was no unified Arabic alphabet. This was resolved during the rule of caliph Abd al-Malik, who made Arabic the official language of his empire and codified it into a single alphabet. This was eventually developed into calligraphy by Ibn Muqla in the 9th century, which was perfected by the 11th century calligrapher Ibn al-Bawwab.

---

1. Based on paragraph 1, it can be inferred that
   - Ⓐ bookmaking flourished because of the varieties of writing styles.
   - Ⓑ printing presses were probably imported around the 15th century.
   - Ⓒ there were no other channels for artistic expression in the Arab world.
   - Ⓓ the upper class did not support bookmaking.

2. The author mentions "Ibn Muqla" in paragraph 2 to indicate who
   - Ⓐ developed the Arabic handwriting system
   - Ⓑ collected the Quran into a single volume
   - Ⓒ made Arabic the official language of Islam
   - Ⓓ codified the Arabic alphabet

3. According to paragraph 2, what was one problem of spreading the Quran?
   - Ⓐ Verbally spreading the word was slow.
   - Ⓑ Most of the recorded Quran were illegible.
   - Ⓒ Calligraphy was not perfected until the 11th century.
   - Ⓓ There was no unified Arabic alphabet.

3 ➡ [■A] What contributed most to the expansion of books throughout the Muslim world was an innovation from China that was introduced in the 9th century: paper. [■B] Muslim forces that captured Chinese prisoners in Samarkand who knew how to make paper allowed this to happen. [■C] Their method of paper production involved three main steps. [■D] First, pulp was extracted from various plant types by boiling them down in water. Next, a fine mesh screen was used to catch these fibers and form a thin layer of pulp. Finally, these screens were carefully dried to make flexible sheets of paper. Despite the labor intensive process, this method actually produced writing material much more quickly and inexpensively than the prior method of curing goat hides. Qurans were soon being produced with pages made of this paper, and later other secular and scientific ideas were also spread through such books.

4 ➡ The first books produced in this way were religious texts, but later history, scientific treatises, poetry, and romantic literature were also written down and transformed into books. Many of these secular texts were just as richly decorated as the Quran, and many people were employed in their manufacture. They often featured leather covers that were embossed with gold in geometric and floral patterns. For the Qurans, this usually involved a fairly consistent pattern with a circle or oval at the center of the design that symbolized the sun. Of course, the degree of decoration varied, with books that were made for important patrons or public use being the richest, whereas those for personal use were often less ostentatious. These books became valuable trade goods, and often could be found far from where they were produced.

5 ➡ As paper spread through the Arab world, it revolutionized more than just bookmaking. Parchments were limited in size by the animals killed to make the original leather, but paper was limited only by the size of the screen it was dried upon. This meant that huge, incredibly detailed

4. The word "extracted" in paragraph 3 is closest in meaning to

   Ⓐ converged
   Ⓑ purified
   Ⓒ accumulated
   Ⓓ removed

5. According to paragraph 4, what was the result of a flourishing bookmaking industry?

   Ⓐ Books became trade goods in other parts of the world.
   Ⓑ There was a growth in the number of literature writers.
   Ⓒ Secular texts became more popular than the Quran.
   Ⓓ Lower quality materials were used to keep up with demand.

6. The word "ostentatious" in paragraph 4 is closest in meaning to

   Ⓐ extravagant
   Ⓑ expensive
   Ⓒ decorated
   Ⓓ obnoxious

TOEFL Reading

maps could be produced, and blueprints could be made large enough to clearly show building elements. In addition, the limitations of paper also made it popular for some purposes. Because the paper was so thin and absorbent, ink marks on it were nearly impossible to change, unlike parchment which allowed for corrections, or even worse, fraudulent alterations. For this reason, it quickly became the chief material used for official documents in Baghdad. Paper and its various uses rapidly spread throughout the Muslim world, stretching across northern Africa, and even into Spain, where it was first introduced to Europeans.

7. Which of the sentences below best expresses the essential information in the highlighted sentence in the passage? *Incorrect* answer choices change the meaning in important ways or leave out essential information.

   Ⓐ While parchment allowed for the correction of ink marks, fraudulent alterations on paper were impossible to change because it was so thin and absorbent.

   Ⓑ Paper's resistance to ink allowed for criminal alterations, while corrections on parchment were nearly impossible.

   Ⓒ While alterations could be made on parchment, the thin nature of paper made it impossible for corrections to be made.

   Ⓓ Because it was thin and absorbent, parchment allowed for corrections, sometimes even fraudulent alterations.

8. Based on paragraph 5, what can be inferred about paper?

   Ⓐ Paper was introduced to Europe before the 9th century.

   Ⓑ Using paper increased the sizes of books and documents.

   Ⓒ The concept of drawing up blueprints was nonexistent until the widespread production of paper.

   Ⓓ The Chinese were unwilling to reveal the secrets of manufacturing paper to the Europeans.

9. Look at the four squares [■] that indicate where the following sentence could be added to the passage.

   Paper was originally developed much earlier, but before this time the technology had not spread westward.

   Where would the sentence best fit?

   Click on a square [■] to add the sentence to the passage.

10. **Directions:** An introductory sentence for a brief summary of the passage is provided below. Complete the summary by selecting the THREE answer choices that express the most important ideas in the passage. Some sentences do not belong in the summary because they express ideas that are not presented in the passage or are minor ideas in the passage. **This question is worth 2 points.**

    Development of a unified alphabet and the introduction of paper-making technology allowed the bookmaking industry to flourish in the Middle East.

    -
    -
    -

    Answer Choices

    (A) Arabic calligraphy wasn't perfected until the 11th century, crippling the caliph's effort at spreading the language.
    (B) Widespread production of paper in the Middle East allowed non-religious literature to be made into books, and the use of paper quickly spread to other continents.
    (C) With a unified alphabet, the teachings of Muhammad could be written down, which was more convenient and reliable than the previous oral means.
    (D) Paper had many advantages over animal hides, and it quickly became the preferred writing material for books, blueprints, and official documents.
    (E) The books were richly decorated with gold, with some books being more ostentatious than others.
    (F) While paper was invented much earlier, it wasn't until the 9th century that the technology spread westward.

    Drag your answer choices to the spaces where they belong.
    To remove an answer choice, click on it. To review the passage, click on **View Text**.

Passage 2

Evolution of Cetaceans

1 ➡ Cetaceans, which comprise whales, dolphins, and porpoises, are among the most intriguing marine mammals, renowned for their cognitive complexity, intricate social structures, and profound adaptations to aquatic life. The evolutionary trajectory of cetaceans from terrestrial origins to fully aquatic organisms spans tens of millions of years, characterized by significant morphological and behavioral transformations. This evolutionary narrative begins approximately 50 million years ago during the Eocene epoch, a period noted for its warm global climates and extensive shallow seas. The earliest ancestors of cetaceans were terrestrial artiodactyls, an order of even-toed, hooved animals that includes extant species such as deer, bovines, and hippopotamuses. One of the earliest identified proto-cetaceans is *Pakicetus*, discovered in the sedimentary deposits of what is now Pakistan. Pakicetus exhibited a morphology resembling a small dog-like animal and possessed characteristics indicative of a semi-aquatic lifestyle. Its auditory structures, particularly the involucrum, were adapted for underwater hearing, while its teeth structure reflected a carnivorous diet. These early cetaceans likely inhabited riverbanks, preying on fish and other aquatic organisms while retaining terrestrial locomotion capabilities.

2 ➡ As proto-cetaceans continued their evolutionary progression, they exhibited increasingly specialized adaptations for aquatic existence. *Ambulocetus*, dating to approximately 49 million years ago, represents a critical transitional form. Often referred to as the "walking whale," Ambulocetus possessed robust limbs capable of supporting its body on land, yet its elongated body and tail anatomy suggest proficient swimming capabilities. Its locomotion in water likely mirrored that of modern otters, utilizing its hind limbs and tail for propulsion

1. The author mentions "deer" in paragraph 1 in order to
    ⓐ provide examples of the first proto-cetaceans.
    ⓑ provide an example of a terrestrial artiodactyl.
    ⓒ explain what the first hooved animals looked like.
    ⓓ explain the evolutionary origins of artiodactyls.

2. Which of the following is NOT a characteristic of Rodhocetus as described in the passage?
    ⓐ fin-like appendages
    ⓑ a streamlined body for swimming
    ⓒ robust limbs capable of sprinting
    ⓓ small hind legs

3. In paragraph 2, which of the following can be inferred about *Ambulocetus*?
    ⓐ *Ambulocetus* possessed a physical structure that made it a better swimmer than its predecessors.
    ⓑ *Ambulocetus* is closely related to other terrestrial artiodactyls, such as otters and beavers.
    ⓒ Most subsequent cetaceans inherited their swimming adaptations from *Ambulocetus*.
    ⓓ *Ambulocetus* tails were much larger and more agile than those of the Rodhocetus

TOEFL Reading

through water with considerable agility. The vertebral morphology of Ambulocetus indicates the flexibility necessary for undulating aquatic movement, a precursor to the more specialized movements particular to subsequent cetaceans. Another significant early cetacean is Rodhocetus, dating from around 47 million years ago. Rodhocetus exhibited further aquatic adaptations, such as more fin-like appendages and a streamlined body for efficient swimming in various aquatic environments. Its pelvis and hind limbs were diminished in size compared to earlier ancestors, indicating a definitive shift towards a predominantly aquatic lifestyle.

3 ➡ By approximately 40 million years ago, cetaceans had achieved significant adaptations for a fully aquatic existence. *Basilosaurus*, which flourished around 35-40 million years ago, exemplifies a pivotal stage in cetacean evolution. Unlike its predecessors, Basilosaurus was entirely adapted to marine life, with a serpentine body reaching up to 18 meters in length. Its reduced hind limbs were no longer functional for walking, signifying a complete transition to aquatic life. The placement of Basilosaurus's nostrils had shifted further back on the skull, evolving into a blowhole, an adaptation critical for breathing while swimming. Concurrently, another cetacean, *Dorudon*, emerged. Dorudon, smaller than Basilosaurus displayed advanced adaptations for aquatic life. Its well-developed flippers facilitated maneuverability, while its tail fluke provided powerful propulsion. The reduction of hind limbs and pelvic bones in Dorudon indicates a fully aquatic lifestyle, and its streamlined body morphology suggests it was an agile swimmer, akin to modern dolphins.

4 ➡ The Oligocene epoch, commencing around 34 million years ago, marked a period of significant diversification and specialization for cetaceans. During this epoch, the two major suborders of modern cetaceans began to diverge: *Odontoceti* and *Mysticeti*. Odontocetes, or toothed whales, developed sophisticated

4. According to paragraph 2, how did Rodhocetus further evolve cetaceans toward aquatic life?

   (A) Their teeth exhibited an increased carnivorous diet.
   (B) Their bodies grew longer, and their tails morphed into a more flap-like shape.
   (C) Their limbs demonstrated an increase in amphibious tendencies.
   (D) Their hind legs were less adapted toward terrestrial movement.

5. The word "concurrently" in paragraph 3 is closest in meaning to

   (A) conversely
   (B) contrarily
   (C) simultaneously
   (D) jointly

6. Which of the following best expresses the essential information in the highlighted sentence? Incorrect answer choices change the meaning in important ways or leave out essential information.

   (A) Not only did Dorudon completely evolve away from the use of its hind limbs, but its body shape indicated a dexterous swimmer, similar to modern dolphins.
   (B) The combination of hind limb reduction and a more aerodynamic body points to Dorudon living fully underwater as an agile swimmer, similar to modern dolphins.
   (C) A more streamlined body enabled Dorudon to swim more adeptly, much like modern dolphins, while smaller hind limbs and pelvic bones signify a complete move to an aquatic lifestyle.
   (D) A more streamlined body suggests Dorudon to have been agile swimmers, much like modern dolphins, and shrinking hind limbs and pelvic bones point to a fully aquatic lifestyle.

echolocation capabilities, facilitating navigation and predation. [■A] Fossil evidence from early odontocetes, such as *Squalodon*, reveals the development of complex cranial structures and specialized auditory ossicles that. [■B]

5 ➡ Mysticetes, or baleen whales, evolved a distinctive feeding strategy. Rather than teeth, they developed baleen plates composed of keratin, which they used for filter feeding. [■C] This adaptation allowed them to efficiently consume large quantities of small prey such as krill and plankton. [■D] Fossil evidence from early mysticetes, such as *Janjucetus*, indicates a transitional phase where teeth and baleen structures coexisted, signifying an evolutionary shift towards filter feeding. The advent of baleen facilitated the exploitation of abundant marine food resources, leading to the evolution of large body sizes seen in species like the blue whale, the largest known animal to have ever existed. Hence, the cetaceans of today owe their unique adaptations to millions of years of evolution, a gradual change that saw land animals evolve into some of the most intelligent and bewildering marine animals today.

7. The word "diverge" in paragraph 4 is closest in meaning to
   A) contradict
   B) split
   C) defy
   D) depart

8. Look at the four squares [■] that indicate where the following sentence could be added to the passage.

   This adaptation conferred a significant evolutionary advantage, allowing odontocetes to detect prey and obstacles with remarkable precision in the marine environment.

   Where would the sentence best fit?

   Click on a square [■] to add the sentence to the passage.

9. According to paragraph 5, how does the lack of teeth benefit *Mysticetes*?
   A) The lack of teeth enables whales to sift through their food more efficiently.
   B) The few teeth they have are used in conjunction with keratin to filter water out of their food.
   C) The absence of teeth provides an advantage when hunting for smaller prey.
   D) Keratin allows for the efficient chewing of krill and plankton.

10. **Directions:** An introductory sentence for a brief summary of the passage is provided below. Complete the summary by selecting the THREE answer choices that express the most important ideas in the passage. Some sentences do not belong in the summary because they express ideas that are not presented in the passage or minor ideas in the passage. *This question is worth 2 points.*

Cetaceans evolved from semi-aquatic artiodactyls into fully-aquatic marine mammals.

- (A) Basilosaurus represented a critical stage in cetacean evolution, as its serpentine body and smaller hind legs reflected a fully aquatic lifestyle.
- (B) The Oligocene period saw the cetacean evolution diverge into two branches: toothed whales and baleen whales.
- (C) Pakicetus' teeth structures were adapted to chew on river prey more efficiently, while their auditory structures revealed the beginnings of echolocation adaptations.
- (D) Ambulocetus was about 4.5 meters long, with flippers that allowed it to move swiftly through the water.
- (E) More aquatic adaptations were seen in Rodhocetus, with flatter appendages that resembled fins.
- (F) Dorudon had significantly larger hind limbs, although its use was limited to swimming, further indicating a move away from terrestrial living.

Drag your answer choices to the spaces where they belong.
To remove an answer choice, click on it. To review the passage, click on **View Text**.

Actual Test 07

정답 및 해석 | P. 76

TOEFL Reading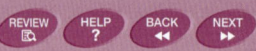

Reading Section Directions

This section measures your ability to understand academic passages in English.

You will have 36 minutes to read and answer the questions 2 passages.

Most questions are worth 1 point but the last question in each set is worth more than 1 point. The directions indicate how many points you may receive.

Within each screen, you can go to the next question by clicking **Next**. You may skip questions and go back to them later. If you want to return to previous questions, click on **Back**.

You can click on **Review** at any time and the review screen will show you which questions you have answered and which you have not answered. From this review screen, you may go directly to any questions you have already seen in the Reading section.

You may now begin the Reading section.

Click on **Continue** to go on.

The Kinetoscope

1 ➡ The Kinetoscope, a forerunner to modern cinema, was developed by Thomas Edison and his assistant William Kennedy Laurie Dickson in the late 19th century. Patented in 1891 and publicly unveiled in 1893, the Kinetoscope represented a significant leap in the development of motion picture technology. Edison, primarily motivated by the commercial potential of motion pictures, envisioned the Kinetoscope as a device for individual viewing. Together with Dickson, the chief engineer, they came up with the idea of a continuous loop of 35mm film running through a viewing machine. This film was perforated along the edges to ensure smooth movement through the mechanism. The Kinetoscope's defining feature was its peephole viewer, through which a single person could watch short, silent films. These films were often less than a minute long, depicting simple scenes like a dancer, a boxing match, or a man sneezing.

2 ➡ The first Kinetoscope parlor, which opened on April 14, 1894 at 1155 Broadway in New York City, marked a significant milestone in the history of motion pictures. This parlor, established by the Holland Brothers, featured ten Kinetoscopes, each offering a different short film. **Patrons were charged 25 cents for access to this novel form of entertainment, which quickly became a popular attraction.** Inside the parlor, visitors would find the Kinetoscopes lined up in two rows, creating an arcade-like atmosphere. Each machine was housed in an oak cabinet, and its contents would be viewed through a peephole. The films shown in these machines were brief, typically lasting around 20 to 30 seconds, and featured a variety of subjects, from vaudeville acts to everyday activities. The novelty of seeing moving images captivated audiences, and the parlor often drew large crowds, including curious onlookers and eager repeat customers. People were shocked and overwhelmed by the novelty

1. According to paragraph 1, which of the following was NOT a functional limitation of the Kinetoscope?

   Ⓐ It could only be viewed by one person at a time.
   Ⓑ It was unable to project films onto a large screen.
   Ⓒ Its films were typically less than 60 seconds long.
   Ⓓ It allowed for limited synchronized sound effects.

2. Which of the following best expresses the essential information in the highlighted sentence? Incorrect answer choices change the meaning in important ways or leave out essential information.

   Ⓐ A low fee of 25 cents was paid to enjoy the novel form of entertainment, which rapidly grew in popularity.
   Ⓑ The new form of entertainment's low cost allowed it to quickly become a popular attraction.
   Ⓒ Talk of the novel form of entertainment was quickly spreading, which customers accessed for 25 cents.
   Ⓓ The intriguing form of entertainment created a sensation among New Yorkers, who were charged 25 cents to access the technology.

3. The word "its" in paragraph 2 refers to

   Ⓐ the machine's
   Ⓑ the oak cabinet's
   Ⓒ the parlor's
   Ⓓ the house's

of the technology, with viewers yelling out loud in amazement from around the parlor. Viewers, engrossed in the films, would reportedly duck and jump, forgetting they were in a parlor watching a motion picture.

3 ➡ The success of the New York Kinetoscope parlor was not just a testament to the public's fascination with moving pictures but also to the potential for commercial exploitation of this new technology. [■A] The profits generated from this parlor model demonstrated that there was a viable market for motion pictures, encouraging further investment and innovation in the field. [■B] This expansion helped to popularize motion pictures and laid the groundwork for the burgeoning film industry. [■C] The Kinetoscope parlor also played a critical role in the cultural landscape of the time, providing a new form of entertainment that was accessible to a broad audience. [■D] Unlike theater or opera, which often catered to more affluent patrons, Kinetoscope parlors were affordable and appealed to people from various social backgrounds. Scholars today view this as the democratization of entertainment, which brought motion pictures to a wider audience. This heavily contributed to the growing popularity of visual media. Finally, the parlor became a social gathering place where people could share the experience of watching moving images, fostering a communal appreciation for this emerging art form. This would become a consumer dynamic within the industry that would continue to this day.

4 ➡ Nonetheless, this social aspect of kinetoscope parlors could not undo the inherent detached nature of the invention: Kinetoscopes could only be viewed by one person at a time. This shortcoming pushed and inspired further innovation in the technology. This eventually led to exploration into projection methods, which would allow images to be displayed to larger audiences all at once. This transition began with the work of inventors such as the

4. What can be inferred about the Kinetoscope in paragraph 2?

   Ⓐ The majority of the Kinetoscope's first viewers became regular customers.
   Ⓑ The Kinetoscope parlor was presented to a public with almost no exposure to motion pictures.
   Ⓒ The Kinetoscope's first audiences were less cultured than ordinary patrons of the visual arts.
   Ⓓ The setup of the Kinetoscope parlor in New York was reminiscent of a game room.

5. Look at the four squares [■] that indicate where the following sentence could be added to the passage.

   Entrepreneurs quickly recognized the opportunity to establish similar parlors in other cities, both in the United States and abroad, many of which were set up and owned by the Holland brothers.

   Where would the sentence best fit?

   Click on a square [■] to add the sentence to the passage.

6. According to paragraph 3, the Kinetoscope's significance is reflected in all of the following EXCEPT

   Ⓐ its profitability
   Ⓑ its appeal to the masses
   Ⓒ its rapid proliferation
   Ⓓ its upper-class clientele

Lumière brothers in France, who developed the Cinématographe in 1895. Unlike the Kinetoscope, the Cinématographe was capable of recording, projecting, and even developing motion pictures, making it more versatile and widely impactful. The invention utilized the same film width of 35mm, which rapidly became the industry standard, while the machine employed a mechanism known as the Maltese cross, which advanced the film strip intermittently, providing smoother motion compared to earlier devices.

5 ➡ On December 28, 1895, the Lumière brothers held their first public screening in Paris. This momentous evening is often regarded as the birth of modern cinema. Ten short films were featured, including the famous "Workers Leaving the Lumière Factory." The success of this screening demonstrated the vast potential of the Cinématographe. More importantly, the Cinématographe further laid the foundation for the development of the film industry, leading to the rise of projection cinema as the dominant cultural force that endures to this day.

7. The author mentions the "Cinématographe" in paragraph 4 in order to

   Ⓐ discuss the Kinetoscope's successor.
   Ⓑ highlight the legacy it left on the cinema industry.
   Ⓒ explain how inventors addressed the Kinetoscope's flaws.
   Ⓓ mention new technologies that were employed.

8. According to paragraph 5, which of the following was an important part of the legacy that the Cinématographe left on the cinema industry?

   Ⓐ It further increased accessibility to motion pictures for middle-class consumers.
   Ⓑ Its concept of projection cinema would come to dominate the industry.
   Ⓒ It set 35mm film as the industry standard once and for all.
   Ⓓ It provided a precedent that transformed movie viewing into a social activity.

9. The word "endures" in paragraph 5 is closest in meaning to

   Ⓐ sustains
   Ⓑ withstands
   Ⓒ prevails
   Ⓓ remains

TOEFL Reading

10. **Directions:** An introductory sentence for a brief summary of the passage is provided below. Complete the summary by selecting the THREE answer choices that express the most important ideas in the passage. Some sentences do not belong in the summary because they express ideas that are not presented in the passage or minor ideas in the passage. **This question is worth 2 points.**

While the Kinetoscope's pioneering technology proved to be popular, the subsequent Cinématographe would set a new standard for the cinema industry.

- Ⓐ The Kinetoscope employed a continuous loop of 35mm film that ran through a viewing machine, which featured a peephole.
- Ⓑ Viewers were often stunned by the new, popular form of entertainment, which featured simple 30 second-or-so films.
- Ⓒ The Kinetoscope's popularity spread quickly to other US states, as well as beyond its borders, to other countries.
- Ⓓ The novel form of entertainment made the visual arts more accessible to people of different classes.
- Ⓔ The Cinématographe was invented by French inventors who improved on the Kinetoscope, namely its limited functionality.
- Ⓕ The Cinématographe's projection technology created the conditions for the development of the movie theater.

Drag your answer choices to the spaces where they belong.
To remove an answer choice, click on it. To review the passage, click on **View Text**.

Railroad Development in the United States

1 ➡ The completion of the Transcontinental Railway in 1869 was a watershed event in United States history. Prior to the construction of railways, the primary means of transportation other than horses was by water. Boats traversed rivers and canals hauling both cargo and passengers. However, this meant that only cities that were on major waterways could benefit, and goods had to be transported by wagon to reach towns that were not. The earliest railways were short, dedicated routes that were used to connect things like quarries to rivers, and they were pulled by horses. When the steam engine was applied to railways in England, Americans were quick to follow suit. The first steam railways were built to connect cities in New England, but they soon spread both south and westward.

2 ➡ By 1850, approximately 14,400 kilometers of tracks had been laid down, but it was during the following decade that construction really began in earnest. By 1860, there was about 48,000 kilometers of railroad tracks, which meant that the United States had the most tracks in the world. The idea for a railroad that would connect the Atlantic and Pacific coasts dates back to 1832, but it did not receive government approval until 1862. The railway was built in three sections: from Oakland, California to Sacramento, California, from Sacramento to Promontory Summit, Utah, and from Omaha, Nebraska to Promontory Summit. When the two lines met at Promontory Summit, Utah, they were connected with a ceremonial golden spike on May 10, 1869.

3 ➡ The benefits of railway construction were many, but the most significant was their effect on the economy. [■A] They allowed the rapid transportation of food and other products to areas that previously had little to no access to such items. [■B] Previously, dairy products

---

1. The word "dedicated" in paragraph 1 is closest in meaning to
   - Ⓐ reserved
   - Ⓑ staunch
   - Ⓒ resolute
   - Ⓓ purposeful

2. Based on paragraph 2, it can be inferred that
   - Ⓐ the construction of the Transcontinental Railway lasted for more than 10 years.
   - Ⓑ England had the most tracks in the world before the development of the Transcontinental Railway.
   - Ⓒ the government dictated the route of the railroad that would connect the Atlantic and Pacific coasts.
   - Ⓓ the construction of the Transcontinental Railway began from both California and Nebraska simultaneously.

had to be produced and consumed locally, but now they could be transported long distances, allowing people to also increase production. [■C] Most of the farmers in the western territories had practiced subsistence agriculture before, selling what little surplus they produced to local markets or using it for barter with neighbors. [■D] The railways allowed them to plant cash crops that they could send all over the country. Along with improvements in plow and harvester technology, this allowed the farms in the Midwest to expand rapidly, transforming the prairie into oceans of wheat and corn.

4 ➡ The railroads also facilitated settlement of the vast reaches of the West. Prior to the completion of the Transcontinental Railway, the only way to reach the West Coast was by wagon trail or by sailing around South America, both of which took many months. By rail, it could be achieved in a matter of days. The railroads also helped these people keep in touch with their families back east as mail came to be transported by train. Settlers flooded into the West, displacing Native Americans as they rapidly established cities and towns. Towns that already existed along the route also grew in response as they became important layovers where trains were supplied with fuel and water. As populations swelled, more states were admitted to the Union, and maps had to be redrawn to reflect the new boundaries.

5 ➡ The extensive rail system also proved to have significant military value. During the American Civil War, both sides transported troops to the front by train whenever possible, and many battles were fought in order to secure vital railway hubs. The North's ability to exploit its more extensive railway network was an important factor in its ultimate victory in 1865. Their importance is further clarified by General Sherman's infamous March to the Sea, wherein his troops specifically targeted railroad tracks for destruction to economically weaken the Confederacy. Later, they helped transport

3. According to paragraph 4, what effect did railroad construction have on the West?
   Ⓐ Existing towns along the railroad became important hubs.
   Ⓑ Displaced Native Americans established new cities and towns.
   Ⓒ It forced mail to be transported along wagon trails during the period of railroad construction.
   Ⓓ Maps had to be redrawn to include locations where trains stopped to replenish their supplies.

4. Why does the author mention "Indian Wars" in paragraph 5?
   Ⓐ To discuss the negative effects of targeting railroad tracks for destruction
   Ⓑ To explain the role General Sherman played in the military after the American Civil War
   Ⓒ To provide further support for the argument that the railroads had significant military value
   Ⓓ To provide an earlier example of how railroads played a strategic role in warfare

5. Based on paragraph 5, it can be inferred that
   Ⓐ the South's railway network was more extensive than the North's.
   Ⓑ General Sherman fought in the South's army.
   Ⓒ the March to the Sea was a failed military operation.
   Ⓓ the South's lack of infrastructure contributed to its defeat.

TOEFL Reading

mounted cavalry throughout the West during the many conflicts of the Indian Wars.

6 ➡ By 1880, there were 17,800 locomotives transporting freight and 22,200 of them transporting passengers all over the country. The industrialists who owned these railways became incredibly wealthy as some of the larger companies spanned across many states. However, the federal government viewed such complete control as monopolistic, and it disapproved of some of the owners' excesses, particularly when they were lax about regulations. Congress responded to the situation by establishing the Interstate Commerce Commission, which controlled their business activities through heavy regulation. This was effective for a while, but then disaster struck.

7 ➡ In 1893, railroad overbuilding and unstable railroad financing resulted in the largest economic crisis ever at that time. By the middle of 1894, one quarter of the railroad companies had failed, and as they collapsed, they took a series of banks with them. This led to a distrust of the railroad companies that only intensified when the remaining owners joined forces to gain control of the railroad tracks left without management. Eventually, the invention of the automobile created competition that the railroads couldn't cope with, and passenger trains dwindled. In the United States today, most of the trains carry only freight.

6. The word "freight" in paragraph 6 is closest in meaning to

   Ⓐ weapons
   Ⓑ vehicles
   Ⓒ cargo
   Ⓓ mail

7. According to paragraph 7, what is true about the railroad companies?

   Ⓐ The railroad companies were owned by the same group of people that owned the banks.
   Ⓑ The Interstate Commerce Commission was successful in regulating the railroad companies.
   Ⓒ The federal government bought railroad tracks that were left without management.
   Ⓓ Railroad companies eventually allocated more locomotives to transporting freight than passengers.

8. Which of the sentences below best expresses the essential information in the highlighted sentence in the passage? *Incorrect* answer choices change the meaning in important ways or leave out essential information.

   Ⓐ Distrust led owners of remaining railroad companies to gain control of tracks left without management.
   Ⓑ Distrust of railroad companies arose when railroad company owners sold tracks that were left without management.
   Ⓒ This resulted in distrust of railroad companies which grew stronger after other company owners teamed up to buy the abandoned tracks.
   Ⓓ Distrust grew as other railroad company owners fought to gain control over railroad tracks that were left without management.

TOEFL Reading

9. Look at the four squares [■] that indicate where the following sentence could be added to the passage.

    Seafood could also be transported further inland than ever before.

    Where would the sentence best fit?

    Click on a square [■] to add the sentence to the passage.

10. **Directions:** An introductory sentence for a brief summary of the passage is provided below. Complete the summary by selecting the THREE answer choices that express the most important ideas in the passage. Some sentences do not belong in the summary because they express ideas that are not presented in the passage or are minor ideas in the passage.
    This question is worth 2 points.

    The Transcontinental Railway, which was completed in 1869, greatly impacted the United States, which already had the most tracks in the world by the mid-19th century.

    -
    -
    -

    Answer Choices

    (A) Despite the government's efforts to regulate the monopoly, railroad company owners retained their dominance until it was broken by the automobile.
    (B) Prior to railway construction, farmers could not attempt mass production because produce had to be consumed locally, with any surplus being sold to neighbors.
    (C) Not only did increased accessibility encourage settlers to rush into the West, but the railway system also proved to be of strategic military value.
    (D) The construction of the railway began in 1862, and it eventually spanned across the continent, connecting the cities in New England to Promontory Summit.
    (E) The railway system allowed farmers to increase crop production as products could be transported to other areas rapidly.
    (F) During the American Civil War, General Sherman focused on destroying railway tracks to prevent troops from being transported to the frontlines.

    Drag your answer choices to the spaces where they belong.
    To remove an answer choice, click on it. To review the passage, click on **View Text**.

PAGODA TOEFL
Actual Test
READING

PAGODA TOEFL

Actual Test

READING

PAGODA TOEFL Actual Test Reading

3rd Edition

해설서

TOEFL® is a registered trademark of Educational Testing Service (ETS).
This publication is not endorsed or approved by ETS.

PAGODA Books

PAGODA TOEFL
Actual Test Reading

3rd Edition

파고다교육그룹 언어교육연구소 l 저

해설서

PAGODA Books

Actual Test 01

본서 | P. 72

Passage 1 Flightless Birds

1. Ⓑ	Vocabulary	6. Ⓒ	Negative Fact
2. Ⓒ	Negative Fact	7. Ⓒ	Fact
3. Ⓓ	Negative Fact	8. Ⓓ	Sentence Simplification
4. Ⓑ	Inference	9. Ⓒ	Insertion
5. Ⓓ	Rhetorical Purpose	10. Ⓐ, Ⓒ, Ⓕ	Summary

Passage 2 Groundwater

1. Ⓐ	Vocabulary	6. Ⓒ	Inference
2. Ⓐ	Inference	7. Ⓐ	Rhetorical Purpose
3. Ⓑ	Vocabulary	8. Ⓓ	Sentence Simplification
4. Ⓓ	Fact	9. Ⓒ	Insertion
5. Ⓓ	Fact	10. Ⓐ, Ⓒ, Ⓕ	Summary

● 내가 맞은 문제 유형의 개수를 적어 보고 어느 유형에 취약한지 확인해 봅시다.

문제 유형	맞은 개수
Sentence Simplification	2
Fact / Negative Fact	6
Vocabulary	3
Reference	0
Rhetorical Purpose	2
Inference	3
Insertion	2
Summary	2
Category Chart	0
Total	20

Passage 1

Flightless Birds

1 → Birds that currently live or used to live on many continents have lost the ability to fly at various points in their evolutionary histories. Such evolution seems paradoxical, since flight is a trait that so many animals from different classes have developed wholly independently. Indeed, convergent evolution would seem to argue against the whole idea of losing such an advanced ability. [■A] However, evolution is not about achieving advanced traits, but rather about developing the traits that are necessary to survive in a given habitat. [■B] Therefore, birds that have lost this ability must have done so because flight did not give them an advantage in their habitat. [■C] Flight became an unnecessary expenditure of energy, so their bodies gradually lost the structures that were needed for flying. A group of large, flightless birds called ratites no longer needed to fly because they did not need to migrate for food or warmth, or because they had no predators from which they needed to escape. [■D] They developed larger bodies supported by strong legs and laid larger eggs.

2 → Many flightless bird species are classified into the ratite group due to the many physical features they share. These birds include the ostriches of Africa, rheas of South America, and the emus and cassowaries of Australia, all of which are very large birds with extremely small wings, long legs and long necks. Other extinct species that are placed in this group are the moa of New Zealand and the elephant bird of Madagascar, which disappeared in the last few thousand years, most likely because of human activity. Although flightless birds all possess vestigial wings, their breast bones lack the ridge that flight muscles attach to in flying bird species. These birds have totally abandoned flight and rely upon their powerful legs for movement and defense.

3 → The largest of the flightless birds went extinct millions of years ago, but they were truly impressive specimens. When the dinosaurs disappeared, niches in many habitats were vacated, and birds were often the animals that filled them before mammals took their place. This resulted in some truly giant birds that replaced both large herbivores and predators. One example of this is *Titanis walleri*, which was a member

of the Phorusrhacidae family of the Americas also known as "terror birds." This hunter stood at 2.5 meters tall and would have weighed around 150 kilograms. It had powerful legs it used to hunt its prey, both for chasing the animals and knocking them to the ground. It also had a massive, hooked beak that was well-suited to tearing flesh. Another ancient bird called the Diatryma was included in the same group, but scientists now believe it was a large herbivore. Although it was of similar size and had a powerful beak, recent data shows that its diet consisted primarily of tough plant matter. For this reason, it would have needed a large caecum, an organ used to digest such a diet, which would have made flight difficult.

4 ➡ The wide distribution of ratite species has long puzzled scientists. For many decades, the most popular theory was that they descended from a common flightless ancestor. The continents that they live on, Africa, Australia and South America, were once connected into one landmass called Gondwana that split apart about 180 million years ago. This would have isolated the animals and allowed them to evolve independently. However, geologic evidence shows that the supercontinent of Gondwana broke apart far too long ago for that to be the case. A recent genetic survey of ratite species supports the more likely theory that the flightless giants evolved from a common ancestor that could fly. Members of this species spread across the world to the already divided continents, and then lost their ability to fly.

5 ➡ However, members of the ratite family are not exclusively large. The kiwi of New Zealand and the tinamou of South America are ratites with stout, robust bodies despite their diminutive size. Still, they have another important trait that they share with other ratites: very large eggs. It makes sense for the ostrich to lay the biggest egg as the largest bird in the world, but the kiwi actually lays the largest egg relative to its own body size, and the ostrich egg is the smallest in comparison to the size of the adult bird. It remains unclear why kiwis lay such large eggs, but there are two possibilities. Either kiwis have always been small and their eggs have grown, or kiwis used to be much larger, and their eggs have not shrunk very much. Either way, a large egg provides definite survival advantages for kiwi chicks. They hatch with an extra

supply of yolk that they can live off of for over two weeks, which means they are born pretty much ready to run. This makes it possible for them to better evade flying predators, so it might be worth carrying such outsized eggs.

1. **Vocabulary**
The word "paradoxical" in paragraph 1 is closest in meaning to
Ⓐ inevitable
Ⓑ **contradictory**
Ⓒ arbitrary
Ⓓ mundane

2. **Negative Fact**
Which of the following is NOT mentioned in paragraph 1?
Ⓐ What convergent evolution is
Ⓑ What caused some birds to be flightless
Ⓒ **How flightless birds survived**
Ⓓ How evolutionary changes in birds took place

3. **Negative Fact**
According to paragraph 2, all of the following are common physical features of ratites EXCEPT
Ⓐ long necks
Ⓑ long legs
Ⓒ vestigial wings
Ⓓ **ridge-shaped chest bones**

4. **Inference**
Which of the following can be inferred about terror birds from paragraph 3?
Ⓐ *Titanis walleri* was the largest land predator in the Western Hemisphere when it lived.
Ⓑ **They were ultimately unable to compete with mammalian predators.**
Ⓒ They lived alongside the dinosaurs and competed with them for food.
Ⓓ They were not as fast and agile as birds that hunt while flying.

5. **Rhetorical Purpose**

Why does the author mention "Diatryma" in paragraph 3?

Ⓐ To cast doubt on its being classified as a "terror bird"
Ⓑ To explain why "terror birds" had large digestive organs
Ⓒ To draw a line between a giant bird and a large herbivore
Ⓓ **To introduce a bird that was mistakenly categorized**

6. **Negative Fact**

In paragraph 4, which of the following is NOT mentioned about Gondwana?

Ⓐ It was an ancient supercontinent that broke up about 180 million years ago.
Ⓑ It incorporated the current continents of Africa, Australia, and South America.
Ⓒ **It started to split when magma from below the Earth's crust began pushing upward.**
Ⓓ Its breakup is believed to have isolated the animals living on it.

7. **Fact**

According to paragraph 5, what advantage do huge eggs bring to the kiwi?

Ⓐ Their large size prevents predators from eating them easily.
Ⓑ They give kiwi chicks a competitive edge over flying birds.
Ⓒ **The chicks do not need to be fed after they hatch.**
Ⓓ A female can only lay one egg at a time, which requires less energy.

8. **Sentence Simplification**

Which of the sentences below best expresses the essential information in the highlighted sentence in the passage? *Incorrect* answer choices change the meaning in important ways or leave out essential information.

Ⓐ The ostrich has the largest egg compared to the body of the adult bird, while the kiwi has the smallest compared to its body.
Ⓑ Although it is a much smaller bird, the kiwi actually lays larger eggs than the ostrich does.
Ⓒ Since it is the largest bird in the world, it is not surprising that the ostrich lays the largest egg, but the kiwi actually lays a very large egg as well.
Ⓓ **The ostrich actually has the smallest egg compared to the adult's body although it is the largest bird, whereas the kiwi has the largest egg compared to its body.**

5.

3단락에서 글쓴이가 "디아트리마"를 언급하는 이유는 무엇인가?

Ⓐ 그것이 공포새로 분류되는 것에 대한 의구심을 제기하기 위해
Ⓑ 공포새들이 큰 소화기관을 가졌던 이유를 설명하기 위해
Ⓒ 거대 새와 거대 초식동물을 비교하기 위해
Ⓓ 잘못 분류된 새를 소개하기 위해

6.

4단락에서 다음 중 곤드와나에 대해 언급되지 않은 것은 무엇인가?

Ⓐ 약 1억 8천만년 전에 분열된 고대의 초대륙이었다.
Ⓑ 현재의 아프리카, 호주, 남아메리카 대륙을 포함했다.
Ⓒ 지구의 지각 아래에서 올라온 마그마가 위로 밀기 시작했을 때 분열되기 시작했다.
Ⓓ 그것의 분열로 인해 그곳에 살던 동물들이 고립되었다고 여겨진다.

7.

5단락에 따르면, 거대한 알이 키위새에게 가져다 주는 이점은 무엇인가?

Ⓐ 크기가 커서 포식자들이 쉽게 먹을 수 없게 한다.
Ⓑ 새끼 키위새가 나는 새들과의 경쟁에서 우위에 서게 한다.
Ⓒ 새끼 새들이 부화한 이후에 먹이를 받아먹을 필요가 없다.
Ⓓ 암컷이 한 번에 하나의 알만 낳을 수 있으므로 에너지를 덜 필요로 한다.

8.

다음 중 지문의 음영 표시된 문장의 핵심 정보를 가장 잘 표현한 문장은 무엇인가? 오답은 의미를 크게 왜곡하거나 핵심 정보를 누락하고 있다.

Ⓐ 타조는 성체의 몸에 비해 가장 큰 알을 낳는 반면, 키위는 몸에 비해 가장 작은 알을 낳는다.
Ⓑ 비록 키위가 타조보다 훨씬 더 작은 새이지만, 사실상 타조보다 더 큰 알을 낳는다.
Ⓒ 세계에서 가장 큰 새이기 때문에, 타조가 가장 큰 알을 낳는 것이 놀랍지 않지만, 키위도 역시 아주 큰 알을 낳는다.
Ⓓ 타조는 가장 큰 새임에도 불구하고 사실상 성체의 크기에 비해 가장 작은 알을 낳는 반면, 키위는 몸에 비해 가장 큰 알을 낳는다.

9. Insertion

Look at the four squares [■] that indicate where the following sentence could be added to the passage.

Flight became an unnecessary expenditure of energy, so their bodies gradually lost the structures that were needed for flying.

Where would the sentence best fit? **[■ C]**

10. Summary

Directions: An introductory sentence for a brief summary of the passage is provided below. Complete the summary by selecting the THREE answer choices that express the most important ideas in the passage. Some sentences do not belong in the summary because they express ideas that are not presented in the passage or are minor ideas in the passage. *This question is worth 2 points.*

Many species of birds like the ratites have lost the ability to fly as they adapted to the habitats in which they live.

Ⓐ Many of the early flightless birds evolved to fill niches that had been left vacant by the dinosaurs when they went extinct.
Ⓒ Scientists originally thought that ratites were flightless when the continents separated, but they have since learned that their ancestors must have flown across the oceans.
Ⓕ The smallest ratite species is the kiwi, which lays disproportionally large eggs.

Ⓑ *Titanis walleri* was the largest of the "terror birds" at 2.5 meters tall.
Ⓓ Ratite species live in Australia, Africa, and South America today.
Ⓔ Some scientists believe that the ancestors of modern kiwis must have been much larger than their descendants.

9.

지문에 다음 문장이 들어갈 수 있는 위치를 나타내는 네 개의 사각형[■]을 확인하시오.

나는 것은 에너지를 불필요하게 소모하기 때문에, 그들의 몸은 점차 나는 것에 필요한 구조를 잃게 되었다.

이 문장이 들어가기에 가장 적합한 곳은? [■C]

10.

지시문: 지문을 간략하게 요약한 글의 첫 문장이 아래 제시되어 있다. 지문의 가장 중요한 내용을 표현하는 세 개의 선택지를 골라 요약문을 완성하시오. 일부 문장들은 지문에 제시되지 않았거나 지문의 지엽적인 내용을 나타내기 때문에 요약문에 포함되지 않는다. *이 문제의 배점은 2점이다.*

주금류와 같은 많은 종의 새들이 자신들이 사는 서식지에 적응하면서 나는 능력을 잃게 되었다.

Ⓐ 초기의 날지 못하는 많은 새들이 공룡이 멸종되면서 남기고 간 적소를 채우는 것으로 진화했다.
Ⓒ 원래 과학자들은 대륙이 분리될 당시 주금류는 날지 못했다고 생각했으나, 그 이후에 그들의 조상이 바다를 건너 날아온 것이 틀림없다는 것을 알게 되었다.
Ⓕ 가장 작은 주금류 새는 키위이며, 이들은 불균형하게 커다란 알을 낳는다.

Ⓑ 티타니스 왈레리는 키가 2.5미터로 공포새 중 가장 컸다.
Ⓓ 주금류는 오늘날 호주, 아프리카, 남아메리카에서 서식한다.
Ⓔ 일부 과학자들은 현대 키위새의 조상들이 그들의 자손들보다 틀림없이 훨씬 더 컸을 것이라고 믿는다.

어휘

1. **advanced** adj 진보한, 선진의, (발달 단계상) 후기의 | **predator** n 포식자, 포식 동물
2. **be classified into** ~로 분류되다 | **extinct** adj 멸종된, 더 이상 존재하지 않는 | **possess** v 소유하다, 보유하다 | **vestigial** adj 남아 있는 | **abandon** v 버리다, 유기하다, 포기하다
3. **specimen** n 견본, 표본 | **knock** v 때리다, 타격하다 | **massive** adj 거대한, 엄청난 | **beak** n 부리 | **tear** v 찢다, 뜯다 | **herbivore** n 초식 동물
4. **distribution** n 분포, 분배 | **landmass** n 광대한 토지, 대륙 | **geologic** adj 지질학상의, 지질의
5. **stout** adj 튼튼한, 통통한 | **robust** adj 강건한, 원기 왕성한, 팔팔한 | **diminutive** adj 아주 작은 | **in comparison to** ~와 비교할 때 | **outsized** adj 대형의

Passage 2

Groundwater

1 ➡ Water, the lifeblood of our planet, exists not only in visible bodies like rivers and lakes but also in hidden reserves beneath the Earth's surface—groundwater. Porous rock formations, such as sandstone and limestone, serve as one type of natural reservoir, harboring vast quantities of groundwater within their interconnected pore spaces. Known as aquifers, these formations vary in permeability and depth, influencing their capacity to store and transmit water. Unconfined aquifers, closer to the surface and replenished by rainfall, are vital for sustaining wells and springs. [■A] In contrast, confined aquifers, situated between impermeable layers, store significant volumes of pressurized water, serving as essential sources for irrigation, industry, and municipal supply. [■B]

2 ➡ Considering this, understanding the geological and absorptive characteristics of these formations is crucial for predicting groundwater behavior and optimizing water resource management strategies. [■C] For instance, sandstone, with its high porosity and permeability, can store substantial volumes of water and facilitate rapid groundwater flow. [■D] Conversely, limestone, characterized by interconnected networks of fractures and cavities, acts as a highly productive aquifer, albeit with variations in permeability due to differing degrees of karstification. Hence, there is always the need for accurate surveying of an area's geology in order to ensure that water is managed efficiently.

3 ➡ Soil, often referred to as Earth's skin, also plays a pivotal role in regulating water distribution and replenishing groundwater reservoirs. When precipitation infiltrates the soil, it is absorbed and retained within the soil matrix, forming soil moisture. The water-holding capacity of soil is influenced by various factors, including texture, structure, organic matter content, and land management practices. Soils rich in organic matter demonstrate superior water retention capabilities, fostering microbial activity and enhancing groundwater recharge.

4 ➡ Agricultural practices significantly impact soil moisture dynamics and groundwater recharge rates. Conventional tillage practices can disrupt

soil structure, increase surface runoff, and reduce infiltration, thereby hindering groundwater recharge. In contrast, conservation practices such as cover cropping, reduced tillage, and agroforestry can enhance soil health, promote infiltration, and mitigate runoff, ultimately replenishing groundwater reservoirs and sustaining water availability during dry periods. For instance, the concept of "managed aquifer recharge" (MAR) involves intentionally augmenting natural groundwater replenishment processes. MAR techniques include the injection of excess surface water or treated wastewater into aquifers, the construction of recharge basins and infiltration galleries, and the implementation of land use practices that enhance infiltration. By strategically managing soil moisture and promoting groundwater recharge, municipalities can alleviate water scarcity concerns and enhance the resilience of water supply systems.

5 ➡ Another critical source of groundwater is wetlands, encompassing a diverse array of ecosystems such as marshes, swamps, and bogs. They are invaluable natural assets due to their multifaceted roles in water storage, purification, and habitat provision. These waterlogged landscapes function as natural sponges, absorbing excess water during high flow periods and slowly releasing it during dry spells, thereby mitigating floods and droughts. Moreover, wetlands serve as highly effective filtration systems, trapping sediments, nutrients, and pollutants, thereby improving water quality before it reaches downstream ecosystems. The hydrology of wetlands is intricately linked to groundwater dynamics, with wetlands often serving as critical recharge areas for adjacent aquifers. The presence of shallow groundwater tables within wetland ecosystems sustains unique plant communities adapted to waterlogged conditions and provides essential habitat for a diverse array of aquatic and terrestrial species. Furthermore, wetlands act as carbon sinks, sequestering organic matter and reducing greenhouse gas emissions, thereby contributing to climate change mitigation efforts.

6 ➡ Finally, permafrost, perennially frozen ground found in polar and subpolar regions, represents a unique and significant component of the Earth's cryosphere. Permafrost regions store vast reserves of frozen water within their icy matrix, making them

재충전을 방해할 수 있다. 반면, 덮개 작물 재배, 경작 감소, 산림농업과 같은 보존 관행은 토양 건강을 증진시키고 침투를 촉진하며 유출을 완화해 궁극적으로 지하수 저장소를 재충전하고 건조한 시기에 물 가용성을 유지할 수 있다. 예를 들어, '지하수 재충전 관리'(MAR) 개념은 자연 지하수 재충전 과정을 의도적으로 증대시키는 것을 포함한다. MAR 기술은 초과 표면수나 처리된 폐수를 대수층에 주입하는 것, 재충전 유역과 침투 갤러리 건설, 침투를 강화하는 토지 이용 관행 구현 등을 포함한다. 토양 수분을 전략적으로 관리하고 지하수 재충전을 촉진함으로써, 시는 물 부족 문제를 완화하고 물 공급 시스템의 복원력을 향상시킬 수 있다.

5 ➡ 지하수의 또 다른 중요한 공급원은 습지, 늪, 늪지대와 같은 다양한 생태계를 포함하는 습지대다. 이들은 물 저장, 정화, 서식지 제공 등 다면적인 역할 덕분에 매우 가치 있는 자연 자산이다. 이러한 물에 잠긴 지형은 천연 스펀지처럼 작동하여 높은 유량 시기에 초과 물을 흡수하고 건조기에는 천천히 방출하여 홍수와 가뭄을 완화한다. 또한 습지는 퇴적물, 영양소, 오염물질을 가두어 수질을 개선하고 하류 생태계에 도달하기 전에 물을 정화하는 매우 효과적인 여과 시스템으로 작동한다. 습지의 수문학은 지하수 역학과 밀접하게 연결되어 있으며, 습지는 종종 인접 대수층의 중요한 재충전 지역으로 작용한다. 습지 생태계 내 얕은 지하수층의 존재는 물에 잠긴 조건에 적응한 독특한 식물 군집을 유지하며, 다양한 수생 및 육상 종들에게 필수적인 서식지를 제공한다. 더 나아가, 습지는 유기물을 격리하고 온실가스 배출을 줄이는 탄소 흡수원으로 작용하여 기후 변화 완화에도 기여한다.

6 ➡ 마지막으로, 영구적으로 얼어 있는 북극 및 아북극 지역의 영구 동토층은 지구의 빙권에서 독특하고 중요한 요소를 구성한다. 영구 동토층 지역은 그 얼음 매트릭스 내에 방대한 양의 동결된 물을 저장하고 있어, 지구 전체의 수문 순환에서 필수적인 구성 요소로 작용한다. 그러나 기후 변

essential components of the global hydrological cycle. However, with rising temperatures due to climate change, permafrost degradation has accelerated, leading to the release of stored water and alterations in hydrological processes. In addition, thawing permafrost results in land subsidence, increased runoff, and changes in groundwater flow patterns, posing significant challenges for infrastructure, ecosystems, and indigenous communities in northern regions. Furthermore, the release of greenhouse gasses trapped within permafrost, particularly methane and carbon dioxide, exacerbates global warming, creating a feedback loop that further accelerates permafrost thaw and climate change impacts.

7 ➡ Understanding the dynamics of permafrost and its interactions with groundwater systems is essential for predicting and mitigating the impacts of climate change on water resources in polar and subpolar regions. Integrated research efforts combining field observations, remote sensing, and numerical modeling can enhance our understanding of permafrost hydrology and inform adaptation strategies to mitigate the impacts of permafrost thaw on water resources, infrastructure, and ecosystems.

1. Vocabulary

The word "harboring" in paragraph 1 is closest in meaning to

Ⓐ retaining
Ⓑ bearing
Ⓒ protecting
Ⓓ possessing

2. Inference

According to paragraph 2, what can be inferred about limestone?

Ⓐ **Groundwater flow through limestone is typically slower than what is seen in sandstone.**
Ⓑ Limestone tends to be a much more productive aquifer than sandstone because of its diminished porosity.
Ⓒ Its network of chambers and pockets makes limestone an abundant source of groundwater.
Ⓓ Limestone's significantly higher levels of karstification render it more permeable than sandstone.

3. Vocabulary

The word "infiltrates" in paragraph 3 is closest in meaning to

Ⓐ pressures
Ⓑ **penetrates**
Ⓒ purifies
Ⓓ pervades

4. Fact

According to paragraph 4, how do managed aquifer recharge (MAR) practices positively impact soil's groundwater storage function?

Ⓐ The implementation of land use practices enhances soil runoff quality.
Ⓑ MAR is often used in conjunction with agroforestry and cover cropping to maintain reservoir health.
Ⓒ Infiltration galleries are constructed to increase the permeability of soil.
Ⓓ **The practice of inserting surface water into aquifers helps keep soil aquifers sustainable.**

5. Fact

According to paragraph 5, how do wetlands regulate water levels in their areas?

Ⓐ Water level regulation serves a critical role in the maintenance of wetland ecosystems and their unique plant life.
Ⓑ The diversity of wetland sediment creates the perfect setting for effective reservoir activity and regulation.
Ⓒ Wetlands clean water in reservoirs by trapping impurities and other foreign bodies.
Ⓓ **Wetlands are able to take in surplus water, which is later gradually discharged in periods of drought.**

6. Inference

What can be inferred about wetland plant and animal life in paragraph 5?

Ⓐ Wetland conditions create unique habitats that have led to the emergence of several amphibious species.
Ⓑ Many of the plants and animals that inhabit wetlands cannot be found in any other part of the world.
Ⓒ **Shallow groundwater tables create unusual conditions that have forced plants to adapt to saturated topographies.**
Ⓓ Some of the wetland animal species have learned to adapt to intermittent periods of flooding and dry spells.

3.

3단락의 "infiltrates(침투하다)"와 의미상 가장 가까운 것은?

Ⓐ 압박하다
Ⓑ 침투하다
Ⓒ 정화하다
Ⓓ 만연하다

4.

4단락에 따르면, 관리된 대수층 재충전(MAR) 방식은 토양의 지하수 저장 기능에 어떻게 긍정적인 영향을 미치는가?

Ⓐ 토지 이용 방식을 구현함으로써 토양 유출수의 질이 향상된다.
Ⓑ MAR은 종종 임업 및 피복작물 재배와 함께 사용되어 저수지 건강을 유지한다.
Ⓒ 토양의 투과성을 높이기 위해 침투 갤러리가 건설된다.
Ⓓ 대수층에 지표수를 주입하는 방식은 토양 대수층을 지속 가능하게 유지하는 데 도움을 준다.

5.

5단락에 따르면, 습지는 어떻게 그 지역의 수위를 조절하는가?

Ⓐ 수위 조절은 습지 생태계와 그 독특한 식물 생명을 유지하는 데 중요한 역할을 한다.
Ⓑ 습지 퇴적물의 다양성은 효과적인 저수지 활동과 규제를 위한 완벽한 환경을 조성한다.
Ⓒ 습지는 불순물과 기타 이물질을 포착하여 저수지의 물을 정화한다.
Ⓓ 습지는 잉여 수분을 흡수하여 가뭄 시기에 서서히 방출한다.

6.

5단락에서 습지 동식물에 대해 추론할 수 있는 것은 무엇인가?

Ⓐ 습지 환경은 독특한 서식지를 만들어 여러 양서류 종의 출현을 이끌어냈다.
Ⓑ 습지에 서식하는 많은 식물과 동물들은 세계의 다른 어느 곳에서도 발견되지 않는다.
Ⓒ 얕은 지하수위는 식물이 포화 지형에 적응할 수밖에 없는 비정상적인 조건을 만들었다.
Ⓓ 일부 습지 동물 종은 간헐적인 홍수와 건기의 변화를 견디도록 적응했다.

7. Rhetorical Purpose

Why does the author mention indigenous communities in paragraph 6?

Ⓐ to point out global warming's effects on permafrost zones and their inhabitants
Ⓑ to bring to attention a population that is affected by changes in permafrost
Ⓒ as a call to action to address climate change
Ⓓ to add to a list of ways thawing permafrost impacts polar and subpolar regions

8. Sentence Simplification

Which of the following best expresses the essential information in the highlighted sentence? Incorrect answer choices change the meaning in important ways or leave out essential information.

Ⓐ Scientists are combining field observations, remote sensing, and numerical modeling to better inform the public so that new adaptation strategies can create a more sustainable future for permafrost biomes.
Ⓑ The success of permafrost thaw mitigation strategies will depend on the quality of the integrated research and modeling currently being carried out.
Ⓒ Mitigating permafrost thaw reduces its impact on water resources, infrastructure, and ecosystem, which will be possible through enhanced understanding via a cohesive effort of field research, remote sensing, and numerical modeling.
Ⓓ **Fully grasping permafrost hydrology and creating more effective adaptation strategies through an integrated approach to research can help minimize the effects of permafrost thaw.**

9. Insertion

Look at the four squares [■] that indicate where the following sentence could be added to the passage.

The porosity and permeability of these rocks determine the rate at which water can flow through them, with well-connected pore spaces facilitating rapid recharge and extraction.

Where would the sentence best fit? [■ C]

7.
6단락에서 글쓴이가 "원주민 공동체"를 언급하는 이유는 무엇인가?

Ⓐ 영구 동토대와 그 거주자들에게 미치는 지구 온난화의 영향을 지적하기 위해
Ⓑ 영구 동토층의 변화로 영향을 받는 인구에 주목하기 위해
Ⓒ 기후 변화에 대응하기 위한 행동 촉구로서
Ⓓ 영구 동토층이 녹는 것이 극지 및 아극지 지역에 미치는 영향을 나열하기 위해

8.
다음 중 강조된 문장에서 본질적인 정보를 가장 잘 표현한 것은 무엇인가? 오답은 의미를 크게 왜곡하거나 핵심 정보를 누락하고 있다.

Ⓐ 과학자들은 현장 관찰, 원격 감지, 그리고 수치 모델링을 결합하여 대중에게 더 나은 정보를 제공하여 새로운 적응 전략이 영구 동토층 생태계를 더 지속 가능한 방향으로 이끌 수 있도록 하고 있다.
Ⓑ 영구 동토층 해빙 완화 전략의 성공은 현재 진행 중인 통합 연구 및 모델링의 품질에 달려 있다.
Ⓒ 영구 동토층 해빙을 완화하면 물 자원, 인프라, 생태계에 미치는 영향을 줄일 수 있으며, 이는 현장 연구, 원격 감지, 수치 모델링의 통합 노력을 통해 향상된 이해를 통해 가능하다.
Ⓓ 영구 동토층 수문학을 완전히 이해하고 통합된 연구 접근을 통해 보다 효과적인 적응 전략을 수립함으로써 영구 동토층 해빙의 영향을 최소화할 수 있다.

9.
지문에 다음 문장이 들어갈 수 있는 위치를 나타내는 네 개의 사각형[■]을 확인하시오.

이러한 암석의 다공성과 투수성에 따라 물이 흐르는 속도가 결정되며, 잘 연결된 기공 공간은 빠른 재충전 및 추출을 용이하게 한다.

이 문장이 들어가기에 가장 적합한 곳은? [■ C]

10. Prose Summary

Directions: An introductory sentence for a brief summary of the passage is provided below. Complete the summary by selecting the THREE answer choices that express the most important ideas in the passage. Some sentences do not belong in the summary because they express ideas that are not presented in the passage or minor ideas in the passage. *This question is worth 2 points.*

One of the most important sources of freshwater on the planet, groundwater can be found in various types of topographical landscapes, with each type presenting its own unique capabilities in holding groundwater.

> (A) **Aquifers are able to hold substantial amounts of groundwater, although the absorptive qualities of the aquifer depends on the level of porosity inherent to the different rock formations found in the aquifer.**
> (C) **Soil is also an important source of groundwater, as it absorbs precipitation, albeit at various levels depending on the makeup of the soil.**
> (F) **Permafrost is another distinct component in Earth's groundwater resources, in which polar and subpolar climates result in the conditions for the ground to retain frozen water.**

(B) Limestone and sandstone are excellent examples of the differing levels of permeability found in aquifers, since the two feature differing levels of karstification.
(D) Although agricultural practices sometimes diminish soil's capacity as a reservoir, various strategies, such as the implementation of the concept of MAR, have shown the potential to counter some of the impacts of agricultural activity on the soil.
(E) Wetlands are a unique source of groundwater and have many critical functions, including acting as a carbon sink, creating conditions for unique wildlife, and absorbing excess water.

10.

지시문: 지문을 간략하게 요약한 글의 첫 문장이 아래 제시되어 있다. 지문의 가장 중요한 내용을 표현하는 세 개의 선택지를 골라 요약문을 완성하시오. 일부 문장들은 지문에 제시되지 않았거나 지문의 지엽적인 내용을 나타내기 때문에 요약문에 포함되지 않는다. **이 문제의 배점은 2점이다.**

지구상에서 가장 중요한 담수 자원 중 하나인 지하수는 다양한 지형에 존재하며, 각 지형은 고유한 지하수 보유 능력을 가지고 있다.

> (A) 대수층은 상당한 양의 지하수를 보유할 수 있지만, 대수층의 흡수 특성은 대수층 내에 있는 암석 형성의 다공성 수준에 따라 다르다.
> (C) 토양 또한 중요한 지하수원으로, 강수량을 흡수하지만 토양 구성에 따라 다양한 수준에서 흡수한다.
> (F) 영구 동토층은 지구의 지하수 자원에서 또 다른 독특한 구성 요소로, 극지 및 아극지 기후가 땅에 얼어붙은 물을 유지할 수 있는 조건을 만든다.

(B) 석회암과 사암은 대수층에서 서로 다른 수준의 투과성을 보이는 훌륭한 예시로, 두 암석은 서로 다른 카르스트화 수준을 특징으로 한다.
(D) 농업 관행은 때때로 토양의 저수 기능을 저해하지만, MAR 개념의 구현과 같은 다양한 전략은 농업 활동이 토양에 미치는 일부 영향을 상쇄할 수 있는 잠재력을 보여주었다.
(E) 습지대는 독특한 지하수원으로, 탄소 흡수원 역할을 하고, 독특한 야생 동물 서식 조건을 만들며, 초과 수분을 흡수하는 등 중요한 기능을 수행한다.

어휘

1. **lifeblood** n 생명선 | **porous** adj 다공성의 | **permeability** n 투과성 | **irrigation** n 관개 | **municipal** adj 시의 | **supply** n 공급
2. **geological** adj 지질학적인 | **absorptive** adj 흡수성의 | **substantial** adj 상당한 | **facilitate** v 촉진하다 | **rapid** adj 빠른 | **fracture** n 균열 | **cavity** n 빈 공간 | **karstification** n 카르스트화
3. **soil** n 토양 | **pivotal** adj 중요한 | **replenish** v 보충하다 | **precipitation** n 강수량 | **moisture** n 수분 | **texture** n 질감 | **organic** adj 유기물 | **retention** n 보유 | **microbial** adj 미생물의

4 **agricultural** adj 농업의 | **dynamics** n 역학 | **tillage** n 경작 | **runoff** n 유출수 | **hinder** v 방해하다 | **agroforestry** n 임업 | **mitigate** v 완화하다 | **reservoir** n 저수지 | **injection** n 주입 | **excess** n 초과 | **scarcity** n 부족 | **resilience** n 회복력
5 **wetlands** n 습지 | **ecosystem** n 생태계 | **marsh** n 늪 | **invaluable** adj 매우 귀중한 | **multifaceted** adj 다면적인 | **drought** n 가뭄 | **filtration** n 여과 | **sediment** n 퇴적물 | **pollutant** n 오염물질 | **aquatic** adj 수생의 | **terrestrial** adj 육지의
6 **permafrost** n 영구 동토층 | **perennially** adv 영구적으로 | **polar** adj 극지의 | **hydrological** adj 수문학적인 | **degradation** n 악화 | **subsidence** n 침하 | **methane** n 메탄 | **carbon dioxide** n 이산화탄소 | **exacerbate** v 악화시키다 | **thaw** v 해빙
7 **integrated** adj 통합된 | **observation** n 관찰 | **numerical** adj 수치적인 | **enhance** v 강화하다 | **hydrology** n 수문학

Actual Test 02

본서 | P. 81

Passage 1 The Fall of the Mayan Civilization

1. Ⓐ	Inference	6. Ⓓ	Fact
2. Ⓐ	Negative Fact	7. Ⓒ	Vocabulary
3. Ⓒ	Sentence Simplification	8. Ⓑ	Fact
4. Ⓓ	Fact	9. Ⓒ	Insertion
5. Ⓒ	Rhetorical Purpose	10. Ⓒ, Ⓓ, Ⓕ	Summary

Passage 2 Altruism in Meerkats

1. Ⓓ	Fact	6. Ⓓ	Inference
2. Ⓑ	Sentence Simplification	7. Ⓑ	Vocabulary
3. Ⓓ	Vocabulary	8. Ⓒ	Negative Fact
4. Ⓐ	Rhetorical Purpose	9. Ⓓ	Insertion
5. Ⓐ	Fact	10. Ⓑ, Ⓒ, Ⓓ	Summary

● 내가 맞은 문제 유형의 개수를 적어 보고 어느 유형에 취약한지 확인해 봅시다.

문제 유형	맞은 개수
Sentence Simplification	2
Fact / Negative Fact	7
Vocabulary	3
Reference	0
Rhetorical Purpose	2
Inference	2
Insertion	2
Summary	2
Category Chart	0
Total	20

Passage 1

The Fall of the Mayan Civilization

1 ➡ The Mayan civilization that once covered much of modern day Guatemala and Southern Mexico was inarguably one of the greatest civilizations ever to exist in Pre-Columbian America. Their settlements date back to around 2,000 BCE, and some existed until the Spanish conquest of the region. They are known for their monumental step-pyramids, stonemasonry, understanding of astronomy and mathematics, and a fully developed hieroglyphic writing system. Their civilization reached its peak during what is called its Classical Period, extending from 250 CE to around 900 CE, when their cities reached their highest state of development. However, their flourishing society suffered a catastrophic collapse at this time from which they never fully recovered. Many theories have been suggested to explain such a sudden decline, including natural disasters, war, and plague. While these may have contributed to the overall decline, the root cause appears to have been an interconnected series of events involving agriculture, conflict, and climate change.

2 ➡ In the Classical Period, the Maya experienced rapid expansion and their population reached into the millions. Most of their large religious and political complexes were built during this time, and their civilization developed into a large politically and economically interconnected society comprised of many small kingdoms and empires. By the 8th century, populations surrounding the central lowlands had reached new peaks of size and density. This was also the area that held the most political influence. Their growing aristocracy, who enjoyed luxuries and the best food, are believed to have expanded rapidly. The outlying kingdoms served as the primary centers for trade, and they brought in goods from throughout Mesoamerica. While relationships with their neighbors were not always peaceful, and warfare did indeed occur, they were generally friendly. The greatest danger to the Maya, although they were probably oblivious to the fact, came from within.

3 ➡ Early in the Classical Period, from about 440 to 660 CE, the area the Maya lived in experienced significantly higher rainfall than it had in the past. This

extended wetter period allowed them to expand their agriculture and produce unprecedented amounts of food. The food surplus allowed the population to grow, and fueled the civilization's rapid expansion. The Maya used permanent farms and raised terraces for cultivation, and their usual method of crop rotation involved fallow cycles, leaving the land uncultivated in order to allow it to recover. However, the increased rainfall would have meant that the minerals and nutrients in the soil of their farms would be replenished more quickly by the mountain runoff, and the temptation to shorten fallow cycles must have been nearly irresistible in a climate that fostered such growth. In addition, the Maya began cutting down expanses of rainforest to clear land for farming and to provide lumber and firewood, reducing the amount of groundcover. Since they raised little livestock, they were also rapidly depleting the area of the animals they relied on for meat. The Maya were overtaxing the carrying capacity of their environment, but they would not realize this until it was too late.

4 ➡ As their civilization continued to expand throughout the 8th and 9th centuries, the advantageous rainfall began to lessen. As this trend continued, pressures began to grow within Mayan society. The large urban centers with their aristocratic populations were a huge drain on agriculture, so as the output decreased, they had to compensate by importing food. This transferred the burden out onto the surrounding communities, which increased competition and conflict between cities and regions. As the societal and economic divide between the peasants and the aristocrats widened further, the lower classes began to revolt against the established order, and food shortages only worsened the situation. Their whole society was teetering on the brink of an abyss.

5 ➡ Then around 1,000 CE, the already faltering civilization was struck by a true disaster: a prolonged drought struck the southern regions. [■A] The drought was a symptom of a global shift in climate that seriously affected other areas in the world, but for the Mayan civilization it was devastating. [■B] Their practice of clearing forest exacerbated the problem in two ways. The land that had been cleared was poor for farming, and the lack of trees disrupted the normal evaporation cycle. [■C] Therefore, when

the drought reduced rainfall by 25 to 40%, their agricultural system became completely unsustainable. Internal warfare escalated as supplies dwindled, and eventually their whole system collapsed. [■D] The Mayan civilization was ultimately a victim of its own unchecked expansion. The drought did not completely destroy their culture as some of the city states in the north survived and continued to expand, but they too fell after the arrival of the Spanish.

1. **Inference**

Based on paragraph 1, what can be inferred about the Mayan civilization?

Ⓐ **Nobody truly knows how the Mayan civilization collapsed.**
Ⓑ The golden age of the Mayan civilization began with the ending of the Classical Period.
Ⓒ Most of the Mayan population lived in cities.
Ⓓ The Mayan civilization eventually recovered from the Spanish conquest.

2. **Negative Fact**

According to paragraph 2, which of the following is NOT true of the Classical Period?

Ⓐ **It was a period of constant warfare with their neighbors.**
Ⓑ It was a period during which the number of aristocrats grew.
Ⓒ It was a period of flourishing trade.
Ⓓ It was a period during which many buildings were constructed.

3. **Sentence Simplification**

Which of the sentences below best expresses the essential information in the highlighted sentence in the passage? *Incorrect* answer choices change the meaning in important ways or leave out essential information.

Ⓐ The increased rainfall quickly diminished the minerals and nutrients in the soil, so it was hard for them to shorten their fallow cycles.
Ⓑ The farmers resisted the temptation to shorten fallow cycles because the increased rainfall fostered growth on the farms where minerals and nutrients were replenished.

Ⓒ **The farmers probably wanted to shorten rest periods because the increased rainfall replenished their farms and made it easier to grow crops.**
Ⓓ The farmers began to use shorter rest periods for their farms because the soil was washed away by water coming from the surrounding countryside.

4. **Fact**
According to paragraph 3, what is one possible cause for the increase in population?
Ⓐ Significantly higher rainfall
Ⓑ Shorter fallow cycle
Ⓒ Reduced expanses of rainforest
Ⓓ **Increased food production**

5. **Rhetorical Purpose**
What is the main purpose of paragraph 4?
Ⓐ To demonstrate the negative effects of reckless expansion
Ⓑ To discuss the effects of rainfall on competition between large urban centers
Ⓒ **To explain what began the downfall of the Mayan civilization**
Ⓓ To highlight the social divide between peasants and aristocrats

6. **Fact**
According to paragraph 4, what was the likely result of importing food?
Ⓐ It increased the number of aristocrats.
Ⓑ The farmers began to revolt against the traders.
Ⓒ It caused conflicts amongst those in large urban centers.
Ⓓ **The social divide between the upper class and lower class widened.**

7. **Vocabulary**
The word "exacerbated" in paragraph 5 is closest in meaning to
Ⓐ evoked
Ⓑ placated
Ⓒ **aggravated**
Ⓓ controlled

8. Fact

According to paragraph 5, why was the drought especially devastating for the Mayan civilization?

(A) It was a symptom of a global shift in climate.
(B) **Deforestation worsened the drought.**
(C) The Maya fought for water.
(D) It was a result of unchecked expansion.

9. Insertion

Look at the four squares [■] that indicate where the following sentence could be added to the passage.

Therefore, when the drought reduced rainfall by 25 to 40%, their agricultural system became completely unsustainable.

Where would the sentence best fit? [■ **C**]

10. Summary

Directions: An introductory sentence for a brief summary of the passage is provided below. Complete the summary by selecting the THREE answer choices that express the most important ideas in the passage. Some sentences do not belong in the summary because they express ideas that are not presented in the passage or are minor ideas in the passage. *This question is worth 2 points.*

While there are many theories that attempt to explain the fall of the Mayan civilization, there seems to have been several interlinked factors that led to the sudden decline of one of the greatest civilizations ever to exist in Pre-Columbian America.

> (C) **With less rainfall, the farms were not able to produce enough food, resulting in food shortages that applied critical pressure to Mayan society.**
> (D) **The drought was the final straw for the weakened Mayan society, completely collapsing their already dysfunctional agricultural system.**
> (F) **Relying heavily on increased rainfall, the Maya overtaxed the natural resources of the land.**

(A) The Maya reached the peak of their civilization by the 9th century CE.
(B) The widening gap and deepening conflict between the aristocrats worsened the economic situation.
(E) The prolonged drought forced the Maya to import food from surrounding communities.

어휘

1. **cover** ~에 이르다, 포함하다, 덮다 | **inarguably** 논쟁의 여지가 없이, 명백하게 | **settlement** 정착지 | **conquest** 정복 | **monumental** 기념비적인, 엄청난, 대단한 | **understanding** 이해 | **hieroglyphic** 상형 문자의 | **flourishing** 번영하는, 성대한 | **catastrophic** 파멸의, 비극적인 | **collapse** 붕괴 | **decline** 쇠퇴, 감소, 하락, 축소 | **natural disaster** 자연 재해 | **plague** 전염병 | **contribute** ~의 원인이 되다, 기여하다 | **interconnected** 상호 연결된 | **conflict** 갈등, 충돌

2. **expansion** 확장, 발전 | **comprise** ~으로 구성되다[이루어지다] | **aristocracy** 귀족(계층) | **outlying** 외딴, 외진, 외곽의 | **oblivious** ~을 감지하지 못하는

3. **extended** (보통 때나 예상보다) 길어진[늘어난] | **unprecedented** 전례 없는 | **surplus** 과잉, 잉여 | **fuel** 부채질하다 | **cultivation** 재배, 경작 | **replenish** 보충하다, 다시 채우다 | **irresistible** 저항할 수 없는, 너무 유혹적인 | **foster** 조성하다, 발전시키다 | **deplete** 대폭 감소시키다, 고갈시키다 | **capacity** 수용력

4. **advantageous** 이로운, 유리한 | **drain** (많은 시간·돈 등을) 고갈시키는[잡아먹는] 것 | **compensate** 보상하다, 보충하다 | **order** 질서

5. **prolonged** 오래 계속되는, 장기적인 | **devastating** 대단히 파괴적인 | **exacerbate** 악화시키다 | **disrupt** 방해하다, 지장을 주다 | **unsustainable** 지속 불가능한 | **escalate** 확대(증가/악화)되다 | **dwindle** 점점 줄어들다 | **unchecked** 억제하지[손을 쓰지] 않고 놔 둔

Passage 2

Altruism in Meerkats

1 ➡ Meerkats are small members of the mongoose family that live in the Kalahari and Namib Deserts of southern Africa. Scientists have studied them for centuries due to their complex societal structure and their altruism, which they practice to a level not often seen in nature. Meerkats breed cooperatively, which means that a group will consist of a dominant breeding pair and up to 40 male and female assistants who do not breed. These assistants spend most of their time taking care of the young by feeding them, training them, and protecting them from danger. As a social predator, it is not unusual that meerkats should do these things as a group, but the extent they carry this behavior to is remarkable.

2 ➡ Meerkats are primarily insectivores, but they will also eat small reptiles, mammals, fungi, and occasionally birds. The majority of the group will usually go out to gather food together, leaving a few to guard the young. Once the pack locates prey, it is difficult for that animal to escape as meerkats are extremely fast and excellent diggers. [■A] Surprisingly, one of their preferred prey animals is scorpions. [■B] While many members of the mongoose family are immune to various snake and insect venoms, it is unclear how much immunity meerkats possess, but this does not deter them. [■C] When a meerkat pounces on a scorpion, the

arachnid often has no time to prepare a strike, and the meerkat circumvents any attack by swiftly biting off the scorpion's stinger. [■D] Then, it uses sand to wash away any venom that may remain on the scorpion's exoskeleton. The meerkat can then devour the disarmed creature at its leisure, or use it as a teaching tool for the young.

3 → Young meerkats feed on milk like any other mammal as infants, but that milk is not always produced by their mother. If the mother is away hunting, other females will actually lactate to feed the infant young. Once they are weaned, however, they must be taught to forage with the adults. To teach them how to hunt dangerous prey like scorpions or centipedes, the adults will start with dead and disarmed prey. Once the young learn how to eat solid food, they will give them prey that has been disarmed but remains very much alive. After they get used to killing their own food, the adults will then show them how to remove the stinger. At that point, it becomes the young animals' turn, and they either succeed or receive a painful and potentially fatal wound. Apart from this kind of training, the adults normally go to great lengths to protect all of the members of their clan.

4 → While most of the clan goes foraging or tends to the young, a few animals will find a place to act as a sentry, either by standing on their hind legs on high ground or by climbing up into a nearby bush, but this also makes them visible to predators. If a sentry spots danger, it will bark, and the entire clan will flee to the nearest burrows. Some researchers have claimed that since the sentries often are the first animals to run, it shows that this behavior may not be entirely altruistic. However, the first animal to reemerge is usually the same sentry animal, and it will continue to give warning barks until it has confirmed that the surface is safe. This behavior is truly selfless, because the animal is not only exposing itself to potential danger, but also announcing its presence to any nearby predators with its barking.

5 → When the clan is unable to avoid a threat in this way, they exhibit further altruistic behavior. If they are threatened in a group, the adults will bunch together and attack the creature en masse in an action called mobbing. This behavior is meant to scare away the predator by making the group appear to be a single

larger animal. This is not always effective against snakes, and sometimes individuals get bitten. When there is danger, the babysitter will quickly usher the young underground, but this is not always possible. When there is no safe place to hide, she will gather the young into a group and then lie on top of them. Ideally, this will keep them from attracting attention, but it may result in the female sacrificing herself for the lives of the young.

리기도 한다. 위험이 있을 때 새끼를 돌보는 미어캣이 급히 새끼들을 땅속으로 인도하지만, 이것이 항상 가능한 것은 아니다. 숨을 만한 안전한 장소가 없을 때 새끼 돌보는 미어캣은 새끼들을 하나로 모아 그 위에 드러눕는다. 이상적으로 이것은 주의를 끄는 것을 막아주지만, 새끼들의 목숨을 위해 암컷이 자신을 희생하는 결과를 낳을 수도 있다.

1. **Fact**

According to paragraph 1, what sets apart the meerkats from other animals?

Ⓐ They are one of the few mammal species that breed cooperatively.
Ⓑ They are a popular subject of study for scientists.
Ⓒ They are the smallest member of the mongoose family.
Ⓓ They are altruistic to an extent rarely observed.

2. **Sentence Simplification**

Which of the sentences below best expresses the essential information in the highlighted sentence in the passage? *Incorrect* answer choices change the meaning in important ways or leave out essential information.

Ⓐ Because many members of the mongoose family hold immunity to various venoms, meerkats do not fear venomous animals.
Ⓑ Unlike with other members of the mongoose family, we don't know how much immunity meerkats possess, but this isn't an obstacle for the meerkats.
Ⓒ Compared to many members of the mongoose family which have immunity to various venoms, meerkats are not aware if they possess immunity.
Ⓓ While it is unclear how much immunity meerkats possess, other members of the mongoose family are weak against most venoms, and this discourages them.

3. **Vocabulary**

The word "circumvents" in paragraph 2 is closest in meaning to

Ⓐ overcomes
Ⓑ eradicates
Ⓒ preserves
Ⓓ avoids

1.

1단락에 따르면, 미어캣을 다른 동물들과 다르게 만드는 것은 무엇인가?

Ⓐ 공동으로 새끼를 기르는 얼마 안 되는 포유류 중 하나이다.
Ⓑ 과학자들에게 인기 있는 연구 대상이다.
Ⓒ 몽구스과의 가장 작은 동물이다.
Ⓓ 찾아보기 어려울 정도로 이타주의적이다.

2.

다음 중 지문의 음영 표시된 문장의 핵심 정보를 가장 잘 표현한 문장은 무엇인가? 오답은 의미를 크게 왜곡하거나 핵심 정보를 누락하고 있다.

Ⓐ 몽구스과의 많은 동물들이 다양한 독에 대한 면역력을 가지고 있기 때문에 미어캣은 독이 있는 동물을 두려워하지 않는다.
Ⓑ 몽구스과의 다른 동물들과 달리 우리는 미어캣이 얼마만큼의 면역력을 가지고 있는지 모르지만 이것은 미어캣에게 장애가 되지 않는다.
Ⓒ 다양한 독에 면역력을 가진 몽구스과의 다른 동물들과 비교하여, 미어캣은 그들이 면역력을 가지고 있는지 알지 못한다.
Ⓓ 미어캣이 얼마만큼의 면역력을 가지고 있는지 확실하지 않지만, 몽구스과의 다른 동물들은 대부분의 독에 취약하고, 이는 그들을 단념시킨다.

3.

2단락의 단어 "circumvents(피한다)"와 의미상 가장 가까운 것은?

Ⓐ 극복한다
Ⓑ 뿌리뽑는다
Ⓒ 막는다
Ⓓ 피한다

4. **Rhetorical Purpose**

What is the purpose of paragraph 3 as it relates to paragraph 2?

Ⓐ **To describe the training young meerkats go through to participate in hunting mentioned in paragraph 2**
Ⓑ To provide an example of how young meerkats develop the immunity to venoms mentioned in paragraph 2
Ⓒ To explain why meerkats prefer to hunt dangerous prey as mentioned in paragraph 2
Ⓓ To differentiate the feeding practices of young meerkats from those of adults as discussed in paragraph 2

5. **Fact**

According to paragraph 4, what is the reasoning against regarding sentry behavior as altruistic?

Ⓐ **Sentries are the first to enter their burrows.**
Ⓑ Sentries do not participate in high-risk duties such as hunting dangerous prey.
Ⓒ Sentries give false warnings to steal food.
Ⓓ Sentries are safe from predator attacks.

6. **Inference**

Based on paragraph 4, what can be inferred about meerkats?

Ⓐ Meerkats are quite vulnerable to predator attacks.
Ⓑ Meerkats have poor vision.
Ⓒ Meerkats takes turns acting as sentries.
Ⓓ **Meerkats dig many burrows in their territory.**

7. **Vocabulary**

The word "usher" in paragraph 5 is closest in meaning to

Ⓐ move
Ⓑ **lead**
Ⓒ carry
Ⓓ push

8. **Negative Fact**

Which of the following is NOT mentioned in the passage about meerkats?

Ⓐ Defensive mechanisms
Ⓑ Foraging behavior
Ⓒ **Domestication by humans**
Ⓓ Breeding habits

9. Insertion

Look at the four squares [■] that indicate where the following sentence could be added to the passage.

Then, it uses sand to wash away any venom that may remain on the scorpion's exoskeleton.

Where would the sentence best fit? [■D]

10. Summary

Directions: An introductory sentence for a brief summary of the passage is provided below. Complete the summary by selecting the THREE answer choices that express the most important ideas in the passage. Some sentences do not belong in the summary because they express ideas that are not presented in the passage or are minor ideas in the passage. *This question is worth 2 points.*

Meerkats, one of the mostly widely studied mammals living in southern Africa, are well known for their exceptionally altruistic behavior.

> Ⓑ **When sentries spot a predator, they issue a series of distinct barks until the danger has passed.**
> Ⓒ **When meerkats are attacked by predators, they display altruistic behavior by mobbing the predator and placing the safety of their young first.**
> Ⓓ **Every adult member of the group plays a role in feeding, training, and protecting the young, even though they are not their own offspring.**

Ⓐ Male and female assistants in a group do not breed until the dominant pair permits them to.
Ⓔ The training for foraging and hunting for food is done in a multi-step process.
Ⓕ Meerkats bite off the scorpion's stinger first to ensure that the arachnid does not strike them with its venom.

어휘

1 **societal** adj 사회의 | **altruism** n 이타주의 | **breed** v 새끼를 낳다, 기르다 | **cooperatively** adv 협력하여, 협조적으로 | **consist of** ~으로 이루어지다[구성되다] | **predator** n 포식자 | **extent** n 정도[규모] | **carry** v 갖다, (특징을) 지니다, 짊어지다 | **remarkable** adj 놀랄 만한, 놀라운

2 **primarily** adv 주로 | **immune** adj 면역성이 있는 | **deter** v 단념시키다 | **pounce** v 덮치다[덤비다] | **circumvent** v 피하다[면하다] | **venom** n 독 | **devour** v 집어삼키다 | **disarmed** adj 무장 해제된, 무력해진

3 **lactate** v 젖을 분비하다[젖이 나오다] | **wean** v 젖을 떼다 | **forage** v 먹이를 찾다 | **get used to** ~에 익숙해지다 | **potentially** adv 가능성 있게, 잠재적으로 | **fatal** adj 치명적인 | **wound** n 상처, 부상 | **clan** n 집단[무리]

4 **tend to** ~을 돌보다 | **hind** adj 뒤쪽의 | **spot** v 알아채다, 발견하다, 찾다 | **burrow** n 굴 | **claim** v 주장하다 | **reemerge** v 다시 나타나다 | **selfless** adj 이타적인 | **announce** v 알리다, 발표하다 | **presence** n 있음, 존재(함)

5 **exhibit** v 드러내다, 전시하다 | **threaten** v 협박[위협]하다 | **en masse** adv 집단으로[일제히] | **usher** v 안내하다, 인도하다 | **ideally** adv 이상적으로 | **sacrifice** v 희생하다

Actual Test 03

본서 | P. 90

Passage 1 Deep Sea Biology

1. Ⓐ	Vocabulary	6. Ⓑ	Rhetorical Purpose
2. Ⓒ	Sentence Simplification	7. Ⓐ	Negative Fact
3. Ⓒ	Inference	8. Ⓓ	Negative Fact
4. Ⓓ	Fact	9. Ⓒ	Insertion
5. Ⓐ	Fact	10. Ⓐ, Ⓓ, Ⓕ	Summary

Passage 2 New York City Urban Planning

1. Ⓐ	Reference	6. Ⓓ	Fact
2. Ⓑ	Vocabulary	7. Ⓒ	Rhetorical Purpose
3. Ⓐ	Inference	8. Ⓓ	Negative Fact
4. Ⓐ	Fact	9. Ⓑ	Insertion
5. Ⓒ	Sentence Simplification	10. Ⓐ, Ⓑ, Ⓔ	Summary

● 내가 맞은 문제 유형의 개수를 적어 보고 어느 유형에 취약한지 확인해 봅시다.

문제 유형	맞은 개수
Sentence Simplification	2
Fact / Negative Fact	7
Vocabulary	2
Reference	1
Rhetorical Purpose	2
Inference	2
Insertion	2
Summary	2
Category Chart	0
Total	20

Passage 1

Deep Sea Biology

1 ➡ After centuries of exploration, scientists have revealed that life exists nearly everywhere on the surface of the Earth. This includes the deepest trenches in the ocean. However, proof of such life remained elusive for a long time because we lacked the technology to reach such depths. Therefore, many hypotheses that supposed that life could not survive there arose. These ideas were logical and convinced many experts that the reason that specimens could not be collected was because they did not exist. However, as evidence of organisms from the depths mounted, many of these ideas were proven wrong. One of the most famous mistaken theories about deep sea biology was created by Edward Forbes.

2 ➡ Edward Forbes was a naturalist and marine biologist from the Isle of Man who had a short but prolific career. He is best known for his time spent upon the HMS Beacon in the Aegean Sea on its survey voyage and the theory on oceanic life that he developed there. Using a dredging rig, he conducted a study of ocean life at varying depths, and came to the conclusion that life did not exist below 300 fathoms (1 fathom is about 2 meters). This belief became known as the azoic hypothesis and was widely accepted by the scientific community until it was disproven by later expeditions of discovery.

3 ➡ Forbes was invited to take part in the expedition by the commander of the ship, Captain Thomas Graves, in 1841. The majority of the trip was spent in the Greek Islands and Asia Minor, where Forbes devoted his time on land to botany. At sea, however, he was constantly dredging, completing at least 150 dredges at depths from 1 fathom to 130 fathoms. His goal was to catalogue how depth, pressure and the geology of the seafloor affected the sizes and types of organisms present. Unsurprisingly, his dredges proved that organisms became smaller and fewer in number the deeper he searched.

4 ➡ Based upon the specimens and data he recovered, Forbes divided the depths of the ocean into eight fairly distinct zones based upon the fauna present. However, due to the fact that he could only dredge up to a certain depth, he was forced

to extrapolate what conditions were like deeper down. This led him to believe that the deepest ocean abysses were utterly devoid of life. He could not conceive how organisms could withstand the brutal pressure, cold and absolute darkness that would be present, and his dredges seemed to support his logic. So, he called this the azoic zone, which literally means "without life." His hypothesis was greeted with general support, and became a dominant theory until it was proven utterly wrong many years later.

5 ➡ The reasons for his mistaken hypothesis come down to particular details of his investigation: the device he used to collect samples and the location. The dredge Forbes used was actually quite poorly designed for its intended use. The opening on the front of the dredge was actually fairly small, meaning that more animals were deflected by it than were captured. To make matters worse, the net on the back of it that was intended to hold the specimens until they were brought to the surface had holes that were large enough for many smaller organisms to freely pass through. In addition, the Aegean Sea had considerably lower levels of fauna than other seas of comparable size and depth. Combined, these factors actually limited the amount of data he could collect.

6 ➡ Another popular but erroneous hypothesis was created by the French naturalist François Peron. Prior to Forbes's survey of the Aegean, Peron explored the depths of the Baltic Sea, paying particular attention to the temperatures he recorded. He correctly noted that the temperature of the water falls as you descend. Pressure also increases with depth, so he believed that the water at the ocean floor was so cold and dense that there must be ice at the bottom of the ocean. These ideas led him to also conclude that the deep sea was lifeless. Like Forbes, Peron's theory also received wide support, even though it later turned out to be false.

7 ➡ As technology advanced, subsequent exploration of the ocean's depths revealed just how flawed these ideas were. [■A] Improved dredging equipment allowed much more effective collection of specimens, and organisms were found at depths well below 300 fathoms. [■B] Forbes's theory that life could not exist below that mark was shattered by Charles Wyville Thomson in 1868 when he collected specimens from over 2,400 fathoms (4,389 meters).

[■C] Scientists also discovered that the oceans were far deeper than they had ever imagined. The Challenger expedition measured the Mariana Trench in 1875 and found that it was over 4,475 fathoms (8,184 meters) deep. [■D] Today, the trench is known to reach a maximum depth of 5,960 fathoms (10,900 meters), and life has been found even there.

1. **Vocabulary**
The word "elusive" in paragraph 1 is closest in meaning to
Ⓐ **undefined**
Ⓑ apparent
Ⓒ complicated
Ⓓ recognizable

2. **Sentence Simplification**
Which of the sentences below best expresses the essential information in the highlighted sentence in the passage? *Incorrect* answer choices change the meaning in important ways or leave out essential information.
Ⓐ After conducting expeditions of discovery, the scientific community was found to be wrong about the azoic hypothesis.
Ⓑ The discoveries and expeditions made by the scientific community helped to disprove the azoic hypothesis.
Ⓒ **The azoic hypothesis had been considered as true until it was proven to be erroneous by later discoveries.**
Ⓓ It was the scientific community that revealed the error of the azoic hypothesis, which had been widely accepted before.

3. **Inference**
According to paragraph 2, which of the following can be inferred about Edward Forbes?
Ⓐ As an experienced biologist, he took part in the survey voyage of the HMS Beacon.
Ⓑ During the survey in the Aegean Sea, he developed a theory about marine life.
Ⓒ **He became a well-respected member of the scientific community.**
Ⓓ He correctly concluded that there was no life in the deep sea.

4. Fact

According to paragraph 3, why did Forbes participate in the expedition?

- Ⓐ To collect a variety of botanical samples in the Greek Islands and Asia Minor
- Ⓑ To find evidence to support his hypothesis that organisms could not inhabit the deep sea
- Ⓒ To develop an effective dredging device with which to study the seabed ecosystem
- **Ⓓ To research the effects of depth, pressure and the geology under the sea on organisms**

5. Fact

According to paragraph 4, why did Forbes conclude that life did not exist in the deepest ocean?

- **Ⓐ He thought the environment was too tough for organisms to survive.**
- Ⓑ He was unable to discover anything when he reached a certain depth.
- Ⓒ He faced unexpected obstacles while dredging.
- Ⓓ He successfully classified the zones according to species diversity.

6. Rhetorical Purpose

Why does the author mention "the device he used to collect samples and the location" in paragraph 5?

- Ⓐ To describe how poor the technology was in Forbes's time
- **Ⓑ To point out what caused Forbes to draw an erroneous conclusion**
- Ⓒ To explain how Forbes collected samples from the ocean
- Ⓓ To emphasize the difficulty Forbes experienced during his exploration

7. Negative Fact

All of the following are mentioned in paragraph 5 as reasons for Forbes's mistaken hypothesis EXCEPT

- Ⓐ the dredge was originally designed for use on the surface of the sea rather than in the deep sea.
- Ⓑ the device Forbes used had a small hole which made it difficult to capture animals.
- Ⓒ the net of the dredge did not function efficiently and failed to hold tiny organisms.
- Ⓓ the Aegean Sea had lower levels of life compared to other seas.

8. Negative Fact

According to paragraph 6, all of the following are true about Peron's hypothesis EXCEPT

Ⓐ Peron's hypothesis was similar to that of Forbes in that it was lifeless in the deep sea.
Ⓑ Peron found that the temperature becomes lower with depth by recording temperatures in the Baltic Sea.
Ⓒ Peron thought ice was present at the bottom of the ocean due to the low seawater temperature.
Ⓓ Peron's hypothesis was correct in that the high pressure at the ocean floor makes it impossible for organisms to inhabit it.

9. Insertion

Look at the four squares [■] that indicate where the following sentence could be added to the passage.

Scientists also discovered that the oceans were far deeper than they had ever imagined.

Where would the sentence best fit? [■ C]

10. Summary

Directions: An introductory sentence for a brief summary of the passage is provided below. Complete the summary by selecting the THREE answer choices that express the most important ideas in the passage. Some sentences do not belong in the summary because they express ideas that are not presented in the passage or are minor ideas in the passage. *This question is worth 2 points.*

Many hypotheses that have been presented to suggest that no life exists in the deepest ocean have since been disproven.

> **Ⓐ Forbes divided the depths of the sea into eight regions based on the data he had collected and concluded it is lifeless in the abysmal depths of the ocean.**
> **Ⓓ The defective device Forbes used for his research and environmental conditions in the Aegean Sea led Forbes to the incorrect conclusion.**
> **Ⓕ Peron also developed a hypothesis that no living things existed in the depths of the ocean because of the low temperature and high pressure there.**

Ⓑ Forbes found that the size and number of organisms decrease as you descend deeper into the sea.
Ⓒ Forbes's theory had been generally supported in the contemporary scientific field before it was revealed to be wrong.
Ⓔ Peron was the first to discover the link between the pressure and the temperature under the sea.

Ⓑ 포브스는 바다로 더 깊이 내려갈수록 생명체의 크기와 수가 줄어든다는 것을 발견했다.
Ⓒ 포브스의 이론은 잘못되었다는 것이 밝혀지기 전까지 당대 과학계로부터 일반적으로 지지를 받았다.
Ⓔ 페론은 바다 밑의 수압과 수온의 관계를 발견한 첫 번째 인물이었다.

어휘

1 **exploration** n 탐험, 탐사 | **reveal** v 밝히다, 드러내다 | **trench** n 해구, 해자(垓子) | **roof** n 지붕 | **elusive** adj 찾기 힘든 | **depth** n 깊이 | **arise** v 생기다, 발생하다 | **convince** v 납득시키다, 확신시키다 | **specimen** n 표본, 견본 | **evidence** n 증거, 흔적 | **mount** v 서서히 증가하다
2 **prolific** adj 많은, 다작하는, 열매를 많이 맺는 | **dredging rig** 준설 장비 | **varying** adj 바뀌는, 가지각색의 | **disprove** v 틀렸음을 입증하다 | **expedition** n 탐험, 원정
3 **devote** v 바치다, 쏟다, 기울이다
4 **distinct** adj 뚜렷한, 분명한 | **extrapolate** v 추론(추정)하다 | **abyss** n 심연, 깊은 구렁 | **devoid of** ~이 전혀 없는 | **conceive** v 이해하다, 상상하다 | **withstand** v 견뎌[이겨]내다 | **brutal** adj 혹독한, 잔혹한, 악랄한 | **absolute** adj 완전한, 완벽한 | **literally** adv 문자[말] 그대로 | **greet** v 받아이다, 맞다, 환영하다 | **utterly** adv 완전히, 순전히
5 **intended** adj 의도된, 계획된 | **deflect** v 방향을 바꾸다, 피하다[모면하다] | **considerably** adv 많이, 상당히 | **comparable** adj 비슷한, 비교할 만한
6 **erroneous** adj 잘못된 | **descend** v 내려오다, 하강하다 | **dense** adj 밀도가 높은, 빽빽한, 밀집한
7 **flawed** adj 결점[결함/흠]이 있는 | **improved** adj 향상된, 개선된 | **collection** n 수집(품), 소장품 | **shatter** v 산산이 부수다

Passage 2

New York City Urban Planning

1 ➡ Originally settled by the Dutch under the name of New Amsterdam, New York is one of the oldest planned cities in the United States. Like many early colonial cities, it began its existence as a fortification and was constructed along military guidelines. They eventually surrendered it to England, which in turn lost it when the United States achieved its independence. As the city expanded, a great deal of effort went into keeping the city organized. In fact, in 1811, the city council adopted a plan that divided up the mostly undeveloped northern portion of Manhattan Island and employed a strict grid pattern, regardless of terrain. However, due to the city's rampant growth, these measures often proved insufficient, and there were many serious problems involving health, sanitation and safety.

2 ➡ New York City has always been an important port city, but few anticipated the number of immigrants it would receive, and many buildings had to be rapidly constructed to accommodate the new

뉴욕 시의 도시 계획

1 ➡ 뉴암스테르담이란 이름으로 원래 네덜란드인들이 정착한 뉴욕은 미국에서 가장 오래된 계획 도시 중 하나이다. 초기의 많은 식민 도시들처럼 뉴욕도 요새로 존재했고 군사 가이드라인을 따라 건설되었다. 그들은 결국 영국에 뉴욕을 넘겼고, 영국은 다시 미국이 독립을 쟁취했을 때 그곳을 빼앗겼다. 도시가 확장함에 따라 도시를 정리하기 위한 많은 노력이 들어갔다. 사실 1811년에 시 의회는 거의 개발되지 않은 맨해튼섬의 북쪽 지역을 분리하고, 지형에 관계없이 엄격한 격자형을 이용하는 계획을 채택했다. 그러나 도시의 걷잡을 수 없는 발달로 이러한 조치들이 종종 불충분한 것으로 드러났고, 건강, 위생, 안전과 관련된 심각한 문제들이 있었다.

2 ➡ 뉴욕 시는 항상 중요한 항구 도시였지만 그것이 받아들이게 될 이민자의 수를 예측한 사람은 거의 없었고, 많은 건물들이 새로 도착한 사람들을 수용하기 위해 빠르게 지어져야 했다. 1800년 즈음에 도시의 인구는 3만 명에 달

arrivals. By 1800, the city's population had reached 30,000 people, most of whom lived in an area that only comprises a fraction of the modern city. Some historians estimate that New York's population increased at a rate of around 100 percent every ten years, which meant that even more people were forced to live in hastily constructed tenements. Such massive immigration and overcrowding inevitably created conditions that were perfect for infectious diseases to ravage the city. Epidemics of cholera, malaria, and typhoid swept through the population in the early 19th century, killing thousands in some of the worst outbreaks the country has ever seen. The demolition of many apartment buildings and the development of the northern part of the island served to alleviate the overcrowding, but these diseases would return again. One famous case was an outbreak of typhoid in the early 1900s. A woman whom the press labeled Typhoid Mary was a carrier of the disease who caused the deaths of over fifty people while working as a maid.

3 ➡ Along with overcrowding, New York also suffered from an inadequate sanitation system. All of the cabs and wagons that transported people and goods through the city streets were pulled by horses, and an estimated 200,000 of them were living there by the beginning of the 20th century. By necessity, most of these animals lived on the island of Manhattan, often in residential areas. [■A] These animals generated large amounts of waste that piled up throughout the city due to a lack of infrastructure. [■B] Most often, waste was left in the middle of the street, as horse owners were far less likely to clean up after their horses if they were not on their own property. This waste made the streets reek in the summer, and it mixed with heavy snow in the winter, sometimes accumulating in frozen piles up to two meters high. [■C] Not only that, but the horses also were often overworked and otherwise mistreated to the extent that many of them died in the streets, where their bodies would remain since no one had the responsibility of cleaning them up. [■D] This situation was not remedied until 1909, when the Queensboro Bridge was opened to traffic. This allowed the waste to be transported over to rural Queens where it was used to fertilize farmland.

4 ➡ Waste from animals and humans led to an even more serious health problem: contaminated drinking

했는데, 그들 대부분은 현재 도시의 일부에 해당하는 지역에 살았다. 일부 역사학자들은 뉴욕의 인구가 10년마다 약 100퍼센트의 비율로 증가했다고 추산하는데, 이는 점점 더 많은 사람들이 급히 지어진 임대건물에 살아야만 했다는 것을 의미했다. 그러한 엄청난 이민과 과밀 거주는 전염병이 도시에 창궐하기에 완벽한 조건을 불가피하게 만들었다. 19세기 초에 콜레라, 말라리아와 장티푸스 같은 전염병이 사람들을 휩쓸었고, 일부 지역에서는 건국 이래 최악의 발생으로 수천 명이 사망했다. 많은 아파트 건물의 철거와 섬 북부의 개발이 과밀 거주를 완화하기 위해 이루어졌지만, 이런 전염병은 재발하곤 했다. 한 유명한 사례는 1900년대 초의 장티푸스 발생이었다. 언론이 장티푸스 메리라고 꼬리표를 붙인 어떤 여자가 병의 보균자였고, 가정부로 일하는 동안 50명이 넘는 사람들의 죽음을 야기했다.

3 ➡ 과밀 거주와 함께 뉴욕은 또한 부적절한 위생 체계로 고통을 받았다. 도시 거리를 가로질러 사람과 상품을 나르던 모든 택시와 수레들은 말이 끌었는데, 20세기 초까지 약 20만 마리의 말이 거기 살고 있던 것으로 추정된다. 필요에 의해 대부분의 말은 맨해튼섬에, 흔히 주거 지역에 살았다. [■A] 말은 기반 시설의 부족으로 도시 전체에 다량의 배설물을 배출했다. [■B] 대부분의 경우 배설물은 거리 중간에 방치되었는데, 말 주인들이 자신의 땅이 아니면 말의 배설물을 치우려고 하지 않았기 때문이었다. 이 배설물은 여름에는 거리에 냄새가 진동하게 했고, 겨울에는 많은 눈과 섞여 때로는 2미터 이상의 높이로 얼어 있었다. [■C] 그뿐만 아니라 말 역시 일을 과하게 하거나 혹사당하여 많은 말이 거리에서 죽었고, 누구도 그 사체를 치울 책임이 없었으므로 거리에 그냥 버려져 있곤 했다. [■D] 이러한 상황은 퀸즈버러 다리가 개통된 1909년까지 고쳐지지 않았다. 다리의 개통으로 배설물이 퀸즈의 시골 지역으로 옮겨져 농장을 비옥하게 하는 데 사용될 수 있었다.

4 ➡ 동물과 사람이 배출한 쓰레기는 더 심각한 건강 문제를 야기했는데, 그것은 오염된 식수였다. 맨해튼섬은 믿을

water. Manhattan Island had never had a reliable water supply, with its brackish rivers forcing people to rely upon well water. Already insufficient, as the population grew, the aquifer those wells reached into became seriously polluted, which led to severe outbreaks of cholera. To cope with this problem, they had to look far outside of the city to find a viable source of water. The city undertook a large and complex project to bring fresh water from the Croton River to the island. Built between 1837 and 1842, the Old Croton Aqueduct brought water 66 kilometers to reservoirs in the city. Life in the city rapidly improved, but its growth did not slow down, and many additional aqueducts have been built since.

5 ➡ As serious as the health and sanitation issues were, a serious safety issue went largely ignored until disaster struck. After years of construction, the Erie Canal opened, successfully linking the Hudson River to the Great Lakes in 1825. This shipping lane dramatically increased trade in New York, and warehouses sprang up throughout the financial district to accommodate the merchants' goods. Unfortunately, like most of the city's other buildings, these warehouses were made of wood, and a calamitous fire started in a warehouse on the bitterly cold and windy evening of December 16, 1835. Before its flames were finally put out, the Great Fire of New York razed southeastern Manhattan, destroying most of the buildings in Wall Street and the New York Stock Exchange. The builders had ignored the dangers of constructing so many wooden buildings in such close proximity, and the fire took full advantage of their oversight. Following the conflagration, city planners regulated the minimum distance between buildings and created newer, stricter fire prevention policies.

만한 식수 공급처를 가진 적이 없었는데, 염분이 섞인 강물은 사람들이 우물물에 의존하게 만들었다. 이미 불충분한 데다 인구가 늘어나자 그 우물들이 닿아 있는 대수층은 심각하게 오염되었고, 이는 심각한 콜레라 발생으로 이어졌다. 이 문제를 해결하기 위해 사람들은 이용 가능한 수자원을 찾기 위해 도시에서 멀리 떨어진 곳까지 찾아야 했다. 시는 담수를 크로턴강으로부터 맨해튼섬으로 끌어오는 복잡한 대형 프로젝트에 착수했다. 1837~1842년 사이에 건설된 올드 크로턴 송수관은 도시의 저수지로 물을 66킬로미터 끌어왔다. 도시의 삶은 급격히 개선되었지만 도시의 성장은 둔화되지 않았고, 추가로 많은 송수관들이 그 이후로 건설되었다.

5 ➡ 건강과 위생 문제가 심각했던 만큼 또 하나의 심각한 안전 문제가 큰 재난이 닥치기 전까지 대체로 무시되었다. 몇 년간의 공사 후, 1825년에 이리 운하가 개통되어 성공적으로 허드슨강과 5대호를 연결했다. 이 선박 항로는 뉴욕의 교역을 극적으로 증가시켰고, 상품을 수용하기 위해 금융가에 창고들이 속속 지어졌다. 불행히도 도시의 다른 대부분의 건물들처럼 이 창고들은 나무로 만들어졌고, 1835년 12월 16일 저녁, 매우 춥고 바람이 많이 불던 날 한 창고에서 재앙을 초래하는 화재가 발생했다. 불이 완전히 꺼지기까지 뉴욕 대화재는 맨해튼 남동부를 완전히 파괴하며, 월가의 대부분의 건물과 뉴욕 증권 거래소를 파괴했다. 건설자들은 그렇게 많은 목조 건물들을 아주 가깝게 건설하는 것의 위험성을 무시했으며, 화재는 그들의 간과를 충분히 이용했다. 대화재 이후 도시 기획자들은 건물 간의 최소 거리를 규제했고, 더 새롭고 더 엄격한 화재 예방 정책들을 세웠다.

---

1. Reference
The word "They" in paragraph 1 refers to
Ⓐ the Dutch
Ⓑ colonial cities
Ⓒ guidelines
Ⓓ the United States

1.
1단락의 단어 "They(그들)"이 가리키는 것은?
Ⓐ 네덜란드인들
Ⓑ 식민 도시들
Ⓒ 가이드라인
Ⓓ 미국

2. **Vocabulary**

The word "inevitably" in paragraph 2 is closest in meaning to

Ⓐ relentlessly
Ⓑ **unavoidably**
Ⓒ perversely
Ⓓ allegedly

3. **Inference**

Based on paragraph 2, what can be inferred about epidemics in New York City in the early 19th century?

Ⓐ **They caused many people to resettle on the northern part of the island.**
Ⓑ Immigration declined due to the unsanitary conditions.
Ⓒ The authorities were unable to locate the sources of outbreaks.
Ⓓ Population growth slowed because of massive outbreaks of disease.

4. **Fact**

According to paragraph 3, what was the main role of horses in New York?

Ⓐ **Pulling cabs and wagons**
Ⓑ Disposing of waste in residential areas
Ⓒ Fertilizing farmland
Ⓓ Clearing snow in the winter

5. **Sentence Simplification**

Which of the sentences below best expresses the essential information in the highlighted sentence in the passage? *Incorrect* answer choices change the meaning in important ways or leave out essential information.

Ⓐ The population was unable to filter the water from the polluted wells, leading to severe cholera outbreaks.
Ⓑ The wells were used as sewers, polluting the aquifer and causing severe outbreaks of cholera amidst the growing population.
Ⓒ **The aquifer which the wells reached into, already insufficient with population growth, became polluted and led to increased disease.**
Ⓓ As the population grew, the wells could no longer reach the aquifer, which led to epidemics.

2.
2단락의 단어 "inevitably(불가피하게)"와 의미상 가장 가까운 것은?

Ⓐ 가차 없이
Ⓑ 피할 수 없이
Ⓒ 심술궂게
Ⓓ 주장한 바에 의하면

3.
2단락에 근거하여 19세기 초반 뉴욕 시의 전염병에 대해 추론할 수 있는 것은 무엇인가?

Ⓐ 많은 사람들이 섬의 북부에 다시 정착하게 만들었다.
Ⓑ 비위생적인 환경 때문에 이민이 감소했다.
Ⓒ 당국은 전염병 발생의 근원지를 밝혀낼 수 없었다.
Ⓓ 대규모 전염병 발생 때문에 인구 증가가 둔화되었다.

4.
3단락에 따르면, 뉴욕에서 말의 주요 역할은 무엇이었는가?

Ⓐ 택시와 수레 끌기
Ⓑ 주거 지역의 배설물 처리
Ⓒ 농장에 거름 주기
Ⓓ 겨울에 눈 치우기

5.
다음 중 지문의 음영 표시된 문장의 핵심 정보를 가장 잘 표현한 문장은 무엇인가? 오답은 의미를 크게 왜곡하거나 핵심 정보를 누락하고 있다.

Ⓐ 사람들은 오염된 우물들의 물을 정수할 수 없었고, 이는 심각한 콜레라의 발생으로 이어졌다.
Ⓑ 우물들은 하수도로 사용되어 대수층을 오염시키고 늘어나는 인구에 심각한 콜레라의 발생을 야기했다.
Ⓒ 이미 인구 증가로 부족한 상태였던 우물들이 닿아 있던 대수층은 오염되었고 이는 질병 발생 증가로 이어졌다.
Ⓓ 인구가 증가함에 따라 우물들은 더 이상 대수층에 도달할 수 없었고, 이는 전염병으로 이어졌다.

6. Fact

According to paragraph 4, what did the Old Croton Aqueduct achieve?

Ⓐ It linked the Croton River to the Great Lakes.
Ⓑ It provided an ample supply of clean water to the city.
Ⓒ It paved the way for additional population growth.
Ⓓ It improved the quality of life in the city.

7. Rhetorical Purpose

Why does the author mention "Great Fire of New York" in paragraph 5?

Ⓐ To prove that fire has a more disastrous effect on society than poor sanitation
Ⓑ To highlight the unexpected consequences of constructing the Erie Canal
Ⓒ To point out an aspect of urban planning the city planners neglected
Ⓓ To introduce the history of fire safety regulations in New York City

8. Negative Fact

Which of the following is NOT mentioned in the passage as a source of misfortune in New York City?

Ⓐ Massive immigration
Ⓑ Poor sanitation system
Ⓒ Lack of drinking water
Ⓓ Wooden buildings

9. Insertion

Look at the four squares [■] that indicate where the following sentence could be added to the passage.

Most often, waste was left in the middle of the street, as horse owners were far less likely to clean up after their horses if they were not on their own property.

Where would the sentence best fit? [■ B]

10. Summary

Directions: An introductory sentence for a brief summary of the passage is provided below. Complete the summary by selecting the THREE answer choices that express the most important ideas in the passage. Some sentences do not belong in the summary because they express ideas that are not presented in the passage or are minor ideas in the passage. *This question is worth 2 points.*

New York, one of the oldest planned cities in the United States, underwent significant trial and error in tackling problems such as public health, sanitation, and fire safety during its development.

- (A) The huge number of immigrants settling down in New York rapidly increased the city's population, resulting in overcrowding and epidemic outbreaks.
- (B) The lack of a proper sanitation system or a reliable water supply resulted in outbreaks of cholera, prompting the city to transport clean water to the island.
- (E) After the fire in 1835, a greater awareness of fire safety led to stricter regulations about constructing buildings.

- (C) The horse owners did not clean up after their horses, and often left the remains of dead horses on the streets, providing a trigger for epidemic outbreaks.
- (D) Frequent outbreaks of infectious diseases led the city to demolish apartment buildings, and it was effective at curbing the death tolls.
- (F) The building of the Queensboro Bridge allowed the waste accumulated in Manhattan to be transported to Queens, where it was used as fertilizer.

10.

지시문: 지문을 간략하게 요약한 글의 첫 문장이 아래 제시되어 있다. 지문의 가장 중요한 내용을 표현하는 세 개의 선택지를 골라 요약문을 완성하시오. 일부 문장들은 지문에 제시되지 않았거나 지문의 지엽적인 내용을 나타내기 때문에 요약문에 포함되지 않는다. *이 문제의 배점은 2점이다.*

미국에서 가장 오래된 계획 도시 중 하나인 뉴욕은 발전 과정에서 공중 보건, 위생 시설, 화재 안전과 같은 문제들을 해결하는 데 상당한 시행 착오를 겪었다.

- (A) 뉴욕에 정착한 엄청난 수의 이민자들은 도시의 인구를 급증시켰으며, 이는 과밀 거주와 전염병 발생으로 이어졌다.
- (B) 적절한 위생 체계나 믿을 만한 물 공급의 부족은 콜레라의 발생으로 이어졌고 도시로 하여금 깨끗한 물을 맨해튼섬으로 끌어오게 했다.
- (E) 1835년의 대화재 이후, 화재 안전에 대한 더 큰 자각은 건물의 건설에 대한 더 엄격한 규정으로 이어졌다.

- (C) 말 주인들은 말의 배설물을 치우지 않았고, 종종 말의 사체를 거리에 그냥 내버려 두어 전염병 발생의 계기를 제공했다.
- (D) 빈번한 전염성 질병의 발생은 도시로 하여금 아파트 건물을 철거하게 했으며, 그것은 사망자 수를 억제하는 데 효과적이었다.
- (F) 퀸즈버러 다리의 건설은 맨해튼에 쌓인 쓰레기가 퀸즈로 옮겨져 그곳에서 비료로 사용될 수 있게 했다.

어휘

1. **originally** adv 원래, 본래 | **settle** v 정착하다 | **construct** v 건설하다 | **surrender** v 항복하다, 포기하다, 넘겨주다 | **expand** v 확대[확장/팽창]되다 | **undeveloped** adj 미개발된 | **employ** v 고용하다, 이용하다 | **rampant** adj 걷잡을 수 없는, 만연[횡행]하는 | **insufficient** adj 불충분한 | **sanitation** n 위생 시설[관리], 공중 위생
2. **anticipate** v 예상하다, 예측하다 | **accommodate** v 수용하다 | **comprise** v ~으로 구성되다[이뤄지다] | **hastily** adv 급히, 서둘러서 | **inevitably** adv 필연적으로, 불가피하게 | **infectious** adj 전염되는 | **ravage** v 황폐[피폐]하게 만들다, 유린[파괴]하다 | **outbreak** n 발생[발발] | **demolition** n 파괴, 폭파, 철거 | **alleviate** v 완화하다 | **carrier** n 보균자, 나르는[운반하는] 사람[것]
3. **estimated** adj 추측의, 견적의 | **necessity** n 필요(성) | **generate** v 발생시키다, 만들어 내다 | **infrastructure** n 사회[공공] 기반 시설 | **accumulate** v 모으다, 축적하다 | **mistreat** v 학대[혹사]하다 | **fertilize** v 비옥하게 하다, 비료를 주다
4. **reliable** adj 믿을[신뢰할] 수 있는 | **pollute** v 오염시키다 | **cope** v 대처[대응]하다 | **viable** adj 실행 가능한, 성공할 수 있는 | **undertake** v 착수하다 | **reservoir** n 저수지
5. **largely** adv 크게, 대체로, 주로 | **ignore** v 무시하다 | **dramatically** adv 극적으로 | **spring up** 갑자기 생겨나다 | **financial** adj 금융[재정]의 | **calamitous** adj 재앙을 초래하는 | **bitterly** adv 몹시, 비통하게, 격렬하게 | **raze** v 완전히 파괴하다 | **proximity** n 가까움[근접] | **take advantage** ~을 기회로 활용하다, ~을 이용하다 | **oversight** n 실수, 간과 | **conflagration** n 대화재 | **regulate** v 규제하다, 조절하다 | **fire prevention** 화재 예방 | **policy** n 정책

Actual Test 04

본서 | P. 99

Passage 1 The Purpose of Extrafloral Nectar

1. Ⓓ	Fact	6. Ⓒ	Rhetorical Purpose
2. Ⓑ	Sentence Simplification	7. Ⓓ	Fact
3. Ⓑ	Inference	8. Ⓑ	Inference
4. Ⓓ	Negative Fact	9. Ⓓ	Insertion
5. Ⓐ	Vocabulary	10. Ⓒ, Ⓓ, Ⓕ	Summary

Passage 2 History of Theater

1. Ⓐ	Fact	6. Ⓐ	Sentence Simplification
2. Ⓑ	Vocabulary	7. Ⓐ	Inference
3. Ⓓ	Rhetorical Purpose	8. Ⓓ	Insertion
4. Ⓐ	Vocabulary	9. Ⓐ	Rhetorical Purpose
5. Ⓑ	Negative Fact	10. Ⓑ, Ⓓ, Ⓕ	Summary

● 내가 맞은 문제 유형의 개수를 적어 보고 어느 유형에 취약한지 확인해 봅시다.

문제 유형	맞은 개수
Sentence Simplification	2
Fact / Negative Fact	5
Vocabulary	3
Reference	0
Rhetorical Purpose	3
Inference	3
Insertion	2
Summary	2
Category Chart	0
Total	20

The Purpose of Extrafloral Nectar

1 ➡ Many flowering plants produce nectar as a way to attract insects that are beneficial to their life cycle. Most of them produce nectar from the sepal, a structure at the base of the inside of the flower. Any organism that wishes to feed on the nectar has to brush past the flower's reproductive structures, which deposit pollen on the organism that it then transports to another flower. However, many plant species produce nectar on other parts of the plant in what are referred to as extrafloral nectaries, which clearly must serve another purpose. Most of the empirical evidence that has been gathered shows that extrafloral nectaries are a defensive mechanism that attracts insects to protect the plant. As a reward, the insects may freely feed upon the nectar provided.

2 ➡ Nectar is a complex brew of many chemicals which are designed to attract and provide sustenance to other organisms. About 95% of all nectars is natural sugars, but many types contain amino acids. In fact, all of the twenty amino acids that naturally occur in proteins have been found in various nectars. Many of the other compounds present in nectar are designed to attract specific organisms by their scent. These are often volatiles that carry long distances on breezes. However, other chemicals present in some nectars actually discourage the organism from taking a second sip. For example, tobacco plants include some nicotine in their nectar, which is very bitter and less aromatic, meaning that the organism will eagerly feed once, but most likely move on soon afterward. This allows the plant to conserve its nectar, which most plants reabsorb after fertilization to use in seed production.

3 ➡ Unlike flowers, extrafloral nectaries produce nectar continuously, regardless of whether the plant has reproduced. This is due to the fact that they attract insects for an entirely different reason. Scientists have observed ladybird beetles, wasps, and particularly ants feeding on extrafloral nectar, and they all provide protection to the plant as well. Ladybird beetles are voracious predators that are very fond of eating aphids, which are a significant pest because they can reproduce asexually. Parasitic wasps will stun, remove, and lay eggs inside of

caterpillars that consume leaves. Ants provide the most protection as they will attack and consume any insects that attack the plant and are also capable of discouraging larger herbivores from feeding on the plants.

4 ➡ Although such relationships may seem obvious today, they were not always so well understood. Initially, many scientists thought that extrafloral nectaries were purely excretory organs, including Charles Darwin. In fact, his disagreement with Federico Delpino about this led the latter to engage in some of the first serious study of the phenomenon. Many experts at the time argued that the structures were actually hydathodes. Hydathodes are a type of specialized plant tissue that is very similar to stomata. However, they are actually used to secrete excess water instead of regulating gas exchange. Delpino published a paper based on his observations in 1886 that contended that plants deliberately attract ants with this nectar to gain their protection.

5 ➡ [■A] Delpino's work later received support from the research of entomologist William Morton Wheeler and botanist Barbara Bentley. [■B] Based upon his own observations, Wheeler proposed in 1910 that not only did the ants feed on the nectar, but that the plants were actually dependent upon the ants for their survival. [■C] He observed that plants that produced extrafloral nectar were almost entirely unable to reproduce without ants present and often died. [■D] Barbara Bentley conducted an experiment in 1977 that added further support to the theory.

6 ➡ In Bentley's experiment, she deliberately set out to determine whether plants genuinely benefited from ants and vice versa. She compared plants living in a carefully controlled environment free of ants to others in an environment that contained them. She found that after the plants had reproduced, there was a marked difference in the number of viable seeds that they produced. The plants that were exposed to ants produced an average of 215 seeds, whereas the plants in the controlled environment produced a mere 45. The ants protected the flowers throughout their stages of development, thereby providing the plants with a better opportunity to reproduce.

7 ➡ As the research by Wheeler and Bentley shows, these organisms depend upon each other for their

survival. The ants provide the plants with much needed protection, while the plants provide the ants with an easily digestible energy source and protection against their predators. Most insects have parasitic relationships with plants, wherein the plants suffer for the insect's benefit. However, the relationships between extrafloral nectarine plants and their protectors appear to be wholly beneficial to both species. This means that they have evolved to share a mutualistic form of symbiosis. When this occurred or how long it took to happen remains unclear, but their interaction is clearly observable.

1. **Fact**

According to paragraph 1, what is the primary function of extrafloral nectar?

Ⓐ It induces pollination.
Ⓑ It provides nutrients to insects.
Ⓒ It poisons organisms that feed on plants.
Ⓓ **It serves as a defense mechanism.**

2. **Sentence Simplification**

Which of the sentences below best expresses the essential information in the highlighted sentence in the passage? *Incorrect* answer choices change the meaning in important ways or leave out essential information.

Ⓐ Insects will move on to other tobacco plants after feeding on the nectar of one tobacco plant because it includes a certain amount of nicotine in its nectar.
Ⓑ **Because insects feeding on the nectar of tobacco plants find it bitter, they move on after only feeding once.**
Ⓒ Some insects are attracted to the nicotine present in tobacco plants because it is bitter and less aromatic, so they do not move on to other plants after feeding.
Ⓓ Because the nicotine in the nectar of tobacco plants is poisonous, insects will only feed eagerly on the nectar once before moving on.

3. **Inference**

Based on paragraph 2, it can be inferred that

Ⓐ the chemical composition of nectar varies little from plant to plant.
Ⓑ **most plants do not want organisms to feed on their nectar indefinitely.**
Ⓒ nectars contain all the building blocks of proteins.
Ⓓ flowers stop producing nectar after they have been fertilized.

4. **Negative Fact**

All of the following are mentioned in paragraph 3 EXCEPT

Ⓐ ants can defend against animals much larger than them.
Ⓑ aphids, which reproduce asexually, are a significant pest.
Ⓒ the purpose of extrafloral nectaries is different from those in flowers.
Ⓓ **parasitic wasps provide protection against caterpillar eggs.**

5. **Vocabulary**

The word "secrete" in paragraph 4 is closest in meaning to

Ⓐ **emit**
Ⓑ secure
Ⓒ conclude
Ⓓ absorb

6. **Rhetorical Purpose**

What is the function of paragraph 6 as it relates to paragraph 5?

Ⓐ To show similarities between the work of Wheeler and Bentley
Ⓑ To provide support for Delpino's work
Ⓒ **To illustrate what Bentley's experiment was about**
Ⓓ To cast doubt on the validity of Bentley's experiment

7. **Fact**

According to paragraph 6, Bentley conducted the experiment by

Ⓐ introducing different types of insects to each environment.
Ⓑ delaying the stages of development of plants in one environment.
Ⓒ controlling the number of plants in each environment.
Ⓓ **comparing plants in an ant-free environment to those in one with ants.**

8. Inference

Based on paragraph 7, it can be inferred that

Ⓐ extrafloral nectaries are a product of evolution.
Ⓑ **a positive symbiotic relationship between insects and plants is rare.**
Ⓒ over time, the ants developed enzymes that could easily digest the amino acids present in nectar.
Ⓓ more careful observation is needed to fully understand the relationship between extrafloral nectarine plants and their predators.

9. Insertion

Look at the four squares [■] that indicate where the following sentence could be added to the passage.

Barbara Bentley conducted an experiment in 1977 that added further support to the theory.

Where would the sentence best fit? [■ D]

10. Summary

Directions: An introductory sentence for a brief summary of the passage is provided below. Complete the summary by selecting the THREE answer choices that express the most important ideas in the passage. Some sentences do not belong in the summary because they express ideas that are not presented in the passage or are minor ideas in the passage. *This question is worth 2 points.*

While nectar produced inside flowers attracts insects to help pollinate them, nectar produced on other parts of the plant attracts insects to protect the plant.

Ⓒ **While many scientists mistakenly assumed that extrafloral nectaries were excretory organs, Delpino was right in his argument that extrafloral nectar attracts insects to gain their protection.**
Ⓓ **Bentley's experiment, which showed that plants produced more seeds when ants were present, revealed the symbiotic relationship between insects and plants with extrafloral nectaries.**
Ⓕ **Insects such as parasitic wasps and ants feed on extrafloral nectar, consume pests which attack the plant, and deter larger herbivores from feeding on the plant.**

Ⓐ Nectar, which is primarily composed of natural sugars, includes other chemical compounds that give off scents to attract insects.

Ⓑ Both hydathodes and stomata are types of specialized plant tissues, but hydathodes secrete excess water while stomata regulate gas exchange. Ⓔ In fact, plants exposed to ants produced an average of 215 seeds while those in an ant-free environment produced an average of 45 seeds.	Ⓑ 배수 조직과 기공은 둘 다 전문화된 식물 조직들이지만 배수 조직은 여분의 수분을 배출하는 반면 기공은 가스 교환을 조절한다. Ⓔ 실제로 개미들에 노출된 식물들은 평균 215개의 씨앗을 생산한 반면에, 개미가 없는 환경에 있는 식물들은 평균 45개의 씨앗을 생산했다.

어휘

1 **beneficial** adj 유익한, 이로운 | **reproductive** adj 생식[번식]의 | **deposit** v 두다[놓다], 맡기다 | **refer to** 언급[지칭]하다 | **clearly** adv 분명히, 알기 쉽게 | **empirical** adj 경험[실험]에 의거한, 실증적인 | **defensive** adj 방어[수비]의 | **mechanism** n 구조[기제], 방법 | **reward** n 보상
2 **sustenance** n 자양물, 영양(물) | **compound** n 복합체, 화합물 | **volatile** adj 휘발성 물질 | **discourage** v 막다, 의욕[열의]을 꺾다 | **eagerly** adv 열심히, 간절히 | **conserve** v 아끼다, 아껴 쓰다 | **fertilization** n 수정 | **production** n 생산
3 **voracious** adj 식욕이 왕성한, 열성이 대단한 | **pest** n 해충 | **asexually** adv 무성(無性)으로 | **parasitic** adj 기생하는 | **consume** v 먹다, 소모하다 | **capable** adj ~을 할 수 있는, 유능한
4 **purely** adv 순전히, 전적으로 | **excretory** adj 배설[분비]의 | **phenomenon** n 현상 | **specialized** adj 전문적인, 전문화된 | **secrete** v 분비하다 | **excess** adj 여분의, 과도한 | **regulate** v 규제하다, 조절하다 | **contend** v 주장하다 | **deliberately** adv 의도[계획]적으로, 고의로
5 **entomologist** n 곤충학자 | **botanist** n 식물학자
6 **genuinely** adv 진정으로, 성실하게 | **controlled** adj 세심히 관리[통제/조절]된, 아주 조심스런 | **marked** adj 뚜렷이 | **viable** adj 독자 생존 가능한, 실행 가능한, 성공할 수 있는 | **mere** adj 겨우, (한낱) ~에 불과한
7 **suffer** v 시달리다, 고통받다 | **wholly** adv 완전히, 전적으로 | **mutualistic** adj 상리 공생의, 상호 부조론의 | **symbiosis** n 공생(共生) | **interaction** n 상호 작용 | **observable** adj 식별[관찰]할 수 있는

Passage 2

History of Theater

1 ➡ The cultural exchange between ancient Greece and Rome laid the groundwork for the development of Roman theater, with Greek tragedies exerting a profound influence on the evolution of Roman dramatic tradition. Greek tragedies served as a source of inspiration for Roman playwrights, who eagerly embraced and adapted these works for Roman audiences. The enduring themes and universal truths explored in Greek tragedies resonated deeply with Roman spectators, who were drawn to the moral dilemmas, human struggles, and cosmic forces depicted in these timeless narratives. Works by Greek tragedians such as Aeschylus, Sophocles, and Euripides were introduced to Roman audiences through translations and adaptations, offering them a glimpse into the cultural and intellectual world of ancient Greece.

2 ➡ The translation of Greek tragedies into Latin by Roman playwrights was a complex and nuanced

연극의 역사

1 ➡ 고대 그리스와 로마 간의 문화 교류는 로마 연극 발전의 기초를 마련했으며, 그리스 비극은 로마 극 전통의 진화에 깊은 영향을 미쳤다. 그리스 비극은 로마 극작가들에게 영감의 원천이 되었고, 이들은 로마 관객들을 위해 이러한 작품들을 적극적으로 수용하고 각색했다. 그리스 비극에서 탐구된 영원한 주제와 보편적인 진리는 시대를 초월한 이야기에 묘사된 도덕적 딜레마, 인간의 투쟁, 우주의 힘에 매료된 로마 관중들에게 깊은 공감을 불러일으켰다. 아이스킬로스, 소포클레스, 에우리피데스와 같은 그리스 비극 작가들의 작품은 번역과 각색을 통해 로마 관객들에게 소개되었으며, 이는 고대 그리스의 문화적, 지적 세계를 엿볼 수 있는 기회를 제공했다.

2 ➡ 로마 극작가들에 의해 그리스 비극이 라틴어로 번역되는 과정은 단순한 언어적 전환 이상을 요구하는 복잡하

process that involved more than just linguistic conversion. Roman dramatists, such as Ennius and Accius, meticulously adapted these ancient Greek works to suit the tastes and sensibilities of Roman audiences. While striving to retain the essential themes and dramatic elements of the original texts, they also incorporated elements of Roman language, culture, and mythology, ensuring that the translated plays spoke to their intended audience. Ultimately, Roman translators faced the challenge of bridging the cultural and contextual gap between ancient Greece and Rome. They were tasked with navigating the differences in social customs, religious beliefs, and political systems, seeking to make the translated tragedies relevant and accessible to Roman spectators.

3 ➡ As a result, many of the characters in Greek tragedies underwent transformations to better suit the sensibilities of Romans. For example, in Seneca's rendition of "Medea," the character of Medea becomes a more complex and morally ambiguous figure than in the original play by Euripides, who originally depicted her as slightly more emotionally predictable. Seneca portrays Medea as a powerful and cunning woman driven by a mixture of love, revenge, and despair, making her motivations and actions more relatable to Roman spectators. Furthermore, characters in Roman tragedies often embodied the ideals of Roman virtue and piety, reflecting the moral and ethical values of Roman society. For instance, the character of Hercules became a favorite in Roman adaptations of Greek tragedies, appearing as a symbol of strength, heroism, and divine favor, embodying qualities that were highly esteemed in Roman culture.

4 ➡ Roman playwrights also transformed Greek tragedies by enriching them with additional dialogue and soliloquies, thus enhancing the dramatic impact and emotional depth of the plays. By inserting new lines of dialogue and introspective monologues, playwrights provided insights into the inner thoughts and motivations of the characters, allowing audiences to connect more deeply with their struggles and dilemmas. These additions often served to intensify the emotional tension and psychological complexity of the narratives, drawing viewers into the emotional turmoil of the characters' experiences. Through these creative embellishments, Roman playwrights

고 미묘한 과정이었다. 엔니우스와 아키우스 같은 로마 극작가들은 그리스의 고대 작품을 로마 관객의 취향과 감성에 맞추어 신중하게 각색했다. 원작의 핵심 주제와 극적 요소를 유지하려 노력하면서도 로마의 언어, 문화, 신화를 포함해 번역된 작품이 로마 관객들에게 공감될 수 있도록 했다. 궁극적으로 로마 번역자들은 고대 그리스와 로마 간의 문화적, 맥락적 차이를 극복해야 하는 과제에 직면했다. 이들은 사회적 관습, 종교적 신념, 정치 체제의 차이를 헤쳐 나가 번역된 비극을 로마 관중에게 적절하고 접근하기 쉽게 만드는 임무를 맡았다.

3 ➡ 그 결과, 그리스 비극의 많은 인물들은 로마의 감성에 맞게 변형되었다. 예를 들어, 세네카의 공연 메데아에서 메데아는 원래 그녀를 조금 더 정서적으로 예측할 수 있게 묘사한 원작자인 에우리피데스의 묘사보다 더 복잡하고 도덕적으로 모호한 인물로 등장한다. 세네카는 메데아를 사랑, 복수, 절망이 뒤섞인 강력하고 교활한 여성으로 묘사하며, 로마 관객들에게 그녀의 동기와 행동이 더 공감되도록 했다. 또한 로마 비극에서 등장인물들은 종종 로마의 덕성과 경건함을 구현하여 로마 사회의 도덕적, 윤리적 가치를 반영했다. 예를 들어, 헤라클레스는 그리스 비극의 로마 각색에서 로마 문화에서 높이 평가되는 자질을 구현한 힘, 영웅주의, 신의 은총을 상징하는 인기 있는 인물이 되었다.

4 ➡ 로마 극작가들은 대화와 독백을 추가함으로써 그리스 비극을 변형하여 극적 효과와 감정적 깊이를 더했다. 극작가들은 새로운 대사와 내면의 독백을 삽입하여 인물들의 생각과 동기에 대한 통찰을 제공함으로써 관객들이 인물들의 고뇌와 진퇴양난에 더 깊이 공감할 수 있게 했다. 이러한 추가 요소들은 종종 감정적 긴장과 심리적 복잡성을 더욱 강화하여 관객들이 인물들의 감정적 혼란에 더욱 몰입하도록 만들었다. 이러한 창의적인 각색을 통해 로마 극작가들은 그리스 비극에 새로운 생명을 불어넣어 로마 관객들이 더 쉽게 공감할 수 있는 즉각성과 감정적 진정성을 부여했다.

breathed new life into Greek tragedies, infusing them with a sense of immediacy and emotional authenticity that Roman audiences could more readily relate to.

5 ➡ Roman reinterpretations of Greek tragedies reflected the political climate of Rome through their portrayal of power dynamics, political intrigue, and societal tensions. Roman playwrights often infused Greek narratives with elements drawn from contemporary Roman politics, allowing them to comment on the complexities of power and governance in their own society. For example, characters such as Creon or Agamemnon were reimagined as authoritarian rulers or ambitious politicians, grappling with issues of legitimacy, authority, and the abuse of power. [■A] These adaptations served as allegories for the political realities of Rome, where struggles for power, political rivalries, and the machinations of ambitious individuals were commonplace. [■B] Furthermore, Roman playwrights used Greek tragedies to explore themes of justice, law, and the responsibilities of leadership, reflecting the societal anxieties and moral dilemmas of their time. [■C] By reinterpreting Greek tragedies within the context of Roman society, playwrights engaged with pressing questions about the nature of governance, the role of the state, and the obligations of rulers towards their subjects. [■D] These demonstrate how Roman playwrights offered audiences a reflection of their own political realities, prompting them to contemplate the ethical complexities of power and authority in Roman society.

6 ➡ The Roman reinterpretations of Greek tragedies served as a critical juncture in the legacy of Greek tragedies. The works of Greek tragedians continue to be studied around the world. Moreover, the enduring influence of Greek tragedies is evident in the cultural and intellectual achievements of Western civilization, where the principles of tragedy and catharsis continue to inform and inspire artistic expression. However, many argue that Roman translations, adaptations, and reinterpretations further enriched the theatrical value of Greek tragedies, helping to continue a tradition of dramatic excellence.

1. **Fact**

According to paragraph 1, Roman audiences enjoyed Greek tragedies because

Ⓐ **Romans related to many of the Greek tragedies' themes.**
Ⓑ both cultures shared nearly identical cultural values.
Ⓒ Roman tragedies also focused on moral dilemmas and mythical narratives.
Ⓓ translations were adapted to fit the preferences of Roman citizens.

2. **Vocabulary**

The word "timeless" in paragraph 1 is closest in meaning to

Ⓐ aging
Ⓑ **enduring**
Ⓒ continuous
Ⓓ endless

3. **Rhetorical Purpose**

Why does the author mention "Ennius and Accius" in paragraph 2?

Ⓐ to emphasize the challenges Roman dramatists faced
Ⓑ to list some of the tasks translating Greek dramas entailed
Ⓒ to give an example of Roman dramatists involved in translation work
Ⓓ **to describe the work involved in translating Greek tragedies**

4. **Vocabulary**

The word "navigating" in paragraph 2 is closest in meaning to

Ⓐ **maneuvering**
Ⓑ steering
Ⓒ redirecting
Ⓓ defusing

5. **Negative Fact**

According to paragraph 3, which of the following was NOT a change that the character Medea underwent by Roman playwrights?

Ⓐ Seneca added additional emotional volatility to Medea's character.
Ⓑ **Playwrights transformed her personality into a more formulaic mixture of emotions.**
Ⓒ It became more difficult for viewers to interpret Medea's intentions.
Ⓓ Medea's virtue and allegiance became more questionable in the Roman version.

1.

1단락에 따르면, 로마 관객들이 그리스 비극을 즐긴 이유는 무엇인가?

Ⓐ 로마인들은 많은 그리스 비극의 주제에 공감했다.
Ⓑ 두 문화는 거의 동일한 문화적 가치를 공유했다.
Ⓒ 로마 비극도 도덕적 딜레마와 신화적 서사에 중점을 두었다.
Ⓓ 번역된 작품들이 로마 시민들의 취향에 맞게 각색되었다.

2.

1단락의 단어 "timeless(시대를 초월한)"와 의미상 가장 가까운 것은?

Ⓐ 낡아가는
Ⓑ 오래가는
Ⓒ 끊임없는
Ⓓ 끝없는

3.

작가가 2단락에서 "엔니우스와 아키우스"를 언급한 이유는 무엇인가?

Ⓐ 로마 극작가들이 직면한 어려움을 강조하기 위해
Ⓑ 그리스 드라마를 번역하는 과정에서 요구되는 작업을 나열하기 위해
Ⓒ 번역 작업에 참여한 로마 극작가의 예를 들기 위해
Ⓓ 그리스 비극을 번역하는 데 필요한 작업을 설명하기 위해

4.

2단락의 단어 "navigating(헤쳐 나가기)"과 의미상 가장 가까운 것은?

Ⓐ 헤쳐 나가기
Ⓑ 방향을 잡기
Ⓒ 재조정하기
Ⓓ 완화하기

5.

3단락에 따르면, 로마 극작가들에 의해 메데아의 성격에 가해진 변화 중 일어나지 않은 것은 무엇인가?

Ⓐ 세네카는 메데아의 성격에 부가적인 감정적 변동성을 추가했다.
Ⓑ 극작가들은 그녀의 성격을 보다 정형화된 감정의 혼합으로 변화시켰다.
Ⓒ 관객들이 메데아의 의도를 해석하기 더 어려워졌다.
Ⓓ 메데아의 미덕과 충성심이 로마 버전에서 더 의심스러워졌다.

6. Sentence Simplification

Which of the following best expresses the essential information in the highlighted sentence? Incorrect answer choices change the meaning in important ways or leave out essential information.

Ⓐ **Playwrights employed various dramatic techniques, including the addition of dialogues and soliloquies, to enhance the emotional resonance of the characters' experiences, thus intensifying the audience's engagement with their trials and tribulations.**

Ⓑ In order to increase the audience's relatability with the characters, the addition of introspective monologues and extra dialogue became a common technique among playwrights, which facilitated further understanding of the character's introspections and motivations.

Ⓒ One of the greatest challenges for Roman playwrights was to create an authentic connection between viewers and the characters, which was often achieved by providing insight into the characters' struggles and dilemmas through additional dialogue and introspective monologues.

Ⓓ Because the addition of dialogues and internal monologues offered audiences a glimpse into the inner workings of the character's conflicts, it also fostered a stronger emotional connection between the viewers and the characters' experiences.

7. Inference

What can be inferred about the Romans from paragraph 5?

Ⓐ **Many Romans were familiar with Roman politics and the power struggles that were common to their governments.**

Ⓑ Nearly all Roman rulers were despotic and authoritarian.

Ⓒ Many Romans were disgruntled with the state of Roman politics and often displayed their protests publicly.

Ⓓ Politics was an important component of Roman existential philosophy as it related to their sense of justice and societal function.

8. Insertion

Look at the four squares [■] that indicate where the following sentence could be added to the passage.

Oedipus and Antigone were remade into tragic figures confronting the consequences of their decisions in a world fraught with political turmoil and moral ambiguity.

Where would the sentence best fit? [■ D]

6.

다음 중 강조된 문장에서 본질적인 정보를 가장 잘 표현한 것은 무엇인가? 오답은 의미를 크게 왜곡하거나 핵심 정보를 누락하고 있다.

Ⓐ 극작가들은 대사와 독백을 추가하는 등 다양한 극적 기법을 사용하여 등장인물들의 경험에 감정적 공감을 더함으로써 관객이 그들의 시련과 고난에 더욱 몰입할 수 있도록 했다.

Ⓑ 관객이 캐릭터와 더 쉽게 공감할 수 있도록 하기 위해, 내면적 독백과 추가 대화가 극작가들 사이에서 공통적인 기법이 되었고, 이를 통해 캐릭터의 내면적 갈등과 동기를 더 잘 이해할 수 있었다.

Ⓒ 로마 극작가들의 가장 큰 과제 중 하나는 시청자와 등장인물 사이에 진정한 유대감을 형성하는 것이었는데, 이는 종종 추가 대화와 내성적인 독백을 통해 등장인물의 투쟁과 딜레마에 대한 통찰을 제공함으로써 달성되었다.

Ⓓ 대사와 내면의 독백을 추가함으로써 관객은 캐릭터의 갈등의 내면을 엿볼 수 있었으며, 시청자와 캐릭터의 경험 사이에 더 강한 감정적 유대감을 형성할 수 있었다.

7.

5단락에서 로마인들에 대해 추론할 수 있는 것은 무엇인가?

Ⓐ 많은 로마인들은 로마 정치와 그들의 정부에서 흔히 일어나는 권력 투쟁에 익숙했다.

Ⓑ 거의 모든 로마 통치자는 독재적이고 권위적이었다.

Ⓒ 많은 로마인들은 로마 정치 상태에 불만을 품고 종종 공개적으로 항의했다.

Ⓓ 정치가 그들의 정의와 사회적 기능에 대한 로마의 실존적 철학과 관련하여 중요한 요소였다.

8.

지문에 다음 문장이 들어갈 수 있는 위치를 나타내는 네 개의 사각형[■]을 확인하시오.

오이디푸스와 안티고네는 정치적 혼란과 도덕적 모호성으로 가득한 세상에서 그들 결정의 결과와 마주하는 비극적 인물로 재구성되었다.

이 문장이 들어가기에 가장 적합한 곳은? [■ D]

9. Rhetorical Purpose

The author mentions "tragedy and catharsis" in paragraph 6 in order to

Ⓐ **demonstrate the significance of Greek tragedy's influence on Western culture.**
Ⓑ argue Greek tragedy's significance is indebted to the work of Roman reinterpretations.
Ⓒ point out two crucial components common to nearly all Greek tragedies.
Ⓓ add to a list of cultural, political, and philosophical impacts Greece had on the West.

10. Prose Summary

Directions: An introductory sentence for a brief summary of the passage is provided below. Complete the summary by selecting the THREE answer choices that express the most important ideas in the passage. Some sentences do not belong in the summary because they express ideas that are not presented in the passage or minor ideas in the passage. *This question is worth 2 points.*

Roman playwrights modified Greek tragedies in order to make the characters and narratives more relatable to Roman audiences.

Ⓑ **Translating the Greek works required Roman playwrights to infuse the original tragedies with elements of Roman mythology, culture, and society.**
Ⓓ **Roman values such as virtue, piety, and strength were added to or enhanced in characters to result in further contextualization.**
Ⓕ **Political themes of power, justice, and law were also incorporated into Greek tragedies to reflect the Roman political culture and climate.**

Ⓐ Greek tragedies dwelled on many themes and values that were already familiar to Roman audiences.
Ⓒ The character Medea was reinterpreted as a more morally ambiguous and emotionally capricious figure.
Ⓔ The addition of soliloquies enabled more insight into the private thoughts of characters, allowing the audience to connect more with the character.

9.

작가가 6단락에서 "비극과 카타르시스"를 언급한 이유는 무엇인가?

Ⓐ 그리스 비극이 서구 문화에 미친 영향의 중요성을 보여주기 위해
Ⓑ 그리스 비극의 중요성이 로마의 재해석 작업에 기인한다고 주장하기 위해
Ⓒ 거의 모든 그리스 비극에 공통적으로 등장하는 두 가지 중요한 요소를 지적하기 위해
Ⓓ 그리스가 서구에 미친 문화적, 정치적, 철학적 영향을 나열하는 것에 추가하기 위해

10.

지시문: 지문을 간략하게 요약한 글의 첫 문장이 아래 제시되어 있다. 지문의 가장 중요한 내용을 표현하는 세 개의 선택지를 골라 요약문을 완성하시오. 일부 문장들은 지문에 제시되지 않았거나 지문의 지엽적인 내용을 나타내기 때문에 요약문에 포함되지 않는다. *이 문제의 배점은 2점이다.*

로마 극작가들은 그리스 비극을 로마 관객들이 더 공감할 수 있는 캐릭터와 서사로 수정했다.

Ⓑ 그리스 작품을 번역하는 것은 로마 극작가들이 원작 비극에 로마 신화, 문화, 사회의 요소를 주입해야 했다.
Ⓓ 미덕, 경건함, 강인함과 같은 로마의 가치가 캐릭터에 추가되거나 강화되어 추가적인 맥락을 형성했다.
Ⓕ 권력, 정의, 법의 정치적 주제도 그리스 비극에 통합되어 로마의 정치 문화와 기후를 반영했다.

Ⓐ 그리스 비극은 이미 로마 관객들에게 친숙한 많은 주제와 가치를 다루었다.
Ⓒ 메데아라는 인물은 도덕적으로 더 모호하고 감정적으로 변덕스러운 인물로 재해석되었다.
Ⓔ 독백의 추가는 캐릭터의 사적인 생각에 대한 더 많은 통찰력을 제공하여 관객이 캐릭터와 더 연결될 수 있게 했다.

어휘

1. **exchange** n 교류 | **inspiration** n 영감 | **spectator** n 관객 | **dilemma** n 딜레마 | **struggle** n 투쟁 | **narrative** n 서사 | **glimpse** n 엿보기
2. **process** n 과정 | **sensibility** n 감수성 | **theme** n 주제 | **element** n 요소 | **custom** n 관습 | **belief** n 신념 | **system** n 체계
3. **transformation** n 변형 | **rendition** n 해석 | **motivation** n 동기 | **action** n 행동 | **virtue** n 미덕 | **heroism** n 영웅주의 | **favor** n 호의
4. **dialogue** n 대화 | **monologue** n 독백 | **insight** n 통찰 | **tension** n 긴장 | **complexity** n 복잡성 | **authenticity** n 진정성
5. **intrigue** n 모의 | **authority** n 권위 | **allegory** n 우화 | **rivalry** n 경쟁 | **justice** n 정의 | **anxiety** n 불안
6. **legacy** n 유산 | **influence** n 영향 | **principle** n 원칙 | **expression** n 표현 | **tradition** n 전통 | **excellence** n 탁월함

Actual Test 05

본서 | P. 108

Passage 1 Dwarfism in Timberline Vegetation

1. Ⓑ	Vocabulary	6. Ⓑ	Fact
2. Ⓒ	Negative Fact	7. Ⓓ	Insertion
3. Ⓐ	Inference	8. Ⓑ	Fact
4. Ⓓ	Fact	9. Ⓐ	Sentence Simplification
5. Ⓓ	Rhetorical Purpose	10. Ⓑ, Ⓒ, Ⓔ	Summary

Passage 2 Agricultural Pest Control

1. Ⓑ	Negative Fact	6. Ⓓ	Rhetorical Purpose
2. Ⓓ	Sentence Simplification	7. Ⓑ	Vocabulary
3. Ⓒ	Negative Fact	8. Ⓐ	Inference
4. Ⓑ	Fact	9. Ⓒ	Insertion
5. Ⓒ	Fact	10. Ⓑ, Ⓒ, Ⓕ	Summary

● 내가 맞은 문제 유형의 개수를 적어 보고 어느 유형에 취약한지 확인해 봅시다.

문제 유형	맞은 개수
Sentence Simplification	2
Fact / Negative Fact	8
Vocabulary	2
Reference	0
Rhetorical Purpose	2
Inference	2
Insertion	2
Summary	2
Category Chart	0
Total	20

Dwarfism in Timberline Vegetation

1 ➡ Dwarfism among timberline vegetation on mountains represents a unique adaptation to the extreme environmental conditions prevalent at high elevations. Dwarfism refers to the phenomenon whereby trees and other vegetation exhibit stunted growth forms at high elevations near the timberline. This adaptation is a response to the challenging environmental conditions prevalent at these altitudes, including low temperatures, high winds, and limited nutrient availability. Dwarfed individuals of tree species such as pine, spruce, and fir often have reduced stature, slower growth rates, and altered morphological characteristics compared to their counterparts at lower elevations.

2 ➡ One pivotal factor contributing to dwarfism is the short growing season characteristic of mountain environments, where prolonged periods of snow cover and low temperatures limit the window of opportunity for plant growth and development. This abbreviated growing season constrains the duration during which plants can photosynthesize and accumulate biomass, resulting in reduced overall plant size. Furthermore, the physiological processes of plants are significantly influenced by temperature, with low temperatures at high elevations inhibiting metabolic activity and slowing down growth rates. As a consequence, plants invest fewer resources in above-ground growth and allocate more towards essential physiological functions such as maintenance and reproduction. Moreover, the nutrient-poor soils prevalent at timberline impose limitations on plant growth, as shallow and rocky substrates restrict root development and nutrient uptake. Consequently, plants exhibit adaptations such as increased root-to-shoot ratios and enhanced nutrient-use efficiency to cope with nutrient scarcity.

3 ➡ Dwarfism among timberline vegetation on mountains fosters a tapestry of microhabitats, nurturing an array of flora and fauna finely attuned to the harsh conditions of high elevations. Take, for instance, the dense mats of alpine dwarf willows (*Salix herbacea*) and cushion plants like the Arctic bearberry (*Arctostaphylos alpinus*). These diminutive plants create sheltered nooks amidst the rugged

terrain, offering refuge for creatures such as the American pika (*Ochotona princeps*), which relies on the protection provided by such vegetation to weather the intense winds and temperature fluctuations of the alpine environment. Moreover, the intricate root systems of these dwarfed plants enhance soil stability and nutrient availability. Additionally, the presence of stunted conifers in these zones creates vertical structure in the landscape, providing niches for species like the northern flying squirrel.

4 ➡ Plants exhibiting dwarfism at timberline have undergone intricate evolutionary processes resulting in a suite of specialized adaptations primarily focused on leaf morphology. One prominent adaptation involves the reduction in leaf size, a strategic adjustment aimed at conserving water in the arid, windy conditions. This not only decreases the surface area available for transpiration but also minimizes the risk of damage from desiccating winds. [■A] Furthermore, alterations in leaf structure optimize light capture and photosynthetic efficiency, crucial for sustaining growth and metabolism. [■B] These adaptations may include alterations in thickness and shape, and the presence of specialized structures such as hairs or wax coatings. [■C] The increased leaf thickness helps to reduce water loss and provides structural support, while alterations in shape and the presence of surface structures serve to maximize the efficiency of photosynthesis. [■D]

5 ➡ Dwarfism among timberline vegetation encompasses critical implications for the functioning and conservation of mountain ecosystems, serving as both sensitive indicators of environmental change and vital components of these fragile habitats. Due to their specialized adaptations and limited tolerance for environmental fluctuations, dwarfed individuals are particularly vulnerable to disturbances such as climate change, habitat fragmentation, and human activities. Shifts in temperature, precipitation patterns, and snowpack dynamics associated with climate change can directly impact the distribution and abundance of dwarfed vegetation, altering the composition and structure of timberline ecosystems. Habitat fragmentation, often caused by human infrastructure development and land-use practices, further exacerbates the vulnerability of dwarfed

vegetation by isolating populations and reducing genetic connectivity, hindering their ability to adapt and persist in changing environments. Human activities such as logging, grazing, and recreational tourism can also degrade fragile timberline habitats, disrupting plant communities and ecological processes essential for ecosystem functioning. ==Monitoring the distribution and abundance of dwarfed vegetation can provide valuable insights into the ecological impacts of these threats on mountain ecosystems, informing conservation strategies and management decisions aimed at preserving these unique and biodiverse habitats.== Of course, conserving intact timberline habitats is essential for maintaining the biodiversity and ecological integrity of mountain landscapes, ensuring the continued survival of dwarfed vegetation and the myriad species that depend on them for habitat and resources.

---

1. Vocabulary

The word "**prevalent**" in paragraph 1 is closest in meaning to

Ⓐ rampant
Ⓑ **pervasive**
Ⓒ visible
Ⓓ tolerable

2. Negative Fact

According to paragraph 2, all of the following are factors that contribute to dwarfism EXCEPT

Ⓐ seasonal effects on plant growth
Ⓑ poor quality soil
Ⓒ **diversion of resources**
Ⓓ extreme temperature and elevation

3. Inference

Through paragraph 2, we can infer that

Ⓐ **the same dwarf plant at a lower elevation would have shorter roots.**
Ⓑ plants at higher elevations compete less for soil nutrients.
Ⓒ extreme attempts at maximizing resources causes many plants at higher elevations to ultimately fail.
Ⓓ dwarfed plants result from limited opportunities for growth.

4. **Fact**

According to paragraph 3, how do dwarfed plants influence their surroundings?

Ⓐ They alter the microclimates of timberline habitats by raising net temperatures.
Ⓑ They create the conditions for a large array of plants to proliferate in the area.
Ⓒ They provide shelter for wildlife that would otherwise be highly vulnerable to predators.
Ⓓ **Their effects on soil quality and stability create habitats for animals.**

5. **Rhetorical Purpose**

The author mentions "intricate root systems" in paragraph 3 in order to

Ⓐ illustrate a critical function of dwarfed plants in creating natural environments for birds.
Ⓑ emphasize the underappreciated effects of dwarfed plants on their ecosystems.
Ⓒ further explain the structure of dwarfed plants.
Ⓓ **give an example of how dwarfed plants create habitats for animals.**

6. **Fact**

According to paragraph 4, how do smaller leaf sizes benefit dwarfed plants?

Ⓐ They enable plants to survive dry conditions by increasing vaporization.
Ⓑ **Smaller leaf sizes reduce exposure to harmful forces such as strong winds.**
Ⓒ They enhance the plant's photosynthetic capabilities by capturing more sunlight.
Ⓓ A reduction in leaf size leads to an increase in thickness, which in turn increases water conservation.

7. **Insertion**

Look at the four squares [■] that indicate where the following sentence could be added to the passage.

Additionally, some dwarfed species exhibit a phenomenon known as "sun-tracking" or "heliotropism," where leaves adjust their orientation throughout the day to optimize exposure to sunlight.

Where would the sentence best fit? [■ D]

8. Fact

According to paragraph 5, dwarfed plants help scientists better understand the effects of changes in the environment because

Ⓐ a surprising share of human activity is concentrated in timberline habitats.
Ⓑ **dwarfed plants have evolved to survive in such extreme, unique conditions.**
Ⓒ habitat fragmentation disrupts timberline ecosystem sustainability.
Ⓓ environmental changes aggravate the already extreme conditions dwarfed plants have adapted to.

9. Sentence Simplification

Which of the following best expresses the essential information in the highlighted sentence? Incorrect answer choices change the meaning in important ways or leave out essential information.

Ⓐ **Insight gained through monitoring dwarfed mountain plants provides crucial information on the effects of environmental changes, which in turn can inform conservation and preservation efforts.**
Ⓑ One way that dwarfed plants inform conservation and management strategies is by providing climatic data that reflect changes in the surrounding environments as well as the effects of human activity.
Ⓒ By tracking the spread and density of stunted plant life, researchers gain valuable understanding of how environmental pressures affect mountain ecosystems."
Ⓓ Scientists and governments alike have taken advantage of studies on timberline dwarfed plants to inform their conservation strategies and policies regarding these unusual and special habitats.

10. Prose Summary

Directions: An introductory sentence for a brief summary of the passage is provided below. Complete the summary by selecting the THREE answer choices that express the most important ideas in the passage. Some sentences do not belong in the summary because they express ideas that are not presented in the passage or minor ideas in the passage. *This question is worth 2 points.*

Dwarfed plants in timberline habitats are exceptionally distinct in both their features as well as the benefits they provide.

- Ⓑ **These plants survive in harsh climates by diverting more resources to root growth and survival, as opposed to size and breadth.**
- Ⓒ **Dwarfed plants provide habitats for wildlife in a variety of ways, such as through their influence on soil quality and vertical food distributions.**
- Ⓔ **Dwarfism provides clues to experts on ways to prevent climate change and other human-induced changes on natural habitats.**

Ⓐ Dwarfism in plants arises from several unique factors, including seasonal differences and comparatively less available resources.
Ⓓ Changes in leaf size have enabled dwarfed plants to weather the windy, arid conditions common in timberline environments.
Ⓕ Plants such as alpine willows create refuge for animals that need protection from the extreme weather.

- Ⓑ 이러한 식물은 크기와 넓이보다 뿌리 성장과 생존에 더 많은 자원을 집중시켜 가혹한 기후에서 생존한다.
- Ⓒ 왜소화된 식물은 토양의 질과 수직적인 먹이 분포에 대한 영향을 통해 야생 동물들에게 다양한 방식으로 서식지를 제공한다.
- Ⓔ 왜소증은 기후 변화 및 인간이 유발한 다른 환경 변화로부터 자연 서식지를 보호하는 방법에 대한 단서를 전문가들에게 제공한다.

Ⓐ 식물의 왜소증은 계절적 차이와 상대적으로 적은 자원을 포함한 여러 독특한 요인에서 비롯된다.
Ⓓ 잎의 크기 변화는 왜소화된 식물들이 산림 한계선 환경에서 흔한 강풍과 건조한 조건을 견딜 수 있게 해주었다.
Ⓕ 알파인 버드나무 같은 식물들은 극한 날씨로부터 보호가 필요한 동물들에게 피난처를 제공한다.

어휘

1. **dwarfism** n 왜소증 | **timberline** n 산림 한계선 | **vegetation** n 식물 | **elevation** n 고도 | **phenomenon** n 현상 | **nutrient** n 영양소 | **morphological** adj 형태의 | **counterpart** n 상대방
2. **pivotal** adj 중요한 | **constrain** v 제한하다 | **biomass** n 생물량 | **allocate** v 할당하다 | **scarcity** n 부족
3. **microhabitat** n 미소 서식지 | **terrain** n 지형 | **refuge** n 피난처 | **conifer** n 침엽수 | **niche** n 적소
4. **morphology** n 형태학 | **transpiration** n 증산작용 | **desiccate** v 건조시키다 | **metabolism** n 신진대사
5. **ecosystem** n 생태계 | **habitat** n 서식지 | **fluctuation** n 변동 | **fragmentation** n 단편화 | **connectivity** n 연결성 | **degrade** v 훼손하다 | **intact** adj 온전한 | **biodiversity** n 생물 다양성 | **integrity** n 온전함

Agricultural Pest Control

1 → Without the adoption and subsequent development of agriculture, human society would never have been able to develop to the extent that it has, nor could our population have grown so rapidly. In order to farm, humans deliberately disrupt natural ecosystems to create the best possible conditions for the crops they wish to grow. [■A] They remove large numbers of the native species, alter the distribution of water, and enrich the soil with fertilizers. In addition, most farms practice monoculture to a certain extent, which means that one section to all of their land is used to grow the same plants. [■B] Such massive disruption of nature often leads to the explosion of species that consume those plants. [■C] These species that endanger crops are labeled as pests. In order to control pest organisms, farmers typically use chemical or biological controls; however, a more moderate approach appears to be the most effective in the long run. [■D]

2 → Chemical controls are the most widely used method for limiting pest populations today, but they have a surprisingly long past. Around 2,500 BCE, ancient Sumerians used elemental sulfur powder to discourage pests, and a text called the Rig Veda, which dates back to around 4,000 years ago, mentions the use of poisonous plants for similar purposes. By the Renaissance, toxic chemicals like mercury, lead, and arsenic were being widely used to kill pests. Although these chemicals are toxic to humans as well, they were also used in makeup and medicines. At the time, people believed that small doses of poison were good for one's health, and no doubt thought that using them on crops would have little effect on them.

3 → Beginning in the 17th century, people began extracting chemicals from plants to use as pesticides: nicotine sulfide from tobacco, pyrethrum from chrysanthemum flowers, and rotenone from the roots of tropical plants. All of these pesticides existed in nature, even the toxic elemental chemicals. However, in the early 20th century, synthesized chemicals became dominant. The first of these was DDT, which was initially used to control human parasites like mosquitoes and lice. Scientists soon learned

to deliver DDT in any physical form, which led to its widespread use in agriculture. Since then, chemical pesticides have become the dominant control for agricultural pests, and their use has revealed many side effects of pest control.

4 ➡ Any attempt at controlling the population of a pest species entails the risk of affecting other species. Initially, this is caused by disrupting the predator-prey system. Even though local predators are unable to control the pest species, they may still depend upon them for food. However, chemical controls introduce additional problems. Firstly, the pesticides often kill organisms other than the intended pests, including their natural predators. Secondly, continuously exposing pests to chemicals will inevitably cause them to develop a resistance. Through natural immunity or repeated low level exposure, some will always survive to reproduce, and their population will rebound. Nearly every pesticide known to man has been used on mosquitoes, and they have always quickly adapted. Thirdly, pesticides spread into the surrounding environment, particularly through the water system. This can have far-reaching effects on organisms with no connection to the farms whatsoever, like birds that eat fish.

5 ➡ Thus, many farmers have decided to return to nature by introducing predatory species. Again, this is hardly a new idea as the Chinese are credited with deliberately introducing ant hives to their fruit orchards. After noticing that a particular species of ants attacked insects on their citrus trees, they began collecting and transplanting the ants' nests into their trees. Today, many farmers introduce spiders, wasps and other predatory animals to their fields. However, they must take great care with the organisms which they select. The introduction of any non-indigenous species can have serious unforeseen side effects. These organisms often have no natural predators in their new environment, so their population can grow unchecked. In addition, there is no guarantee that they will eat the correct organisms, or even remain in the desired area. This has occurred widely with the cane toad, which often fled farmers' fields due to insufficient ground cover. Since the toads are poisonous, they have had a disastrous impact on local predatory animals with no immunity to their toxin.

화학 살충제는 농업 해충 방제에서 가장 우세하게 되었으며 사용은 해충 방제의 많은 부작용을 드러냈다.

4 ➡ 유해 동물종의 개체수를 억제하려는 어떤 노력도 다른 종에 영향을 미치는 위험을 수반한다. 처음에는 포식자와 피식자 시스템에 혼란을 일으킴으로써 야기된다. 비록 토착 포식동물이 유해 동물종을 억제할 수 없더라도, 그들은 여전히 먹이로서 그것들에 의존한다. 그러나 화학 방제는 부가적인 문제점들을 가져온다. 첫째로, 살충제는 종종 죽이려고 의도했던 해충 이외에 해충의 천적을 포함한 다른 종을 죽인다. 둘째, 지속적으로 해충을 화학물질에 노출시키는 것은 필연적으로 내성을 키우게 만들 것이다. 자연적인 면역이나 반복된 낮은 수치의 노출을 통해 언제나 일부는 번식할 정도로 살아남을 것이며, 개체수는 반등할 것이다. 인간에게 알려진 거의 모든 살충제가 모기에게 사용되었는데, 그들은 항상 빠르게 적응해 왔다. 셋째, 살충제는 이웃하는 환경으로 퍼지는데, 특히 하천의 수계를 통해 퍼진다. 이것은 농장과 아무런 관계도 없는 생물들, 예를 들어 물고기를 먹이로 하는 새들에게까지 널리 영향을 미칠 수 있다.

5 ➡ 따라서 많은 농부들은 천적을 도입함으로써 자연으로 돌아가기로 결정했다. 중국인들이 과수원에 개미집을 일부러 놓아두는 방법을 썼던 것으로 인정받기에 이는 전혀 새로운 생각이 아니다. 특정 개미 종이 감귤류 나무의 벌레들을 공격하는 것을 알아차린 후, 중국인들은 개미 둥지를 모아서 나무에 옮기기 시작했다. 오늘날 많은 농부들이 거미, 말벌, 그리고 다른 포식동물들을 농장에 도입한다. 그러나 생물을 선택함에 있어 매우 조심해야 한다. 어떤 외래종의 도입이라도 예기치 못한 심각한 부작용을 불러일으킬 수 있다. 이러한 생물들은 새로운 환경에 천적이 없어서, 개체수가 제재되지 않은 채 증가할 수 있다. 게다가 목적에 맞는 생물을 먹이로 하거나 심지어 원하는 지역에 남아 있으리라는 보장은 어디에도 없다. 이러한 경우가 수수두꺼비에게서 광범위하게 발생했는데, 그들은 부족한 지표식물로 인해 종종 농장에서 달아났다. 두꺼비는 독성이 있기 때문에 그들의 독에 면역이 없는 토착 포식동물들에게 처참한 영향을 주었다.

6 ➡ In order to avoid such problems and still maintain maximum possible crop yield, many experts recommend an approach called Integrated Pest Management (IPM). IPM involves many tactics, but it begins with determining the threat level to the crops. Merely sighting a possible pest is not sufficient cause to begin using pesticides. The situation should be carefully monitored until an identified pest becomes an economic threat to the farm. At that point, preventative measures like removing the affected plants, rotating crops, or selecting more resistant varieties of a plant are recommended. If these are ineffective, then introducing reliable predator species may be an option, but spraying of broad-spectrum pesticides should only be used as a last resort.

1. **Negative Fact**
All of the following are mentioned in paragraph 2 about past pest control EXCEPT
Ⓐ Sumerians used powdered sulfur to deter pests.
Ⓑ **farmers used toxins that made produce unsafe for consumption.**
Ⓒ ancient farmers were aware of plants that are toxic to pests.
Ⓓ texts on agriculture have been written for over 4,000 years.

2. **Sentence Simplification**
Which of the sentences below best expresses the essential information in the highlighted sentence in the passage? *Incorrect* answer choices change the meaning in important ways or leave out essential information.
Ⓐ At that time, people thought using a little poison on crops was helpful for their health.
Ⓑ At that time, people took small doses of poison for their health by using them on the crops that they grew.
Ⓒ At that time, the poisons which people used on their crops were not very dangerous, so they took them for their health.
Ⓓ **At that time, people thought that using poisons would not affect crops seriously since they were thought to be beneficial when used in small quantities.**

3. **Negative Fact**

According to paragraph 3, all of the following are true about DDT EXCEPT

- Ⓐ DDT replaced natural chemicals from plants that had been used to kill pests.
- Ⓑ DDT was the first synthetic pesticide, and it came to be used widely in the 20th century.
- **Ⓒ DDT was originally synthesized to help agriculture by eliminating insects.**
- Ⓓ DDT was adapted to be available in various physical forms.

4. **Fact**

According to paragraph 4, how does intentional control of pest populations affect the food chain?

- Ⓐ Pesticides make it unnecessary for natural predators to depend upon pests for food.
- **Ⓑ The use of pesticides may kill natural predators as well as pest species.**
- Ⓒ Pesticides affect the whole ecosystem by causing mutations in natural predators.
- Ⓓ Pesticides often weaken the immunity of predators, allowing pests to thrive.

5. **Fact**

According to paragraph 5, the Chinese introduced ant hives to their orchards to

- Ⓐ identify the organisms affecting their trees.
- Ⓑ remove undesired plants from the rows of trees.
- **Ⓒ keep their citrus trees safe from fruit-damaging insects.**
- Ⓓ make their citrus trees more resistant to insects and disease.

6. **Rhetorical Purpose**

Why does the author mention the "cane toad" in paragraph 5?

- Ⓐ To give an example of a species with great adaptability
- Ⓑ To explain how to domesticate introduced species effectively
- Ⓒ To claim that any attempt to control a pest population is fruitless
- **Ⓓ To show the danger of introducing foreign species indiscriminately**

7. Vocabulary

The word "tactics" in paragraph 6 is closest in meaning to

Ⓐ alliances
Ⓑ **strategies**
Ⓒ standards
Ⓓ advantages

8. Inference

What can be inferred about IPM from paragraph 6?

Ⓐ **It was designed to guarantee both ecological safety and productivity improvement.**
Ⓑ It aims to eradicate any kind of pest by introducing predator species.
Ⓒ It puts the highest priority on environmental value and the protection of species.
Ⓓ It was intended to expand agricultural fields and maximize crop yields.

9. Insertion

Look at the four squares [■] that indicate where the following sentence could be added to the passage.

These species that endanger crops are labeled as pests.

Where would the sentence best fit? [■ C]

10. Summary

Directions: An introductory sentence for a brief summary of the passage is provided below. Complete the summary by selecting the THREE answer choices that express the most important ideas in the passage. Some sentences do not belong in the summary because they express ideas that are not presented in the passage or are minor ideas in the passage. *This question is worth 2 points.*

There have been various efforts to raise agricultural productivity by controlling pest organisms throughout human history.

- Ⓑ **In the past, a variety of chemicals from nature were generally used as pesticides.**
- Ⓒ **To avoid the adverse effects of chemical pesticides on the ecosystem, some farmers began to make use of the predator-prey system.**
- Ⓕ **IPM is an approach which requires care for the balance between economic values and the ecosystem.**

ⓐ Thanks to the development of agriculture, mankind could flourish and build civilizations.
ⓓ Before the advent of DDT, people had mainly depended upon specific predator species to discourage pests.
ⓔ These days, the introduction of non-indigenous species is recommended for pest eradication since it has few side effects.

ⓐ 농업의 발달 덕분에 인류는 번창하고 문명을 건설할 수 있었다.
ⓓ DDT의 등장 전에 사람들은 해충을 죽이기 위해 특정 포식종들에 주로 의존했다.
ⓔ 오늘날 외래종의 도입은 부작용이 거의 없기 때문에 해충 박멸에 사용되도록 추천된다.

어휘

1 **adoption** n (아이디어·계획 등의) 채택 | **subsequent** adj 그[이] 다음의, 계속되는, 연속되는 | **extent** n (크기·중요성·심각성 등의) 정도[규모] | **native** adj 원산[토종/자생]의 | **alter** v 바꾸다, 고치다, 변하다, 달라지다 | **distribution** n 분배 (방식), 분포 | **enrich** v (토지를) 비옥하게 하다, 풍요롭게 하다 | **monoculture** n 단일재배 | **consume** v 먹다, 마시다 | **endanger** v 위험에 빠뜨리다, 위태롭게 만들다 | **pest** n 해충, 유해 동물 | **however** adv 하지만, 그러나 | **moderate** adj 보통의, 중간의, 중도의[온건한] | **long run** 장기간

2 **widely** adv 널리, 폭넓게 | **dose** n (약의) 복용량[투여량]

3 **extract** v 뽑다[얻다], 추출하다 | **pesticide** n 살충제 | **elemental** adj 요소의, (물리, 화학) 원소의[같은] | **synthesized** adj 합성화된 | **dominant** adj 우세한, 지배적인 | **parasite** n 기생충, 기생 동물[식물] | **deliver** v 배달하다, 전하다, 넘겨 주다 | **widespread** adj 광범위한, 널리 퍼진 | **side effect** n 부작용

4 **entail** v 수반하다 | **intended** adj 의도된, 계획된, 고의의 | **continuously** adv 계속해서, 연속적으로, 끊임없이 | **immunity** n 면역, 면역력 | **exposure** n 노출 | **survive** v 살아남다, 생존[존속]하다 | **reproduce** v 번식하다 | **rebound** v 반등하다, 되돌아오다 | **far-reaching** adj (효과, 영향 등이) 멀리까지 미치는

5 **hardly** adv 거의 ~ 아니다[없다] | **non-indigenous** adj (어떤 지역) 원산의[토착]이 아닌 | **unforeseen** adj 예측하지 못한, 뜻밖의 | **unchecked** (유해한 것이 더 악화되지 않도록) 억제하지[손을 쓰지] 않고 놔 둔 | **guarantee** v 보장 | **desired** adj 바랐던, 희망했던, 훌륭한 | **disastrous** adj 처참한, 형편없는 | **immunity** n 면역력 | **toxin** n 독소

6 **yield** n (농작물 등의) 산출[수확]량, 총수익 | **recommend** v 추천[천거]하다 | **threat** n 협박, 위협 | **merely** adv 한낱, 그저, 단지 | **identified** adj 확인된, 인정된, 식별된 | **preventative** adj 예방[방지]을 위한 | **measure** n 조치[정책] | **resistant** adj 저항력 있는, ~에 잘 견디는[강한] | **last resort** n 마지막 수단[방책, 수]

Actual Test 06

본서 | P. 117

Passage 1 The Development of Islamic Bookmaking

1. Ⓑ	Inference	6. Ⓐ	Vocabulary
2. Ⓐ	Rhetorical Purpose	7. Ⓒ	Sentence Simplification
3. Ⓓ	Fact	8. Ⓑ	Inference
4. Ⓓ	Vocabulary	9. Ⓑ	Insertion
5. Ⓐ	Fact	10. Ⓑ, Ⓒ, Ⓓ	Summary

Passage 2 Evolution of Cetaceans

1. Ⓑ	Rhetorical Purpose	6. Ⓓ	Sentence Simplification
2. Ⓒ	Negative Fact	7. Ⓑ	Vocabulary
3. Ⓐ	Inference	8. Ⓐ	Insertion
4. Ⓓ	Fact	9. Ⓐ	Fact
5. Ⓒ	Vocabulary	10. Ⓐ, Ⓑ, Ⓔ	Summary

● 내가 맞은 문제 유형의 개수를 적어 보고 어느 유형에 취약한지 확인해 봅시다.

문제 유형	맞은 개수
Sentence Simplification	2
Fact / Negative Fact	5
Vocabulary	4
Reference	0
Rhetorical Purpose	2
Inference	3
Insertion	2
Summary	2
Category Chart	0
Total	20

The Development of Islamic Bookmaking

1 ➡ Bookmaking flourished in the Middle East between the 9th and 15th centuries. Islamic books from this period were finely hand-crafted with luxurious materials and had detailed and artistically wrought covers and interior illustrations. This flowering of literary artistry was the result of two major events in the Muslim world. The first was the development of an official language with a codified alphabet and an accepted writing style. The second was the importation of paper-making technology, which allowed books to be produced on a vaster scale. These books were one of the main venues for artistic expression in the Arab world, and they employed not only calligraphers and painters, but also leather and paper makers and professional binders. This bookmaking industry was financially supported by princes and caliphs and lasted until printing presses were imported.

2 ➡ Islamic bookmaking extends back to the beginning of the religion it supports. According to the teachings of Islam, the Quran was imparted to the Prophet Muhammad by the archangel Gabriel between 610 and 632 CE, and he in turn translated the word of Allah into his own native Arabic. At first, his followers memorized his words and verbally relayed them to others, but this method of spreading the word was inconvenient, and worse yet, unreliable. In order to faithfully repeat his words, his assistants began writing down the Quran on any available material. These were eventually collected together, but a problem emerged: there was no unified Arabic alphabet. This was resolved during the rule of caliph Abd al-Malik, who made Arabic the official language of his empire and codified it into a single alphabet. This was eventually developed into calligraphy by Ibn Muqla in the 9th century, which was perfected by the 11th century calligrapher Ibn al-Bawwab.

3 ➡ [■A] What contributed most to the expansion of books throughout the Muslim world was an innovation from China that was introduced in the 9th century: paper. [■B] Paper was originally developed much earlier, but before this time the technology had not spread westward. Muslim forces that captured Chinese prisoners in Samarkand who knew how to make paper allowed this to happen. [■C] Their

method of paper production involved three main steps. [■D] First, pulp was extracted from various plant types by boiling them down in water. Next, a fine mesh screen was used to catch these fibers and form a thin layer of pulp. Finally, these screens were carefully dried to make flexible sheets of paper. Despite the labor intensive process, this method actually produced writing material much more quickly and inexpensively than the prior method of curing goat hides. Qurans were soon being produced with pages made of this paper, and later other secular and scientific ideas were also spread through such books.

4 ➡ The first books produced in this way were religious texts, but later history, scientific treatises, poetry, and romantic literature were also written down and transformed into books. Many of these secular texts were just as richly decorated as the Quran, and many people were employed in their manufacture. They often featured leather covers that were embossed with gold in geometric and floral patterns. For the Qurans, this usually involved a fairly consistent pattern with a circle or oval at the center of the design that symbolized the sun. Of course, the degree of decoration varied, with books that were made for important patrons or public use being the richest, whereas those for personal use were often less ostentatious. These books became valuable trade goods, and often could be found far from where they were produced.

5 ➡ As paper spread through the Arab world, it revolutionized more than just bookmaking. Parchments were limited in size by the animals killed to make the original leather, but paper was limited only by the size of the screen it was dried upon. This meant that huge, incredibly detailed maps could be produced, and blueprints could be made large enough to clearly show building elements. In addition, the limitations of paper also made it popular for some purposes. Because the paper was so thin and absorbent, ink marks on it were nearly impossible to change, unlike parchment which allowed for corrections, or even worse, fraudulent alterations. For this reason, it quickly became the chief material used for official documents in Baghdad. Paper and its various uses rapidly spread throughout the Muslim world, stretching across northern Africa, and even into Spain, where it was first introduced to Europeans.

1. **Inference**

Based on paragraph 1, it can be inferred that

Ⓐ bookmaking flourished because of the varieties of writing styles.
Ⓑ **printing presses were probably imported around the 15th century.**
Ⓒ there were no other channels for artistic expression in the Arab world.
Ⓓ the upper class did not support bookmaking.

2. **Rhetorical Purpose**

The author mentions "Ibn Muqla" in paragraph 2 to indicate who

Ⓐ **developed the Arabic handwriting system**
Ⓑ collected the Quran into a single volume
Ⓒ made Arabic the official language of Islam
Ⓓ codified the Arabic alphabet

3. **Fact**

According to paragraph 2, what was one problem of spreading the Quran?

Ⓐ Verbally spreading the word was slow.
Ⓑ Most of the recorded Quran were illegible.
Ⓒ Calligraphy was not perfected until the 11th century.
Ⓓ **There was no unified Arabic alphabet.**

4. **Vocabulary**

The word "extracted" in paragraph 3 is closest in meaning to

Ⓐ converged
Ⓑ purified
Ⓒ accumulated
Ⓓ **removed**

5. **Fact**

According to paragraph 4, what was the result of a flourishing bookmaking industry?

Ⓐ **Books became trade goods in other parts of the world.**
Ⓑ There was a growth in the number of literature writers.
Ⓒ Secular texts became more popular than the Quran.
Ⓓ Lower quality materials were used to keep up with demand.

6. **Vocabulary**

The word "ostentatious" in paragraph 4 is closest in meaning to

Ⓐ **extravagant**

1.
1단락에 근거하여 추론할 수 있는 것은?

Ⓐ 서적 제조는 다양한 문체로 인해 번성했다.
Ⓑ 인쇄기는 아마도 15세기 즈음에 수입됐다.
Ⓒ 아랍 세계에 다른 예술적 표현의 통로는 없었다.
Ⓓ 상류층은 서적 제조를 지원하지 않았다.

2.
글쓴이가 2단락에서 언급하는 "이븐 무클라"는?

Ⓐ 아랍어 필기 체계를 개발했다
Ⓑ 쿠란을 한 권의 책으로 모았다
Ⓒ 아랍어를 이슬람교의 공식 언어로 삼았다
Ⓓ 아랍어 알파벳을 성문화했다

3.
2단락에 따르면, 쿠란을 전파하는 것의 한 가지 문제점은 무엇이었는가?

Ⓐ 말씀을 구두로 퍼뜨리는 것은 느렸다.
Ⓑ 기록된 쿠란의 대부분이 알아보기 힘들었다.
Ⓒ 서예는 11세기까지 완성되지 않았다.
Ⓓ 통일된 아랍어 알파벳이 없었다.

4.
3단락의 단어 "extracted(추출했다)"와 의미상 가장 가까운 것은?

Ⓐ 모여들었다
Ⓑ 정화했다
Ⓒ 축적했다
Ⓓ 꺼냈다

5.
4단락에 따르면, 번성하는 서적 제조 산업의 결과는 무엇이었는가?

Ⓐ 서적은 세계의 다른 지역에서 무역품이 되었다.
Ⓑ 문학가들의 수가 증가했다.
Ⓒ 세속적인 서적이 쿠란보다 더 인기있었다.
Ⓓ 수요를 따라잡기 위해 품질이 낮은 재료들이 사용되었다.

6.
4단락의 단어 "ostentatious(호사스러운)"와 의미상 가장 가까운 것은?

Ⓐ 호화로운

Ⓑ expensive
Ⓒ decorated
Ⓓ obnoxious

7. **Sentence Simplification**
Which of the sentences below best expresses the essential information in the highlighted sentence in the passage? *Incorrect* answer choices change the meaning in important ways or leave out essential information.
Ⓐ While parchment allowed for the correction of ink marks, fraudulent alterations on paper were impossible to change because it was so thin and absorbent.
Ⓑ Paper's resistance to ink allowed for criminal alterations, while corrections on parchment were nearly impossible.
Ⓒ **While alterations could be made on parchment, the thin nature of paper made it impossible for corrections to be made.**
Ⓓ Because it was thin and absorbent, parchment allowed for corrections, sometimes even fraudulent alterations.

8. **Inference**
Based on paragraph 5, what can be inferred about paper?
Ⓐ Paper was introduced to Europe before the 9th century.
Ⓑ **Using paper increased the sizes of books and documents.**
Ⓒ The concept of drawing up blueprints was nonexistent until the widespread production of paper.
Ⓓ The Chinese were unwilling to reveal the secrets of manufacturing paper to the Europeans.

9. **Insertion**
Look at the four squares [■] that indicate where the following sentence could be added to the passage.

Paper was originally developed much earlier, but before this time the technology had not spread westward.

Where would the sentence best fit? [■ B]

10. **Summary**
Directions: An introductory sentence for a brief summary of the passage is provided below. Complete the summary by selecting the THREE answer choices that express the most important ideas in the passage. Some sentences do not belong in the summary because they express ideas that are not presented in the passage or are minor ideas in the passage. **This question is worth 2 points.**

Development of a unified alphabet and the introduction of paper-making technology allowed the bookmaking industry to flourish in the Middle East.

- Ⓑ Widespread production of paper in the Middle East allowed non-religious literature to be made into books, and the use of paper quickly spread to other continents.
- Ⓒ With a unified alphabet, the teachings of Muhammad could be written down, which was more convenient and reliable than the previous oral means.
- Ⓓ Paper had many advantages over animal hides, and it quickly became the preferred writing material for books, blueprints, and official documents.

Ⓐ Arabic calligraphy wasn't perfected until the 11th century, crippling the caliph's effort at spreading the language.
Ⓔ The books were richly decorated with gold, with some books being more ostentatious than others.
Ⓕ While paper was invented much earlier, it wasn't until the 9th century that the technology spread westward.

통일된 알파벳의 개발과 종이 제작 기술의 도입은 서적 제조 산업이 중동에서 번성하게 만들었다.

- Ⓑ 중동에서의 대대적인 종이 생산은 비종교적 문학이 책으로 만들어지는 것을 가능하게 했으며, 종이의 사용은 다른 대륙으로 빠르게 퍼져나갔다.
- Ⓒ 통일된 알파벳으로 무함마드의 가르침은 기록될 수 있게 되었는데, 이는 기존의 구두로 전달하는 방식보다 더 편리하고 신뢰할 수 있는 방식이었다.
- Ⓓ 종이는 동물 가죽보다 많은 장점을 갖고 있었으며, 빠르게 책, 청사진과 공문서에 선호되는 필기 재료가 되었다.

Ⓐ 아랍어 서예는 11세기가 되어서야 완성됐으며, 이것은 언어를 널리 알리고자 했던 칼리프의 노력을 좌절시켰다.
Ⓔ 책들은 금으로 화려하게 장식되었으며, 어떤 책들은 다른 것들보다 더 호사스러웠다.
Ⓕ 종이는 훨씬 일찍 발명되었지만 그 기술이 서방으로 퍼진 것은 9세기가 되어서였다.

어휘

1. **flourish** v 번창하다 | **finely** adv 섬세[정교]하게 | **hand-crafted** adj 수공예품인 | **luxurious** adj 아주 편안한; 호화로운, 사치스러운 | **artistically** adv 예술[미술]적으로 | **wrought** adj (철물 등이) 두들겨 만든, 단련한, 꾸민, 수놓은 | **interior** adj 내부의 | **illustration** n 삽화 | **flowering** n 전성기 | **literary** adj 문학의 | **artistry** n 예술가적 기교 | **codified** adj 성문화된 | **accepted** adj 일반적으로 인정된, 용인된 | **importation** n 수입 | **vast** adj (범위·크기·양 등이) 어마어마한[방대한/막대한] | **financially** adv 재정적으로 | **caliph** n 칼리프(과거 이슬람 국가의 통치자를 가리키던 칭호) | **last** v 계속되다

2. **extend** v (시간이) 계속되다, (~까지) 걸치다 | **impart** v (정보·지식 등을) 전하다 | **translate** v 번역[통역]하다, (다른 언어로) 옮기다 | **memorize** v 암기하다 | **verbally** adv 구두로 | **relay** v (정보 등을 받아서) 전달하다 | **inconvenient** adj 불편한[곤란한] | **unreliable** adj 믿을[신뢰할] 수 없는 | **faithfully** adv 충실히, 정확히 | **emerge** v 나오다, 드러나다 | **resolve** v 해결하다 | **perfect** v 완벽하게 하다

3. **innovation** n 혁신, 쇄신, 새로 도입한 것 | **capture** v 포로로 잡다 | **extract** v 뽑다[얻다], 추출하다 | **flexible** adj 신축성[융통성] 있는 | **intensive** adj 집중적인(짧은 시간에 많은 일·활동을 하는) | **inexpensively** adv 값싸게, 많은 비용을 들이지 않고 | **cure** v 보존 처리를 하다 | **secular** adj 세속적인

4. **treatise** n 논문 | **manufacture** n 제조[생산] | **feature** v 특별히 포함하다, 특징으로 삼다 | **emboss** v 양각[돋을새김]하다 | **geometric** adj 기하학의; 기하학적인 | **consistent** adj 한결같은, 일관된 | **ostentatious** adj 대단히 비싼[호사스러운]

5. **revolutionize** v 대변혁[혁신]을 일으키다 | **limit** v 한정[제한]하다 | **incredibly** adv 믿을 수 없을 정도로, 엄청나게 | **detailed** adj 상세한 | **absorbent** adj 잘 빨아들이는, 흡수력 있는 | **fraudulent** adj 사기를 치는[치기 위한] | **alteration** n 변화, 개조 | **stretch** v 뻗어 있다[펼쳐지다 / 이어지다]

Evolution of Cetaceans

1 ➡ Cetaceans, which comprise whales, dolphins, and porpoises, are among the most intriguing marine mammals, renowned for their cognitive complexity, intricate social structures, and profound adaptations to aquatic life. The evolutionary trajectory of cetaceans from terrestrial origins to fully aquatic organisms spans tens of millions of years, characterized by significant morphological and behavioral transformations. This evolutionary narrative begins approximately 50 million years ago during the Eocene epoch, a period noted for its warm global climates and extensive shallow seas. The earliest ancestors of cetaceans were terrestrial artiodactyls, an order of even-toed, hooved animals that includes extant species such as deer, bovines, and hippopotamuses. One of the earliest identified proto-cetaceans is *Pakicetus*, discovered in the sedimentary deposits of what is now Pakistan. Pakicetus exhibited a morphology resembling a small dog-like animal and possessed characteristics indicative of a semi-aquatic lifestyle. Its auditory structures, particularly the involucrum, were adapted for underwater hearing, while its teeth structure reflected a carnivorous diet. These early cetaceans likely inhabited riverbanks, preying on fish and other aquatic organisms while retaining terrestrial locomotion capabilities.

2 ➡ As proto-cetaceans continued their evolutionary progression, they exhibited increasingly specialized adaptations for aquatic existence. *Ambulocetus*, dating to approximately 49 million years ago, represents a critical transitional form. Often referred to as the "walking whale," Ambulocetus possessed robust limbs capable of supporting its body on land, yet its elongated body and tail anatomy suggest proficient swimming capabilities. Its locomotion in water likely mirrored that of modern otters, utilizing its hind limbs and tail for propulsion through water with considerable agility. The vertebral morphology of Ambulocetus indicates the flexibility necessary for undulating aquatic movement, a precursor to the more specialized movements particular to subsequent cetaceans. Another significant early cetacean is Rodhocetus, dating from around 47 million years ago. Rodhocetus exhibited

further aquatic adaptations, such as more fin-like appendages and a streamlined body for efficient swimming in various aquatic environments. Its pelvis and hind limbs, were diminished in size compared to earlier ancestors, indicating a definitive shift towards a predominantly aquatic lifestyle.

3 ➡ By approximately 40 million years ago, cetaceans had achieved significant adaptations for a fully aquatic existence. *Basilosaurus*, which flourished around 35-40 million years ago, exemplifies a pivotal stage in cetacean evolution. Unlike its predecessors, Basilosaurus was entirely adapted to marine life, with a serpentine body reaching up to 18 meters in length. Its reduced hind limbs were no longer functional for walking, signifying a complete transition to aquatic life. The placement of Basilosaurus's nostrils had shifted further back on the skull, evolving into a blowhole, an adaptation critical for breathing while swimming. Concurrently, another cetacean, *Dorudon*, emerged. Dorudon, smaller than Basilosaurus displayed advanced adaptations for aquatic life. Its well-developed flippers facilitated maneuverability, while its tail fluke provided powerful propulsion. The reduction of hind limbs and pelvic bones in Dorudon indicates a fully aquatic lifestyle, and its streamlined body morphology suggests it was an agile swimmer, akin to modern dolphins.

4 ➡ The Oligocene epoch, commencing around 34 million years ago, marked a period of significant diversification and specialization for cetaceans. During this epoch, the two major suborders of modern cetaceans began to diverge: *Odontoceti* and *Mysticeti*. Odontocetes, or toothed whales, developed sophisticated echolocation capabilities, facilitating navigation and predation. [■A] Fossil evidence from early odontocetes, such as *Squalodon*, reveals the development of complex cranial structures and specialized auditory ossicles. [■B]

5 ➡ Mysticetes, or baleen whales, evolved a distinctive feeding strategy. Rather than teeth, they developed baleen plates composed of keratin, which they used for filter feeding. [■C] This adaptation allowed them to efficiently consume large quantities of small prey such as krill and plankton. [■D] Fossil evidence from early mysticetes, such as *Janjucetus*, indicates a transitional phase where teeth and baleen structures coexisted, signifying an evolutionary shift

towards filter feeding. The advent of baleen facilitated the exploitation of abundant marine food resources, leading to the evolution of large body sizes seen in species like the blue whale, the largest known animal to have ever existed. Hence, the cetaceans of today owe their unique adaptations to millions of years of evolution, a gradual change that saw land animals evolve into some of the most intelligent and bewildering marine animals today.

왕고래와 같은 큰 몸집의 진화를 이끌었다. 따라서 오늘날의 고래류는 수천만 년에 걸친 진화에 의해 그들의 독특한 적응을 이루었으며, 이는 육상 동물이 지구에서 가장 지적이고 놀라운 해양 동물로 변모한 과정이다.

1. Rhetorical Purpose

The author mentions "deer" in paragraph 1 in order to

Ⓐ provide examples of the first proto-cetaceans.
Ⓑ **provide an example of a terrestrial artiodactyl.**
Ⓒ explain what the first hooved animals looked like.
Ⓓ explain the evolutionary origins of artiodactyls.

1.

1단락에서 저자가 "사슴"을 언급한 이유는?

Ⓐ 최초의 원시 고래류의 예를 제공하기 위해서이다.
Ⓑ **육상 우제류의 예를 제공하기 위해서이다.**
Ⓒ 최초의 우제류가 어떻게 생겼는지 설명하기 위해서이다.
Ⓓ 우제류의 진화적 기원을 설명하기 위해서이다.

2. Negative Fact

Which of the following is NOT a characteristic of *Rodhocetus* as described in the passage?

Ⓐ fin-like appendages
Ⓑ a streamlined body for swimming
Ⓒ **robust limbs capable of sprinting**
Ⓓ small hind legs

2.

다음 중 본문에서 설명된 로도케투스의 특징이 아닌 것은 무엇인가?

Ⓐ 지느러미와 같은 부속지
Ⓑ 유선형의 수영에 적합한 몸체
Ⓒ **전력 질주가 가능한 튼튼한 팔다리**
Ⓓ 크기가 작은 뒷다리

3. Inference

In paragraph 2, which of the following can be inferred about *Ambulocetus*?

Ⓐ ***Ambulocetus* possessed a physical structure that made it a better swimmer than its predecessors.**
Ⓑ *Ambulocetus* is closely related to other terrestrial artiodactyls, such as otters and beavers.
Ⓒ Most subsequent cetaceans inherited their swimming adaptations from *Ambulocetus*.
Ⓓ *Ambulocetus* tails were much larger and more agile than those of the Rodhocetus.

3.

2단락에서, 다음 중 암불로케투스에 대해 추론할 수 있는 것은 무엇인가?

Ⓐ **암불로케투스는 이전 종보다 더 나은 수영 실력을 갖추게 한 신체 구조를 가지고 있었다.**
Ⓑ 암불로케투스는 수달과 비버와 같은 다른 육상 우제류와 밀접한 관련이 있다.
Ⓒ 이후의 대부분의 고래류는 암불로케투스로부터 수영에 대한 적응을 물려받았다.
Ⓓ 암불로케투스의 꼬리는 로도케투스보다 훨씬 크고 민첩했다.

4. Fact

According to paragraph 2, how did Rodhocetus further evolve cetaceans toward aquatic life?

Ⓐ Their teeth exhibited an increased carnivorous diet.
Ⓑ Their bodies grew longer, and their tails morphed into a more flap-like shape.
Ⓒ Their limbs demonstrated an increase in amphibious tendencies.
Ⓓ Their hind legs were less adapted toward terrestrial movement.

5. Vocabulary

The word "concurrently" in paragraph 3 is closest in meaning to

Ⓐ conversely
Ⓑ contrarily
Ⓒ simultaneously
Ⓓ jointly

6. Sentence Simplification

Which of the following best expresses the essential information in the highlighted sentence? Incorrect answer choices change the meaning in important ways or leave out essential information.

Ⓐ Not only did Dorudon completely evolve away from the use of its hind limbs, but its body shape indicated a dexterous swimmer, similar to modern dolphins.
Ⓑ The combination of hind limb reduction and a more aerodynamic body points to Dorudon living fully underwater as an agile swimmer, similar to modern dolphins.
Ⓒ A more streamlined body enabled Dorudon to swim more adeptly, much like modern dolphins, while smaller hind limbs and pelvic bones signify a complete move to an aquatic lifestyle.
Ⓓ A more streamlined body suggests Dorudon to have been agile swimmers, much like modern dolphins, and shrinking hind limbs and pelvic bones point to a fully aquatic lifestyle.

7. Vocabulary

The word "diverge" in paragraph 4 is closest in meaning to

Ⓐ contradict
Ⓑ split
Ⓒ defy
Ⓓ depart

8. Insertion

Look at the four squares [■] that indicate where the following sentence could be added to the passage.

This adaptation conferred a significant evolutionary advantage, allowing odontocetes to detect prey and obstacles with remarkable precision in the marine environment.

Where would the sentence best fit? [■ A]

9. Fact

According to paragraph 5, how does the lack of teeth benefit *Mysticetes*?

Ⓐ **The lack of teeth enables whales to sift through their food more efficiently.**
Ⓑ The few teeth they have are used in conjunction with keratin to filter water out of their food.
Ⓒ The absence of teeth provides an advantage when hunting for smaller prey.
Ⓓ Keratin allows for the efficient chewing of krill and plankton.

10. Prose Summary

Directions: An introductory sentence for a brief summary of the passage is provided below. Complete the summary by selecting the THREE answer choices that express the most important ideas in the passage. Some sentences do not belong in the summary because they express ideas that are not presented in the passage or minor ideas in the passage. *This question is worth 2 points.*

Cetaceans evolved from semi-aquatic artiodactyls into fully-aquatic marine mammals.

> Ⓐ **Basilosaurus represented a critical stage in cetacean evolution, as its serpentine body and smaller hind legs reflected a fully aquatic lifestyle.**
> Ⓑ **The Oligocene period saw the cetacean evolution diverge into two branches: toothed whales and baleen whales.**
> Ⓔ **More aquatic adaptations were seen in Rodhocetus, with flatter appendages that resembled fins.**

Ⓒ Pakicetus' teeth structures were adapted to chew on river prey more efficiently, while their auditory structures revealed the beginnings of echolocation adaptations.
Ⓓ Ambulocetus was about 4.5 meters long, with flippers that allowed it to move swiftly through the water.

Ⓕ Dorudon had significantly larger hind limbs, although its use was limited to swimming, further indicating a move away from terrestrial living.

Ⓕ 도루돈은 현저하게 더 큰 뒷다리를 가졌지만, 그것의 사용은 수영에 국한되었고, 이는 육상 생활에서 더욱 멀어졌음을 나타낸다.

어휘

1 **cetacean** n 고래류 | **intriguing** adj 흥미로운 | **cognitive** adj 인지의 | **aquatic** adj 수생의 | **trajectory** n 궤적 | **terrestrial** adj 육지의 | **morphological** adj 형태의 | **epoch** n 시대 | **artiodactyl** n 우제류 | **extant** adj 현존하는 | **proto-cetacean** n 원시 고래류 | **sedimentary** adj 퇴적의 | **auditory** adj 청각의 | **involucrum** n 이형 돌출부 | **carnivorous** adj 육식성의 | **locomotion** n 이동

2 **progression** n 진행 | **robust** adj 튼튼한 | **limb** n 팔다리 | **anatomy** n 해부학 | **propulsion** n 추진 | **vertebral** adj 척추의 | **undulating** adj 물결 모양을 만드는 | **appendage** n 부속지 | **streamlined** adj 유선형의 | **pelvis** n 골반

3 **adaptation** n 적응 | **serpentine** adj 뱀 같은 | **functional** adj 기능적인 | **maneuverability** n 기동성 | **fluke** n 고래 꼬리 끝 | **propulsion** n 추진 | **morphology** n 형태

4 **diversification** n 다양화 | **specialization** n 전문화 | **suborder** n 아목 | **diverge** v 갈라지다 | **echolocation** n 반향 정위 | **navigation** n 길찾기 | **auditory ossicle** n 청소골

5 **baleen** n 고래수염 | **filter feeding** n 여과 섭식 | **prey** n 먹이 | **krill** n 크릴 새우 | **coexist** v 공존하다 | **exploitation** n 이용

Actual Test 07

본서 | P. 126

Passage 1 The Kinetoscope

1. Ⓓ	Negative Fact	6. Ⓓ	Negative Fact
2. Ⓐ	Sentence Simplification	7. Ⓒ	Rhetorical Purpose
3. Ⓐ	Reference	8. Ⓑ	Fact
4. Ⓑ	Inference	9. Ⓓ	Vocabulary
5. Ⓑ	Insertion	10. Ⓑ, Ⓓ, Ⓕ	Summary

Passage 2 Railroad Development in the United States

1. Ⓐ	Vocabulary	6. Ⓒ	Vocabulary
2. Ⓓ	Inference	7. Ⓓ	Fact
3. Ⓐ	Fact	8. Ⓒ	Sentence Simplification
4. Ⓒ	Rhetorical Purpose	9. Ⓒ	Insertion
5. Ⓓ	Inference	10. Ⓐ, Ⓒ, Ⓔ	Summary

● 내가 맞은 문제 유형의 개수를 적어 보고 어느 유형에 취약한지 확인해 봅시다.

문제 유형	맞은 개수
Sentence Simplification	2
Fact / Negative Fact	5
Vocabulary	3
Reference	1
Rhetorical Purpose	2
Inference	3
Insertion	2
Summary	2
Category Chart	0
Total	20

Passage 1

The Kinetoscope

1 ▶ The Kinetoscope, a forerunner to modern cinema, was developed by Thomas Edison and his assistant William Kennedy Laurie Dickson in the late 19th century. Patented in 1891 and publicly unveiled in 1893, the Kinetoscope represented a significant leap in the development of motion picture technology. Edison, primarily motivated by the commercial potential of motion pictures, envisioned the Kinetoscope as a device for individual viewing. Together with Dickson, the chief engineer, they came up with the idea of a continuous loop of 35mm film running through a viewing machine. This film was perforated along the edges to ensure smooth movement through the mechanism. The Kinetoscope's defining feature was its peephole viewer, through which a single person could watch short, silent films. These films were often less than a minute long, depicting simple scenes like a dancer, a boxing match, or a man sneezing.

2 ▶ The first Kinetoscope parlor, which opened on April 14, 1894 at 1155 Broadway in New York City, marked a significant milestone in the history of motion pictures. This parlor, established by the Holland Brothers, featured ten Kinetoscopes, each offering a different short film. Patrons were charged 25 cents for access to this novel form of entertainment, which quickly became a popular attraction. Inside the parlor, visitors would find the Kinetoscopes lined up in two rows, creating an arcade-like atmosphere. Each machine was housed in an oak cabinet, and its contents would be viewed through a peephole. The films shown in these machines were brief, typically lasting around 20 to 30 seconds, and featured a variety of subjects, from vaudeville acts to everyday activities. The novelty of seeing moving images captivated audiences, and the parlor often drew large crowds, including curious onlookers and eager repeat customers. People were shocked and overwhelmed by the novelty of the technology, with viewers yelling out loud in amazement from around the parlor. Viewers, engrossed in the films, would reportedly duck and jump, forgetting they were in a parlor watching a motion picture.

3 ▶ The success of the New York Kinetoscope parlor was not just a testament to the public's fascination

with moving pictures but also to the potential for commercial exploitation of this new technology. [■A] The profits generated from this parlor model demonstrated that there was a viable market for motion pictures, encouraging further investment and innovation in the field. [■B] This expansion helped to popularize motion pictures and laid the groundwork for the burgeoning film industry. [■C] The Kinetoscope parlor also played a critical role in the cultural landscape of the time, providing a new form of entertainment that was accessible to a broad audience. [■D] Unlike theater or opera, which often catered to more affluent patrons, Kinetoscope parlors were affordable and appealed to people from various social backgrounds. Scholars today view this as the democratization of entertainment, which brought motion pictures to a wider audience. This heavily contributed to the growing popularity of visual media. Finally, the parlor became a social gathering place where people could share the experience of watching moving images, fostering a communal appreciation for this emerging art form. This would become a consumer dynamic within the industry that would continue to this day.

4 ➡ Nonetheless, this social aspect of kinetoscope parlors could not undo the inherent detached nature of the invention: Kinetoscopes could only be viewed by one person at a time. This shortcoming pushed and inspired further innovation in the technology. This eventually led to exploration into projection methods, which would allow images to be displayed to larger audiences all at once. This transition began with the work of inventors such as the Lumière brothers in France, who developed the Cinématographe in 1895. Unlike the Kinetoscope, the Cinématographe was capable of recording, projecting, and even developing motion pictures, making it more versatile and widely impactful. The invention utilized the same film width of 35mm, which rapidly became the industry standard, while the machine employed a mechanism known as the Maltese cross, which advanced the film strip intermittently, providing smoother motion compared to earlier devices.

5 ➡ On December 28, 1895, the Lumière brothers held their first public screening in Paris. This momentous evening is often regarded as the birth of modern cinema. Ten short films were featured,

수 있다는 가능성을 보여준 것이기도 했다. [■A] 이 상점 모델에서 발생한 수익은 영화에 대한 유망한 시장이 존재한다는 것을 보여주었고, 이는 더 많은 투자와 혁신을 촉진시켰다. [■B] 이러한 확장은 영화를 대중화시키고 영화 산업의 성장에 기반을 마련했다. [■C] 또한, 키네토스코프 상점은 당시 문화적 풍경에서 중요한 역할을 하며 폭넓은 대중에게 접근 가능한 새로운 형태의 오락을 제공하였다. [■D] 연극이나 오페라가 흔히 부유층을 대상으로 했던 것과 달리 키네토스코프 상점은 저렴하여 다양한 사회적 배경을 가진 사람들이 이용할 수 있었다. 오늘날 학자들은 이를 오락의 민주화로 보고 있으며, 이는 영화를 더 넓은 관객에게 가져다준 것이다. 이러한 상점은 시각적 미디어의 인기를 높이는 데 크게 기여하였다. 마지막으로, 상점은 사람들이 영상을 감상하는 경험을 공유할 수 있는 사교의 장이 되었으며, 이는 이 새로운 예술 형식에 대한 공동체적 감상을 촉진하였다. 이는 오늘날까지 지속되는 산업 내 소비자 역학 관계로 자리 잡았다.

4 ➡ 그러나 키네토스코프 상점의 이러한 사회적 측면도 발명 자체의 본질적인 한계, 즉 키네토스코프가 한 번에 한 사람만 볼 수 있다는 점을 극복할 수는 없었다. 이러한 단점은 기술의 추가적인 혁신을 자극하였다. 결국 더 많은 관객이 동시에 이미지를 볼 수 있도록 하는 투사 방식에 대한 탐구로 이어졌다. 이러한 전환은 1895년에 시네마토그래프(Cinématographe)를 개발한 프랑스의 뤼미에르 형제와 같은 발명가들의 작업으로 시작되었다. 키네토스코프와 달리 시네마토그래프는 영화 녹화, 투사, 현상까지 할 수 있어 더욱 다재다능하고 광범위한 영향을 미쳤다. 이 발명품은 동일한 35mm 필름 너비를 사용하였으며, 이는 빠르게 업계 표준이 되었다. 기계는 필름 스트립을 간헐적으로 이동시켜 매끄러운 움직임을 제공하는 몰타 십자 메커니즘을 채택했다.

5 ➡ 1895년 12월 28일, 뤼미에르 형제는 파리에서 최초의 공개 상영회를 열었다. 이 역사적인 저녁은 종종 현대 영화의 탄생으로 여겨진다. 상영은 유명한 "뤼미에르 공장을 떠

including the famous "Workers Leaving the Lumière Factory." The success of this screening demonstrated the vast potential of the Cinématographe. More importantly, the Cinématographe further laid the foundation for the development of the film industry, leading to the rise of projection cinema as the dominant cultural force that endures to this day.

나는 노동자들"(La Sortie de l'Usine Lumière à Lyon)을 포함한 열 개의 단편 영화를 선보였다. 이 상영회의 성공은 시네마토그래프의 엄청난 잠재력을 보여주었다. 더 나아가 시네마토그래프는 영화 산업 발전의 토대를 마련하였으며, 투사 영화의 대중적 문화적 영향력의 상승으로 이어졌다. 이는 오늘날까지 지속되는 주요 문화적 힘으로 자리잡았다.

---

1. **Negative Fact**
According to paragraph 1, which of the following was NOT a functional limitation of the Kinetoscope?
Ⓐ It could only be viewed by one person at a time.
Ⓑ It was unable to project films onto a large screen.
Ⓒ Its films were typically less than 60 seconds long.
Ⓓ **It allowed for limited synchronized sound effects.**

2. **Sentence Simplification**
Which of the following best expresses the essential information in the highlighted sentence? Incorrect answer choices change the meaning in important ways or leave out essential information.
Ⓐ **A low fee of 25 cents was paid to enjoy the novel form of entertainment, which rapidly grew in popularity.**
Ⓑ The new form of entertainment's low cost allowed it to quickly become a popular attraction.
Ⓒ Talk of the novel form of entertainment was quickly spreading, which customers accessed for 25 cents.
Ⓓ The intriguing form of entertainment created a sensation among New Yorkers, who were charged 25 cents to access the technology.

3. **Reference**
The word "its" in paragraph 2 refers to
Ⓐ **the machine's**
Ⓑ the oak cabinet's
Ⓒ the parlor's
Ⓓ the house's

1.
1단락에 따르면, 다음 중 키네토스코프의 기능적 한계가 아니었던 것은 무엇인가?
Ⓐ 한 번에 한 사람만 영상을 볼 수 있었다.
Ⓑ 영상을 대형 스크린에 투사할 수 없었다.
Ⓒ 영상의 길이는 일반적으로 60초 이하였다.
Ⓓ 제한적인 동기화된 음향 효과를 허용했다.

2.
다음 중 지문에 음영 표시된 문장의 핵심 정보를 가장 잘 표현한 문장은 무엇인가? 오답은 의미를 크게 왜곡하거나 핵심 정보를 누락하고 있다.
Ⓐ 저렴한 25센트의 요금을 지불하고 새로운 형태의 오락을 즐길 수 있었으며, 이는 빠르게 인기를 얻었다.
Ⓑ 새로운 형태의 오락은 저렴한 비용으로 빠르게 인기 있는 명소가 되었다.
Ⓒ 25센트를 내고 이용할 수 있는 새로운 형태의 오락이 빠르게 소문을 탔다.
Ⓓ 매력적인 형태의 오락이 뉴요커들에게 큰 반향을 일으켰으며, 이들은 기술을 체험하기 위해 25센트를 지불했다.

3.
2단락의 "its"라는 단어는 무엇을 가리키는가?
Ⓐ 기계의
Ⓑ 오크 나무 캐비닛의
Ⓒ 상점의
Ⓓ 집의

4. **Inference**

What can be inferred about the Kinetoscope in paragraph 2?

Ⓐ The majority of the Kinetoscope's first viewers became regular customers.
Ⓑ **The Kinetoscope parlor was presented to a public with almost no exposure to motion pictures.**
Ⓒ The Kinetscope's first audiences were less cultured than ordinary patrons of the visual arts.
Ⓓ The setup of the Kinetoscope parlor in New York was reminiscent of a game room.

5. **Insertion**

Look at the four squares [■] that indicate where the following sentence could be added to the passage.

Entrepreneurs quickly recognized the opportunity to establish similar parlors in other cities, both in the United States and abroad, many of which were set up and owned by the Holland brothers.

Where would the sentence best fit? [■ **B**]

6. **Negative Fact**

According to paragraph 3, the Kinetoscope's significance is reflected in all of the following EXCEPT

Ⓐ its profitability
Ⓑ its appeal to the masses
Ⓒ its rapid proliferation
Ⓓ **its upper-class clientele**

7. **Rhetorical Purpose**

The author mentions the "Cinématographe" in paragraph 4 in order to

Ⓐ discuss the Kinetoscope's successor.
Ⓑ highlight the legacy it left on the cinema industry.
Ⓒ **explain how inventors addressed the Kinetoscope's flaws.**
Ⓓ mention new technologies that were employed.

8. **Fact**

According to paragraph 5, which of the following was an important part of the legacy that the Cinématographe left on the cinema industry?

Ⓐ It further increased accessibility to motion pictures for middle-class consumers.
Ⓑ **Its concept of projection cinema would come to dominate the industry.**
Ⓒ It set 35mm film as the industry standard once and for all.

Ⓓ It provided a precedent that transformed movie viewing into a social activity.

9. **Vocabulary**

The word "endures" in paragraph 5 is closest in meaning to

Ⓐ sustains
Ⓑ withstands
Ⓒ prevails
Ⓓ **remains**

10. **Prose Summary**

Directions: An introductory sentence for a brief summary of the passage is provided below. Complete the summary by selecting the THREE answer choices that express the most important ideas in the passage. Some sentences do not belong in the summary because they express ideas that are not presented in the passage or minor ideas in the passage. ***This question is worth 2 points.***

While the Kinetoscope's pioneering technology proved to be popular, the subsequent Cinématographe would set a new standard for the cinema industry.

- Ⓑ **Viewers were often stunned by the new, popular form of entertainment, which featured simple 30 second-or-so films.**
- Ⓓ **The novel form of entertainment made the visual arts more accessible to people of different classes.**
- Ⓕ **The Cinématographe's projection technology created the conditions for the development of the movie theater.**

Ⓐ The Kinetoscope employed a continuous loop of 35mm film that ran through a viewing machine, which featured a peephole.
Ⓒ The Kinetoscope's popularity spread quickly to other US states, as well as beyond its borders, to other countries.
Ⓔ The Cinématographe was invented by French inventors who improved on the Kinetoscope, namely its limited functionality.

9.

5단락의 단어 "endures(지속하다)"와 의미상 가장 가까운 것은?

Ⓐ 유지하다
Ⓑ 견디다
Ⓒ 우세하다
Ⓓ 남아 있다

10.

지시문: 지문을 간략하게 요약한 글의 첫 문장이 아래 제시되어 있다. 지문의 가장 중요한 내용을 표현하는 세 개의 선택지를 골라 요약문을 완성하시오. 일부 문장들은 지문에 제시되지 않았거나 지문의 지엽적인 내용을 나타내기 때문에 요약문에 포함되지는 않는다. *이 문제의 배점은 2점이다.*

키네토스코프의 선구적인 기술이 인기를 끌었지만, 이후 시네마토그래프는 영화 산업에 새로운 기준을 세웠다.

- Ⓑ 관객들은 새로운 인기 오락 형식에 놀랐으며, 이는 대략 30초 정도의 단순한 영화로 구성되었다.
- Ⓓ 새로운 형태의 오락은 다양한 계층의 사람들이 시각 예술을 더 쉽게 접근할 수 있게 했다.
- Ⓕ 시네마토그래프의 투사 기술은 영화관 발전의 토대를 마련했다.

Ⓐ 키네토스코프는 작은 구멍이 있는 감상 기계를 통해 연속적인 35mm 필름을 사용했다.
Ⓒ 키네토스코프의 인기는 미국 다른 주와 국경 너머 다른 국가들로 빠르게 확산되었다.
Ⓔ 시네마토그래프는 주로 키네토스코프의 제한된 기능을 개선한 프랑스 발명가들에 의해 발명되었다.

어휘

1. **forerunner** n 전신, 선구자 | **patent** v 특허를 받다 | **unveil** v 공개하다 | **commercial** adj 상업적인 | **perforate** v 구멍을 뚫다 | **peephole** n 작은 구멍 | **depict** v 묘사하다
2. **parlor** n 영업장 | **milestone** n 중요한 단계 | **patron** n 고객 | **novel** adj 새로운 | **vaudeville** n 버라이어티 쇼 | **captivate** v 매료시키다 | **onlooker** n 구경꾼 | **engrossed** adj 몰두한

3 **testament** n 증거 | **exploitation** n 착취, 이용 | **burgeoning** adj 급증하는 | **affluent** adj 부유한 | **democratization** n 민주화 | **communal** adj 공동의
4 **detached** adj 분리된 | **transition** n 전환 | **project** v 투사하다 | **versatile** adj 다재다능한 | **standard** n 기준 | **intermittently** adv 간헐적으로
5 **screening** n 상영 | **momentous** adj 중대한 | **foundation** n 토대 | **dominant** adj 지배적인 | **cultural force** n 문화적 힘 | **endure** v 지속하다

Passage 2

Railroad Development in the United States

1 ➡ The completion of the Transcontinental Railway in 1869 was a watershed event in United States history. Prior to the construction of railways, the primary means of transportation other than horses was by water. Boats traversed rivers and canals hauling both cargo and passengers. However, this meant that only cities that were on major waterways could benefit, and goods had to be transported by wagon to reach towns that were not. The earliest railways were short, dedicated routes that were used to connect things like quarries to rivers, and they were pulled by horses. When the steam engine was applied to railways in England, Americans were quick to follow suit. The first steam railways were built to connect cities in New England, but they soon spread both south and westward.

2 ➡ By 1850, approximately 14,400 kilometers of tracks had been laid down, but it was during the following decade that construction really began in earnest. By 1860, there was about 48,000 kilometers of railroad tracks, which meant that the United States had the most tracks in the world. The idea for a railroad that would connect the Atlantic and Pacific coasts dates back to 1832, but it did not receive government approval until 1862. The railway was built in three sections: from Oakland, California to Sacramento, California, from Sacramento to Promontory Summit, Utah, and from Omaha, Nebraska to Promontory Summit. When the two lines met at Promontory Summit, Utah, they were connected with a ceremonial golden spike on May 10, 1869.

3 ➡ The benefits of railway construction were many, but the most significant was their effect on the economy. [■A] They allowed the rapid transportation

of food and other products to areas that previously had little to no access to such items. [■B] Previously, dairy products had to be produced and consumed locally, but now they could be transported long distances, allowing people to also increase production. [■C] Seafood could also be transported further inland than ever before. Most of the farmers in the western territories had practiced subsistence agriculture before, selling what little surplus they produced to local markets or using it for barter with neighbors. [■D] The railways allowed them to plant cash crops that they could send all over the country. Along with improvements in plow and harvester technology, this allowed the farms in the Midwest to expand rapidly, transforming the prairie into oceans of wheat and corn.

4 ➡ The railroads also facilitated settlement of the vast reaches of the West. Prior to the completion of the Transcontinental Railway, the only way to reach the West Coast was by wagon trail or by sailing around South America, both of which took many months. By rail, it could be achieved in a matter of days. The railroads also helped these people keep in touch with their families back east as mail came to be transported by train. Settlers flooded into the West, displacing Native Americans as they rapidly established cities and towns. Towns that already existed along the route also grew in response as they became important layovers where trains were supplied with fuel and water. As populations swelled, more states were admitted to the Union, and maps had to be redrawn to reflect the new boundaries.

5 ➡ The extensive rail system also proved to have significant military value. During the American Civil War, both sides transported troops to the front by train whenever possible, and many battles were fought in order to secure vital railway hubs. The North's ability to exploit its more extensive railway network was an important factor in its ultimate victory in 1865. Their importance is further clarified by General Sherman's infamous March to the Sea, wherein his troops specifically targeted railroad tracks for destruction to economically weaken the Confederacy. Later, they helped transport mounted cavalry throughout the West during the many conflicts of the Indian Wars.

6 ➡ By 1880, there were 17,800 locomotives transporting freight and 22,200 of them transporting passengers all over the country. The industrialists who owned these railways became incredibly wealthy as some of the larger companies spanned across many states. However, the federal government viewed such complete control as monopolistic, and it disapproved of some of the owners' excesses, particularly when they were lax about regulations. Congress responded to the situation by establishing the Interstate Commerce Commission, which controlled their business activities through heavy regulation. This was effective for a while, but then disaster struck.

7 ➡ In 1893, railroad overbuilding and unstable railroad financing resulted in the largest economic crisis ever at that time. By the middle of 1894, one quarter of the railroad companies had failed, and as they collapsed, they took a series of banks with them. This led to a distrust of the railroad companies that only intensified when the remaining owners joined forces to gain control of the railroad tracks left without management. Eventually, the invention of the automobile created competition that the railroads couldn't cope with, and passenger trains dwindled. In the United States today, most of the trains carry only freight.

1. **Vocabulary**
The word "dedicated" in paragraph 1 is closest in meaning to
Ⓐ reserved
Ⓑ staunch
Ⓒ resolute
Ⓓ purposeful

2. **Inference**
Based on paragraph 2, it can be inferred that
Ⓐ the construction of the Transcontinental Railway lasted for more than 10 years.
Ⓑ England had the most tracks in the world before the development of the Transcontinental Railway.
Ⓒ the government dictated the route of the railroad that would connect the Atlantic and Pacific coasts.
Ⓓ **the construction of the Transcontinental Railway began from both California and Nebraska simultaneously.**

3. **Fact**

According to paragraph 4, what effect did railroad construction have on the West?

Ⓐ **Existing towns along the railroad became important hubs.**
Ⓑ Displaced Native Americans established new cities and towns.
Ⓒ It forced mail to be transported along wagon trails during the period of railroad construction.
Ⓓ Maps had to be redrawn to include locations where trains stopped to replenish their supplies.

4. **Rhetorical Purpose**

Why does the author mention "Indian Wars" in paragraph 5?

Ⓐ To discuss the negative effects of targeting railroad tracks for destruction
Ⓑ To explain the role General Sherman played in the military after the American Civil War
Ⓒ **To provide further support for the argument that the railroads had significant military value**
Ⓓ To provide an earlier example of how railroads played a strategic role in warfare

5. **Inference**

Based on paragraph 5, it can be inferred that

Ⓐ the South's railway network was more extensive than the North's.
Ⓑ General Sherman fought in the South's army.
Ⓒ the March to the Sea was a failed military operation.
Ⓓ **the South's lack of infrastructure contributed to its defeat.**

6. **Vocabulary**

The word "freight" in paragraph 6 is closest in meaning to

Ⓐ weapons
Ⓑ vehicles
Ⓒ **cargo**
Ⓓ mail

7. **Fact**

According to paragraph 7, what is true about the railroad companies?

Ⓐ The railroad companies were owned by the same group of people that owned the banks.
Ⓑ The Interstate Commerce Commission was successful in regulating the railroad companies.

3.

4단락에 따르면, 철도 부설은 서부에 어떤 영향을 미쳤는가?

Ⓐ 철도를 따라 자리잡고 있는 기존의 마을들이 중요한 거점이 되었다.
Ⓑ 쫓겨난 북미 원주민들이 새로운 도시와 마을을 건설했다.
Ⓒ 철도가 부설되는 기간 동안 마차 길을 따라서 우편물이 운송되도록 했다.
Ⓓ 열차가 물자를 보충하기 위해 멈추었던 위치를 포함시키기 위해 지도가 다시 그려져야 했다.

4.

글쓴이가 5단락에서 "인디언 전쟁"을 언급하는 이유는 무엇인가?

Ⓐ 철도 파괴를 목적으로 삼는 것의 부작용을 논하기 위해
Ⓑ 남북전쟁 후 군대에서의 셔먼 장군의 역할을 설명하기 위해
Ⓒ 철도가 중대한 군사적 가치를 지녔다는 주장에 대한 근거를 더 제시하기 위해
Ⓓ 철도가 전쟁에서 어떻게 전략적 역할을 했는지에 관한 이전의 예를 제시하기 위해

5.

5단락에 근거하여 추론할 수 있는 것은?

Ⓐ 남부의 철도 네트워크는 북부의 것보다 더 광범위했다.
Ⓑ 셔먼 장군은 남부 군대에서 싸웠다.
Ⓒ 대행진은 실패한 군사 작전이었다.
Ⓓ 남부의 사회 기반시설 부족이 패배의 원인이 되었다.

6.

6단락의 단어 "freight(화물)"와 의미상 가장 가까운 것은?

Ⓐ 무기
Ⓑ 탈것
Ⓒ 화물
Ⓓ 우편물

7.

7단락에 따르면, 다음 중 철도 회사에 대해 사실인 것은 무엇인가?

Ⓐ 철도 회사들은 은행을 소유했던 사람들과 똑같은 집단에 의해 소유되었다.
Ⓑ 주간 통상위원회는 철도 회사들을 규제하는 데 성공했다.

- Ⓒ The federal government bought railroad tracks that were left without management.
- Ⓓ **Railroad companies eventually allocated more locomotives to transporting freight than passengers.**

8. Sentence Simplification

Which of the sentences below best expresses the essential information in the highlighted sentence in the passage? *Incorrect* answer choices change the meaning in important ways or leave out essential information.

- Ⓐ Distrust led owners of remaining railroad companies to gain control of tracks left without management.
- Ⓑ Distrust of railroad companies arose when railroad company owners sold tracks that were left without management.
- Ⓒ **This resulted in distrust of railroad companies which grew stronger after other company owners teamed up to buy the abandoned tracks.**
- Ⓓ Distrust grew as other railroad company owners fought to gain control over railroad tracks that were left without management.

9. Insertion

Look at the four squares [■] that indicate where the following sentence could be added to the passage.

Seafood could also be transported further inland than ever before.

Where would the sentence best fit? [■C]

10. Summary

Directions: An introductory sentence for a brief summary of the passage is provided below. Complete the summary by selecting the THREE answer choices that express the most important ideas in the passage. Some sentences do not belong in the summary because they express ideas that are not presented in the passage or are minor ideas in the passage. *This question is worth 2 points.*

The Transcontinental Railway, which was completed in 1869, greatly impacted the United States, which already had the most tracks in the world by the mid-19th century.

Ⓐ **Despite the government's efforts to regulate the monopoly, railroad company owners retained their dominance until it was broken by the automobile.**
Ⓒ **Not only did increased accessibility encourage settlers to rush into the West, but the railway system also proved to be of strategic military value.**
Ⓔ **The railway system allowed farmers to increase crop production as products could be transported to other areas rapidly.**

Ⓑ Prior to railway construction, farmers could not attempt mass production because produce had to be consumed locally, with any surplus being sold to neighbors.
Ⓓ The construction of the railway began in 1862, and it eventually spanned across the continent, connecting the cities in New England to Promontory Summit.
Ⓕ During the American Civil War, General Sherman focused on destroying railway tracks to prevent troops from being transported to the frontlines.

Ⓐ 독점을 규제하려는 정부의 노력에도 불구하고 철도 회사 소유주들은 자동차로 무너질 때까지 우세를 점했다.
Ⓒ 개선된 접근 용이성이 정착민들로 하여금 서부로 몰려들게 했을 뿐만 아니라, 철도 시스템은 또한 전략상 중요한 군사적 가치도 지닌 것으로 증명되었다.
Ⓔ 철도 시스템은 상품이 다른 지역으로 신속히 운송될 수 있게 되면서 농부들이 작물 생산량을 늘릴 수 있게 해 주었다.

Ⓑ 철도 부설 이전에는 농작물이 지역적으로 소비되고, 여분의 농산물은 이웃에게 판매되어야만 했기 때문에 농부들은 대량 생산을 시도할 수 없었다.
Ⓓ 철도 부설은 1862년에 시작되었고, 마침내는 대륙 전역에 걸쳐 이어졌고 뉴잉글랜드의 도시들과 프로먼토리 서밋을 연결시켰다.
Ⓕ 남북전쟁 시기에 셔먼 장군은 군대가 전선으로 수송되는 것을 막기 위해 철로를 파괴하는 데 중점을 두었다.

어휘

1. **completion** n 완성, 완료 | **transcontinental** adj 대륙횡단의 | **watershed** adj 분수계[분기점]를 이루는, 획기적인 n 분수령 | **primary** adj 주된 | **transportation** n 운송, 수송 | **traverse** v 가로지르다 | **haul** v 운반하다, 끌다 | **cargo** n 화물 | **benefit** v 혜택[이익]을 얻다 | **dedicated** adj 특정 작업용으로 만들어진, 전용의 | **quarry** n 채석장 | **follow suit** 전례를 따르다
2. **in earnest** 본격적으로 | **ceremonial** adj 의식용의
3. **previously** adv 이전에 | **consume** v 소비하다 | **inland** adv 내륙으로 | **territory** n 지역, 구역, 영역 | **subsistence agriculture** 자급 농업 | **surplus** n 잉여 농산물, 잉여, 과잉 | **barter** v 물물교환하다 | **cash crop** 환금성 작물 | **plow** n 경작 | **rapidly** adv 신속히 | **transform** v 변형시키다, 완전히 바꿔놓다[탈바꿈시키다]
4. **facilitate** v 용이하게 하다 | **displace** v 쫓아내다 | **in response (to)** ~에 대응하여 | **layover** n 기착지, 도중차 | **swell** v 늘다, 팽창하다 | **boundary** n 경계선
5. **value** n 가치 | **troop** n 부대, 병력 | **front** n 전선 | **secure** v 확보하다 | **hub** n 중심지 | **exploit** v 활용하다 | **extensive** adj 광범위한 | **clarify** v 명확히 하다 | **ultimate** adj 궁극적인 | **infamous** adj 악명 높은 | **target** v 목표로 삼다, 겨냥하다 | **weaken** v 약화시키다 | **mounted** adj 말에 탄, 기동의 | **cavalry** n 기사 | **conflict** n 충돌, 갈등, 전투

PAGODA TOEFL
Actual Test
READING

PAGODA TOEFL Actual Test Reading | 해설서